80-870

HV8665   Toch, Hans
.T6   Living in prison.

LIVING
IN
PRISON

Living in Prison

The Ecology of Survival

Hans Toch

With contributions by
John Gibbs
John Seymour
Daniel Lockwood

THE FREE PRESS
A Division of Macmillan Publishing Co., Inc.
NEW YORK

Collier Macmillan Publishers
LONDON

The Free Press
A Division of Macmillan Publishing Co., Inc.
866 Third Avenue, New York, N.Y. 10022

Collier Macmillan Canada, Ltd.

First Free Press Paperback Edition 1979

Library of Congress Catalog Card Number: 77-4570

Printed in the United States of America

Casebound printing number

2 3 4 5 6 7 8 9 10

Paperbound printing number

1 2 3 4 5 6 7 8 9 10

Library of Congress Cataloging in Publication Data

Toch, Hans.
    Living in prison.

    Bibliography: p.
    Includes index.
    1. Prisons. 2. Prison psychology. 3. Prisoners.
I. Title.
HV8665.T6   365'.3   77-4570
ISBN 0-02-932680-X
ISBN 0-02-932940-X pbk.

FOR MY MOTHER,
my most devoted reader
and
FOR MICHELLE,
who'll soon be reading

Contents

Acknowledgments

THIS BOOK OWES MUCH to many persons. Its existence is a testimonial to the trust and faith, the help and commitment of an awesome range of friends, acquaintances, and strangers. In a very direct way, the effort is the product of a supportive and receptive environment.

The work on which the book is based was underwritten by the National Institute of Law Enforcement and Criminal Justice, Law Enforcement Assistance Administration, U.S. Department of Justice. NILECJ funded the project under its Innovative Research Program, through a grant entitled "Interventions for Inmate Survival."

More proximate assistance came to us from the New York Department of Correctional Services. Without the help of prison staff and clients, ranging from commissioners and wardens to correctional officers and inmates, we could not have done what we have done. I am grateful for the readiness with which time was set aside for us, arrangements were cheerfully made, hospitality extended, facilities opened, and (most important) thoughts and impressions were shared. Our contribution must remain comparatively minuscule compared to the toll in inconvenience we have exacted.

When I say "we," I intend the pronoun literally. This book is a true group product. Among my closest associates were John Gibbs, John Seymour, Daniel Lockwood, Robert Johnson, James Fox, and our secretaries, Barbara Meilinger and Kathy Schmidt. Team–mates once-removed were the members of our Research Advisory Committee, Donald Kenefick, Robert Rommel, Victor Rosenblum, and Ezra Stotland. This advisory group functioned as a roving seminar in which we could test ideas and in which we frequently evolved or perfected them. Cynthia Jackson, our project monitor, was another valued team member, as was Commissioner Edward Elwin, who helped in designing and implementing our project.

Part of this book is based on intensive interviews conducted in New York State prisons. These interviews were made possible through the cooperation of Commissioner Elwin and Commissioner William Ciuros, and through the support of superintendents and wardens at Coxsackie, Green Haven, Attica, Elmira, Auburn, and Comstock (Great Meadows). Inmates and staff contributed to many of our concepts and much of our thinking. In the sort of research we do, it is impossible to separate the roles of subject, informant, and colleague.

Our psychometric data derive from several agencies. We are grateful for the cooperation of Larry Karacki, U.S. Bureau of Prisons; Warden Bill Kay, FCI Lexington; Commissioner William Robinson and Dr. R. Belford, Pennsylvania Bureau of Corrections; Thomas Riemer, Robert Brooks, Hugh O'Hare, Paul Wiehm, and Martin Greengrass, of the Connecticut Department of Correction; Dr. L. A. Bennett and Raymond Fowler, of the California Department of Corrections; and Warden Edwin LaVallee, Gene Beaubriand, and F. Welch, of the New York State Reception Center at Clinton Prison.

My major indebtedness is to the late Hadley Cantril. While working on this book, I have rediscovered the bridge that link's Cantril's thinking to mine. It would be pleasant to hope that this book may reflect positively on that personal heritage.

HANS TOCH

Albany, N.Y.
February 1977

LIVING
IN
PRISON

1

Transactions of Man and Environment

THE LINK BETWEEN MAN AND ENVIRONMENT holds a position in the social sciences similar to that of virtue in society. We love to preach and teach it, but we often ignore it in practice.

In both cases the fault lies with the complexity of life. It is easy to say that man is inextricably linked to his surroundings, but inextricability is a hard thing to study. The tools and modes of thought we are most familiar with center on personality or behavior and on social context or influence. And no matter what we say, we are tied to the assumption that man and environment can be *independently* defined and can be thought of apart from each other. The notion is thus engraved in me that I am the same sitting at my typewriter as at my dinner table and that the typewriter I am pounding is identical to the tool it may have been to previous owners.

In one sense, the typewriter and I do lead independent existences, but in another sense we are interlinked.[1] Different aspects of me are brought out by my work than by my dinner, and the "typewriter" connotations evoked in my mind are different from those produced for other typists. The typewriter *as a feature of my personal environment* is unique to me and relates to my typing experience, my attitudes toward work, and all sorts of feelings and expectations. The same machine that to one person symbolizes eight daily hours of slavery to another may be a bridge to the gods. No outsider could "describe" the typewriter as a feature of my environment

[1] The relationship may be more salient in other cultures than in our own. Mai-mai Sze, in discussing the technology of Chinese painting, tells us that "a [Chinese] painter often has favorite brushes and comes to know them so well they take on part of his personality; he finds that a particular worn brush is good, for instance, for drawing the jagged outlines of rocks in a kind of brushstroke that cannot be produced by any other brush. In short, the brush is the painter's and scholar's chief means of individual expression, capable of reflecting traits of character and temperament, and so, in effect, an extension of his personality" (Sze, 1959, pp. 65–66).

by noting its (venerable) age, counting its keys, or otherwise measuring it. Similarly, no one could understand me as a "user" of my environment simply by assessing my motives, attitudes, or personal idiosyncracies.

Dewey and Bentley (1949) coined the term "transaction" to describe the closeness of man–environment links. What Dewey and Bentley suggested is that man relates to his world as a buyer relates to a seller. Lacking a buyer, the seller might not sell, or he might sell at a higher or lower price; the buyer might go through life unsold-to or might find a better buy around the corner. A given physical or social milieu is a different psychological environment for everyone who operates in it; a person feels and acts differently if he is translated from one setting to another.

Those are important notions for environmental psychology, which studies man in his intimate and generic settings. Some pioneers of the emerging discipline (Ittelson *et al.*) note that

> . . . environment perception does not spring directly from the objective properties of the world out there, but rather, from that world transformed into a psychological environment by a perceiving and cognizing organism. In a very general sense of the term, it is an essentially creative process, actively carried out by the individual who is himself immersed in the perceptual situation. The adequacy of these perceptions is assessed not by comparing them with some hypothetically independent environment, but rather by their utility in aiding the individual in achieving his own personal and social goals [p. 113].

Students of environmental psychology are more mindful than the rest of us of the uniqueness and the relativity of man–environment links. But the difficulty of translating such notions into researchable questions produces a lag between theory and practice.[2] We have a great deal of data about pollution, room arrangements and architecture, and humane or authoritarian settings; we know how people react to stress situations and how they suffer or recover. But we know little about the uniqueness and variability of responses to the same setting or about differential impacts of settings on the same person.

The consequences of ignoring such matters are troublesome. We design environments to serve people who often seem ungrateful. Multiple-purpose schoolrooms are converted into conventional classrooms; model housing units become vandalized shells; recreation areas "recreate" rapists and muggers.

---

[2] Stern notes that "what is clear and generally agreed upon is that it is a psychological environment with which we are working, and the constructs that are needed will be essentially psychological.

"Various psychologists . . . have adopted such a transactional viewpoint in principle. But few have gone beyond the point of expanding on the theoretical necessity of such a position. At best, attention has been called to general classes of phenomena, but the specific dimensions to be subsumed within them have been left unspecified." (P. 5).

Man's unique purposes assert themselves in defiance of the most soundly conceived predictions. We offer city dwellers fresh air and find them nostalgic for asphalt; we bring farmers to the facilities of cities and watch them feel lost. We discover the wisdom of the cigarette commercial which tells us that men can be translated to new environments ("you can take . . . out of the country") but that human perceptions and expectations are unresponsive to manipulation (you can't take the country out of . . .).

Where environments are designed for human aggregates, they are imposed on diverse subgroups. We recall a designer's dream car, the Edsel, calculated to meet the needs of male and female drivers. That vehicle became an ecological disaster—a vehicle for mythical hermaphrodites (Hayakawa).

"Desirable" and "undesirable" features of environment are "desirable" or "undesirable" for averaged and hypothetical clients. Even extremes of pain are welcomed by some as tests of strength, opportunities for self-cleansing, masochistic rewards, or sources of existential meaning. In some cases, one man's meat is another's poison; on the average, "meaty" and "poisonous" qualities differ from one of us to the next.

While such considerations may prove trivial for "luxury" qualities in environments, they are crucial where the world impinges and intrudes. It may not matter that a hilarious play is a delight to me and a bore to my companion; it does matter if a school stultifies some students or if surgery traumatizes some patients to the point of death.

Stress environments are environments in which transactional junctures are of critical personal import. Transactions mark the difference between psychological survival and nonsurvival, between growth and discomfort, or even agony. To assume universal impact may mean that we worry about persons who manage nicely and overlook the suffering of others who go under.

This danger exists if we define stress as stimuli and (less so) where we infer it from people's responses. Stress *stimuli* are uninviting situations such as hurricanes, shellings, icebergs, concentration camps, surgery, migration, unemployment, submersion (with blinders and earphones), blood-curdling films, and dentists' waiting rooms; these experiences have been found to produce widely different impacts on people, no matter how we measure their effects (Lazarus; Appley and Trumbull; McGrath).

Stress *responses* are (among other things) emergency body changes ranging from perspiration and blood-pressure level to hormones found in urine. Such indices, if they are reliable, show a "defensive" reaction by our organism at the time of measurement. The trouble is that we never know what the reaction is inspired by or what goes on inside the organism other than the change that we measure.

Even lower animals under stress can tell us a great deal if we listen to them and if we observe them. A postoperative dog's urine chemistry may change, but this fact is not half so revealing as the dog's plaintive, low-key complaints and its pitiful retreat into privacy and isolation. When the animal moves and eats again, it tells us as much as (or more than) does the chemical composition of its blood or the electroconductivity of its fur.

We discover that as we extend our inquiry into organismic responses from the simple to the complex, we obtain more than the *indicators* of stress we start with. We see, gradually, the *psychological connotations* of stress, the feelings, perceptions, and concepts that are the mirrors of the organism's despair. With verbal communication and refined behavior in man, we obtain information about stress connotations that are very detailed and that are, in some respects, unique to each person.

In exploring connotations of stress, we enter the transactional realm of the experience. We discover that the same disaster caps despondency in one person, poses moral issues (or guilt reactions) in others, and brings welcome escape to still others. We see the experience as ranging in salience, meaning, and impact to the extent that it leaves some persons unaffected and others paralyzed.

It is easy to ignore transactions in everyday life, but never under stress. I can see my typewriter as an object, but thumbscrews or arctic weather are always intimate experiences. To describe a stressor, we must consider its "stressing" injuries; we cannot define a man's freezing to death in terms of degrees Celsius, nor can we equate starvation with the meals a person misses.

Stress is a man–environment laboratory in the same sense in which neuroses were the laboratory of mental health. Stress challenges man's capacity to adapt. By so doing, it highlights ways in which we process information, assess it, and react to it; it highlights the plasticity and vulnerability of man; it traces human options, with their constraints and limits. Stress is the testing ground of man's frailty and his capacity to resist.

The study of stress transactions can be, and must be, more than research. Freud cured patients as he gained insights, and we can relieve stress as we begin to understand it. The concerns of men under stress are immediate and tangible, and we must respond to those concerns, if we can, as we learn what they are. Such has been the history of "real life" research in combat, isolation, and disaster.

In an earlier book (Toch, 1975), I explored the prisoner's experience of stress and tried to map personal breakdowns as they evolve for inmates in crisis. Such data are designed to help "crisis interventionists," whose task it is to ameliorate suffering and restore the perspective of stress victims. But crisis interventionists do not attack the occasions for crisis (the stressors), nor do they arrange or rearrange the stressed person's life.

In proposing to study stress transactions we enter a new and different realm, which is that of trying to *prevent* stress through ecological interventions. By knowing which features of the environment are stressful (or ameliorative) to which persons, we can appropriately modify a person's environment, alter the person's relationship to the environment, or translate people from one set of circumstances to another. Such interventions are familiar to us from daily life. We may be neat or casual with different roommates, respect dietary preferences and special sensibilities in conversation, play Bach cantatas for one guest and rock or folk music for the next. These are moves that take cognizance of environmental preferences, aversions, requirements, and allergies. They are efforts to accommodate to known needs with congruent responses.

In institutional settings, we often assume that we have no way of making environments individually or personally congenial. Instead, we try to reduce harshness and stress "across the board." We lower noise in assembly lines, arrange rest for troops, repaint lunchrooms, sugarcoat algebra lessons, play canned music, and act cheerful. Such responses are generic because we assume that efficient organizations effect their improvements wholesale. We also assume (mostly unconsciously) that what is good for the goose (or ourselves) must be good for the gander ("the average person").

The transactional perspective is different. It assumes human uniqueness and expects important needs to vary significantly within the same context. The perspective implies that both organizational effectiveness and personal happiness can be maximized through orchestrated diversity. If we can identify differences in the personal worlds that people need for survival, we can deploy organizational options for the best "fit." Any organization—any environment—has "options." My desk is thus placed to face the window to provide me with a view. Hypothetically, I might prefer a different view, such as the Oregon coastline or the Croatian alps. But this is not an "option" for me. What *is* an option is to place the desk elsewhere, gaining freedom from distraction (by facing a wall) or a safe feeling (a protected back). The unimpeded vista of dirty New England snow that cheers me depresses the person next door. Our *choice* of seating permits each of us to shape our environments in ways that matter to us.

This book addresses the issue of *significant variations in the environmental requirements* of different people. In later chapters (10, 11, and 14) we return to the question of how such requirements can be satisfied to reduce personal stress.

The Impact of Prison Environments

Our research laboratory for the study of environmental impact is the prison. Since prisons are designed to deter criminal misbehavior, society has no compunction about confining people there, away from their loved ones, in very limited space and in stultifying routines. Prisons are meant to be uncomfortable, to be much less than desirable. Nowadays, however, we also strive to make prisons (1) not flagrantly inhumane and (2) not psychologically harmful. And to the extent that officials may wish to rehabilitate inmates, they want prisons to be therapeutic, or at least conducive to self-betterment. Most of all, society wants prisons to be *secure,* so as to keep inmates dependably inside. That goal determines the isolated location, quarantined insulation, and fortress architecture of prisons and shapes their "custodial" staffing patterns.

The walls and goals of prison do not make a neat or logical package. They do not paint a psychologically coherent picture in the sense of describing the experience we want inmates to have in prison. While stress is a built-in feature of prisons, so are its positive goals, such as humaneness, protection, and self-improvement. And, while therapy may be out of fashion, we want prisons to be "sane" places; we also want prisons to furnish tangible tools of self-reform to inmates who desire our support and are able to use it (Morris).

There are 300,000 persons housed in American prisons. This makes The Prison a mammoth human industry, and its product (the inmate) an important national product. It is therefore disheartening that we have facts —discouraging facts—about the failure of prisons to affect crime rates and to rehabilitate offenders.

None of us is sure why prisons fail. One reason we don't understand the effects of prisons is that we don't understand the personal impact of prisons. Only inmates have the experience of imprisonment, and inmates who write about prison are neither dispassionate nor representative. They are men who have dealt with their experience by drawing meaning from it. This is specialized adaptation, and it makes inmate-authors unique in the same sense in which Bruno Bettelheim and Viktor Frankl were unique as concentration camp inmates.

One fact is clear: While some men adapt eagerly to challenges of the prison environment, there are others who suffer tangibly or struggle visibly while confined. All three groups are of interest to us, because they can give us different perspectives about attributes of prisons and about needs of inmates. They can tell us in turn about man–environment transactions that are congruent (in which milieu attributes respond to people's needs), incongruent (where attributes are in conflict with needs), or negotiable (where there is coping going on).

Such transactions are hard to describe if we preclassify prison environments or if we prejudge inmate adaptation. Parochial views of prison environments cover a wide spectrum and include portraits of prisons as (1) cafeterias of remediation efforts, (2) hotbeds of violence, (3) schools of crime, (4) concentration camps for the disadvantaged, and (5) repositories of revolutionaries.

More sophisticated preclassifications of prison focus on the "pains" of imprisonment—the stresses involved in being an inmate in prison. Sykes, for example, has traced the discomforts of male inmates to deprivation of liberty, the absence of goods and services, the loss of sexual companionship, a decrease in autonomy, and a lessening of security. Such deficits, according to Sykes, translate into self-doubts and reduced feelings of self-esteem. The same picture has been traced for the female inmate by Giallombardo. The pains are similar, though the indices of self-esteem among women (centered on relationships) differ from those for male inmates.

Most environmental descriptions of prison focus on descriptive attributes (such as crowding, monotony, lack of privacy) that are plausibly relevant to inmate life (Nagel; Flynn). But plausibility is not enough. It never tells us whether the attributes *deemed noxious by the observer* are in fact noxious or harmful to all inmates, most inmates, or an appreciable minority of inmates. It is also not obvious that addressing ecological deficiencies that are located by observers makes a dent on attributes of prison that are deemed important by inmates.

A Norwegian colleague (Mathiesen) studied morale in two contrasting prisons located near Oslo. One setting, Botsfengslet, is damp, stark, and ugly. Inmates reside in dungeons, receive lukewarm meals through trap doors, share no contact, and get almost no attention from staff. The second setting, Ila, is attractive, modern, and well staffed. The walls are pastel-colored, the living areas are individualized and attractive, dining rooms are small, and supervision is unobtrusive. No ecologist worth his salt would consider living in Botsfengslet, but inmates prefer it by a heavy margin. They prefer it because it has clear criteria, known rules, and an unambiguous (nonrehabilitative) philosophy.

The point is that Norwegian inmates have a prepotent concern about predictability and structure that must be considered in designing prisons for such inmates. This task is simple, but most environments are multidimensional, and the concerns of people who inhabit environments are also multidimensional. This makes it hard to predict and to prevent stress. Transactions are intersections of many stimuli and needs. They cannot be anticipated unless we "map" environments and people in detail.

In simple situations we accommodate simple needs by manipulating simple attributes of milieus. We design homes without stairs for the old and infirm; we install chairlifts or ramps where stairlessness is precluded. We place bathrooms near bedrooms, cupboards in kitchens, and lights near chairs.

But complexity means that obscure environmental features can have impact on hidden human needs, particularly where situations or people are unfamiliar to us. Where our experience is no guide, we invoke logic. This means that we assign people motives that make sense to us and are surprised when men "betray" us by having needs of their own. For example, logic tells us that solitary confinement is onerous. We enter a prison as reforming warden. We call in the press and announce that one must expunge harsh, anachronistic medieval relics of questionable legality such as segregation cells. Accompanied by a contingent of photographers, we proceed to close down the maximum security wing of our institution. We are surprised to discover that some of the inmates we have liberated refuse to move out of their cells and that when they are gently moved, they lock themselves into minimum security cells. We also learn that some inmates "arrange" disciplinary infractions so as to be put away. We belatedly find out that some of our clients feel unsafe in prison. We also learn that some inmates find punishment settings congenial, low-pressure, and prestigeful.

The converse of the coin may be our assumption that persons who talk about suicide must be segregated to keep them from destroying themselves. Having implemented this program, we find that segregation increases despondency and self destructive motives. We learn (belatedly) that suicidologists recommend contact and communication as requisites for suicide prevention.

Even knowledge does not solve our problem, because (1) we can affect only a small part of any environment; (2) we must accommodate other values besides reducing stress; (3) we must balance any individual's many needs against each other, and (4) we must set off one person's needs against those of others. We may close segregation units, for example, to benefit the *majority* of inmates, though *some* inmates are short-changed, and we may isolate suicidal patients to prevent civil suits by their relatives.

Transactions are more easily visualized in the abstract than they can be engineered in practice—particularly in the context of organizational constraints. Shellshock can be eliminated by abolishing wars, but the most humane general cannot do this. He may try rotating personnel and run out of personnel to rotate. He may end up organizing ballgames or inventing unnecessary patrol activities to reduce boredom.

To "maximize" the congruence of people and environments we must exercise new options or use old options in new ways. This means that we must abandon traditional ways of defining environments. Traditional perspectives highlight structural (or "outside-perceived") features rather than those seen by clients. Ila, the Norwegian institution I have cited, for example, is seen as "therapeutic." To reduce inmate stress we must also see this prison as "unpredictable" and must reduce the structurelessness of its regime. We may similarly find ourselves using a classroom as a social mixer, a machine shop as a source of loving supervision, a living area as a haven of privacy, and punishment as therapy.

Before we realign environments we must know what the transactional possibilities or the "human" attributes of our environments are. That requires a "phenomenological" approach to the study of environments, which tells us how people who operate in an environment or who live in it perceive it and adjust to it. Such an approach not only tells us about existing transactions but highlights the problems we must address by realigning transactions to reduce stress and maximize "match."

A Transactional Approach to Prisons

In setting out to study prisons as environments, we are concerned with understanding life in prison and particularly with the stress of inmates who have trouble surviving in prisons. Recent past experiences (Toch, 1975) have confirmed for us that adjustment problems in prison are neither rare nor confined to extreme groups of generally vulnerable persons. Though stress intersects with vulnerability, many of the crises and much of the despair and suffering of prisoners can be averted. Similar inmates survive in the same settings; inmates who survive in one setting break down in another; situations that are stressful to some inmates have no impact on other inmates.[3] It seems that there is a plausible potential for arranging prison environments to reduce or ameliorate stress by inventorying resources and realigning them. But to consider environmental realignments presupposes knowledge of "pinpointed" areas of stress and of stress-reducing aspects of environments.

To attack this sort of mapping is difficult because it entails in-depth inquiry into subjective stress while at the same time it calls for findings that can be generalized and used. To short-change clinical inquiry means to lose sight of the suffering that is the essence of the problem, but to perpetually approach each man *de novo* is impossible where we must act quickly and on a large scale.

We shall solve this problem by obtaining in–depth portraits and then combining them into pictures of larger groups. We proceed from the unique to the general sequentially, by moving from a full-blooded phenomenology of inmate views to a description of the dimensions of environments that appear significant to large numbers of inmates. In this approach, the tasks we set ourselves include the following:

1. to explore the personal connotations of prison environments for inmates, in an effort to reconstruct their "reality worlds" as faithfully as possible

[3] These facts are not unrelated; we'll see in our exploration of prison life that some inmates flourish at the expense of others, and that an inmate's mode of adaptation may bring another inmate stress.

2. to search for shared environmental concerns, for dimensions of "reality worlds" that "cut across" persons and that are differentially satisfied in different environments [4]
3. to look at differences in the distribution of such environmental concerns so as to try to understand the origins of human needs in the experiences of different groups of persons
4. to develop shorthand means of "diagnosing" the personal concerns that enter into environmental transactions

And because of our interest in stress and survival, we also set out

5. to examine the special concerns or "stress transactions" of men who have experienced or are experiencing difficulties
6. to study ameliorative properties of environments or subenvironments that seem to reduce stress

These tasks are not modest. Before we finally folded our tents, we conducted nine hundred interviews (seven hundred with inmates and two hundred with staff) and administered the special instrument we had developed as a mapping tool to 2,650 inmates in five major prison systems. If we accomplished the tasks we had set ourselves, we managed to do so thanks to generous financial sponsorship, much help from one correctional agency, and selfless assistance from researchers across the country. Most important, we enjoyed the confidence of the inmates we interviewed, who saw the point of our efforts and who shared our hopes for reform.

The Mechanics of Inquiry

To gain an overview of inmate concerns with prisons, we interviewed random samples of prison inmates in five (out of the seven) New York maximum-security institutions for male offenders. We did not include the female prison, Bedford Hills, because it is a small, self-contained world of its own. Male offenders are dispersed to a number of settings with different program options, which can be mapped as a correctional "system." All New York female inmates—including the reformatory population—

---

[4] This goal and the preceding one were dear to the heart of Murray (1938, 1945), who shares the paternity of environmental psychology with Lewin and Barker. Our efforts to reconstruct "reality worlds" correspond to Murray's notion of *beta press,* which (unlike *alpha press*) is a purely subjective environment. Our "environmental concerns" are Murray's *sentiments,* his "tendencies to be attracted or repelled by . . ." Like Murray, we assume that environmental concerns are conditioned by *needs,* some of which are stronger than others ("primary") and may become obsessive (*prepotent*). When we speak of qualities of the environment that are responsive (or unresponsive) to human concerns we are referring to Murray's *cathexes.*

are intermixed at Bedford Hills. The institution deserves a separate and different study, which must be aimed at projecting an expanded range of assignments for its heterogeneous population.

We drew our random samples from prison housing rosters, aiming at a 4 percent sample of population. We also conducted interviews in each prison with stratified random samples of inmates located in definable sub-environments (work, program, and living arrangements). Both sets of samples yielded a total of 418 completed interviews.[5]

In these interviews we explored as fully as possible the reactions of inmates to significant aspects of their world. Each interview was tape-recorded and included an orally administered instrument, the Self-Anchoring Striving Scale, which was originated by Cantril (1965), and which we modified for use as a rating scale for prison settings. The scale, according to Cantril, is a "technique for tapping the unique reality world of an individual and learning what it has in common with that of others." In responding to the scale, "a person is asked to define on the basis of *his own* assumptions, perceptions, goals, and values the two extremes or anchoring points of the spectrum on which some scale measurement is desired—for example, he may be asked to define the top and bottom of the scale as the best and worst. This self-defined continuum is then used as our measuring instrument" (p. 22).

Our version of Cantril's instrument (with discretion allowed for variations in wording) includes the following:

A: Everyone who serves time in prisons prefers some types of institutions to others. When you think about what really matters to you when you have to serve time, what would the *best possible* prison be like, for you? In other words, if you have to be confined for a time, what would the institution have to look like—what would it have to offer, for you to be happy there? Take your time answering; such things aren't easy to put into words.

PERMISSIBLE PROBES: What would you need in an institution, to serve the easiest bit, or have the most profitable time? What is missing in some places you have been (besides women) that could have made you happier?

OBLIGATORY PROBE: Anything else?

• • •

B: Now, taking the other side of the picture, what are the things you *hate most* about some prisons? If you imagine the *worst possible* institution,

[5] The five institutions were sampled as follows: At Attica we drew a random sample of 60 and a stratified sample (which we derived from predefined subsettings) of 30; at Auburn the random sample totaled 69 and the stratified sample 22; at Coxsackie, we interviewed 43 and 45 inmates, respectively; at Elmira, 39 and 36; at Green Haven, 60 and 24. The two prisons we did not cover were the Great Meadows Correctional Facility and Clinton Prison.

as far as *you* are concerned, what would it be like? What qualities would it have? What would it look like, and feel like?

PERMISSIBLE PROBES: What would make you most miserable in prison? What would make it hardest to do time? What would be your idea of a nightmare prison?

OBLIGATORY PROBE: Anything else?

• • •

Here is a picture of a ladder. Suppose we say that the top of the ladder (POINTING) represents the best possible institution for you, and the bottom (POINTING) represents the worst possible institution for you,

C. Where on the ladder (MOVING FINGER RAPIDLY UP AND DOWN LADDER) would you place (NAME OF PRISON) as far as you personally are concerned?

D: Why wouldn't you place (NAME OF PRISON) lower than you have? In what ways is it better than the worst institution?

E. Why wouldn't you place (NAME OF PRISON) higher than you have? In what ways is it worse than the best institution?

• • •

F. One last question. When you first began to serve time, would you have ranked (NAME OF PRISON) *higher* or *lower* than you have now? (IF HIGHER OR LOWER) Where would you have ranked it?

Why is that?

The interview took place in a private room or office, or in a secluded corner of a public facility. Most inmates did not anticipate the purpose of their callout; the objectives of the research were therefore summarized for each inmate, with opportunities for questions. Each man was assured of anonymity and was asked whether he agreed to help us and whether he objected to being tape-recorded.[6] Very few inmates balked at being in-

---

[6] We have kept the promise we made to each subject to protect his anonymity. All inmates were assigned research-relevant code numbers. Each interviewee was given a composite "name," which includes his institution of origin and the sample from which he was drawn. We shall use these codes below in identifying inmates when we quote them, except where we deal extendedly with the same person (pp. 46–50) or where we draw data from a single sample (Chapter 11). It may help the reader to know that the first section of the code usually refers to a correctional institution. "El" thus means Elmira; "Att" means Attica; "GH," Green Haven; "Cox," Coxsackie, and "Au," Auburn. A second set of letters is used where there is a need to distinguish various types of institutional samples from each other. Here "R" and "R2" stand for random; "N" for niche, "T" for transfer, and "S" for stratified. Some settings are explicitly identified: "C-2" refers to the C-2 Company at Coxsackie; "Actec" is the abbreviation for an institution (now extinct) that contained the therapeutic community Diagnostic and Treatment Center #4. "P" and "PC" identify inmates in protection and members of our protection control sample; "VR" refers to the staff-referred "victimization referral" sample.

terviewed, and none requested that we discontinue recording. Randomized substitutes were invoked where an inmate could not be reached or did not respond to repeated callouts.

Our samples are representative of the prisons in which they were drawn. With respect to the entire New York adult male maximum-security population, we suffer some underrepresentation of older, long-term offenders because of the two prisons we could not cover. There is also underrepresentation of the nonserious, short-term offenders who are residents of medium or minimum security settings. This group, however, is small.

Our random interviews started with descriptive questions ("How long have you been here at . . . ?) and explored the inmate's perceptions of his prison ("What is this place like as a place to do time?" "How is this place different from . . . ?"). The interview contained a variety of questions tapping environmental concerns ("What kinds of things are important to you that you find [lack] here?" "What are the good points of doing time here? The advantages?" "What are the disadvantages of being in . . . ? What about . . . makes it harder for you to do time?") Following our exploration of the inmate's prison concerns (and of his feelings about subenvironments) we administered our version of the Cantril scale. The inmate was then asked about serious problems he might have experienced while in prison.

A different schedule was used for samples of "stressed inmates." We located these samples of inmates inside and outside ameliorative environments. The inmates in special settings included (1) the population of an "elderly and handicapped unit" (N = 29); (2) the population of a "specialized treatment unit" for men with emotional-adjustment problems (N = 24); (3) the populations of two protection or protective-segregation companies and a sample from a third protective company (N = 53); (4) the population of a segregated gallery (informally designated the "weak company") in an institution for youthful inmates (N = 30). We also interviewed inmates who were known to staff as having suffered from peer aggression (N = 34) or as having experienced personal crises (N = 28), and we talked to two random samples of inmates to gain baseline estimates of stress (N = 31).

The interviews all contained (1) exploratory questions about noteworthy crises or problems; (2) sequential breakdowns of incidents, perceptions, and feelings; (3) questions about coping strategies; (4) exploration of residual stress, including problems experienced at the time of interview; and (5) questions about requests made by the inmate for assistance, and about assistance he had obtained. We also asked about the person's contemporary environment and his reactions to it.

We spoke to a sample of inmates who had requested transfer from one institution to another (N = 34), using the random interview schedule. We also questioned samples of inmate "experts," including men who were assumed to have been sources of stress for their peers. The results of these interviews are background data, and we are not including them as data sources.[7]

We approached staff members as informants in relation to every aspect of our research problem. In addition, we talked to random samples of officers to get baseline estimates of stress prevalence among prison inmates. These samples of custodial personnel (primarily housing-block guards) were drawn from three major prisons. The combined sample (N = 81) includes the most experienced officer from every housing tier or block of each prison. Only one guard refused to talk to us, but our efforts to record the interviews met with resistance and had to be abandoned 50 percent of the time. As a compromise, we took notes during each interview and dictated summaries after each session.

The officer interviews proved fascinating. The guards gave us no epidemiological indicators but told us much about the range of resources in prison. While some officers were very concerned with mental-health problems, others were not. Widely different pictures of inmates were drawn by officers located in the same, or similar, assignments. Among guards who manned housing units, for example, estimates of crisis prevalence ranged from 0 to 65 percent. The same disparity emerged for officers assigned to special units. One officer in a prison mental-observation ward, for example, noted that all the men on the tier had experienced personal crises in the preceding six months; another officer on the same shift reported a 10 percent crisis rate over the same time period. Similarly, one officer in a punishment (restricted) division described in detail three recent crises experienced by inmates, while his partner assessed the unit as completely crisis-free.

What makes such facts interesting is that estimates of stress go hand in hand with accounts of incidents that the officers had observed and responded to. While there are men who discount stress indicators because they see them as contrived or inconsequential, there are others who are perceptive and sensitive to cues of stress, and who resonate to them. Such officers (who comprised 20 percent of our sample) made such statements as:

In the gym . . . because of the team sport activity and the restricted situation, you can recognize a man real fast if he doesn't participate. This is one of the ways you can tell. If something is bothering him we'll talk

---

[7] We have described the use of inmate research informants to explore parameters of a problem in a spirit of colleagueship (Toch, 1967). Though subjects are generally guaranteed confidentiality, this guarantee is more crucial where we share insights and discuss problem areas that touch on past transgressions of informants.

to him about it and help him if we can and refer him to someone or call someone else.

● ● ●

This is one advantage of having them all the time in the division, you see them all the time and you get to know them. It's the same way if you get an inmate that respects you, you ask them to do something and they'll do it, no problems. So okay, one day you come in and ask him to do something and he's pretty nasty and just about goes and tells you to screw yourself. Now, you know this is not right. You know that right away. You know that something is wrong. Myself, I'll go up to them and say, "You've got problems?" And they may say, "I just got a Dear John letter" or "I just got news that so-and-so died." Or something like that. You can spot it. Or if you have one that's a loudmouth all the time and then, all of a sudden, just like that, he's quiet, and then you know something is wrong. This is when a guy needs a kind word from somebody, because he's hurting.

We asked officers what they had done as well as what they had observed. Many incidents of officer intervention were full of extraordinary detail, and they documented skills both in crisis intervention and in the invoking of other personnel. The following summary is typical:

The incident this officer describes involves a man he says was "sitting kinda funny, slumped over in a depressed manner in his cell looking anything but casual." The officer said this stood out to him because it was just an unnatural way to sit in your cell. So the guard asks, "Are you all right?" At first the inmate gives a half-hearted reply indicating that he's all right and the guard pursues it by saying "well, when I finish my round I'll drop back and see you." And apparently when he drops back there's a certain amount of beating around the bush and then the inmate comes out and tells him that he just got a letter saying that his wife had a Caesarean section and he's a father. But that's all he said. And he doesn't know whether his wife and baby are healthy or well and he's extremely upset by this and uncertain as to what's happening. In addition, he approached another staff member that day regarding his problem and was rebuffed, so he is upset about this as well. . . . Now the officer does a number of things that appear to help this inmate. For one, he addresses the man's feelings of resentment by explaining the constraints under which staff operate—there being a low number of guards and a heavy work load. The guard also tried to point out that the particular officer who treated him very roughly that day might have been caught at a bad time. The officer may not have been trying to be a prick to this inmate. Now as far as the major difficulty that the inmate was experiencing (that is, the uncertainty about his wife and child), the guard saw his most appropriate role there as writing a letter to the counselor and personally notifying the midnight supervisor of the difficulty. The counselor subsequently got in touch with the inmate and clarified the situation. One week later the inmate went out of his way to thank the guard for his concern.

Matching environments with clients includes the deployment of social environments, including staff. Human resources must be selected and placed in terms of skills and interests that match the needs of their clients. This matching includes the degree of the staff's responsiveness to stress cues and its desire to be helpful or to make appropriate referrals.

Analyzing Environments

If we are concerned about environmental "matches" and "mismatches" we must first classify man–environment transactions so that we can pinpoint where they are congruent and where they are incongruent.[8] We must specify what a man requires that his environment furnishes, and what he needs that is absent from his environment.

Our interviews provide portraits of what is valuable and noxious to inmates in prison settings. To understand and compare these portraits, we have to dimensionalize and dissect them. This task, for us, involved immersing ourselves in inmate interview protocols to see whether the preferences and aversions recorded there could be meaningfully "grouped." The result of our efforts was a set of eight hypothetical environmental concerns, which, briefly defined, are as follows:

PRIVACY — A concern about social and physical overstimulation; a preference for isolation, peace and quiet, absence of environmental irritants such as noise and crowding.

SAFETY — A concern about one's physical safety; a preference for social and physical settings that provide protection and that minimize the chances of being attacked.

STRUCTURE — A concern about environmental stability and predictability; a preference for consistency, clear-cut rules, orderly and scheduled events and impingements.

SUPPORT — A concern about reliable, tangible assistance from persons and settings, and about services that facilitate self-advancement and self-improvement.

---

[8] Our use of the term "congruent" is similar to that of Stern, who uses the word to describe environments that respond to personal needs, "producing a sense of satisfaction and fulfillment for the participant" (p. 8). Stern talks of *dissonant* person–environment relationships as resulting in "discomfort and stress."

EMOTIONAL
FEEDBACK

A concern about being loved, appreciated and cared for; a desire for intimate relationships that provide emotional sustenance and empathy.

SOCIAL
STIMULATION

A concern with congeniality, and a preference for settings that provide an opportunity for social interaction, companionship, and gregariousness.

ACTIVITY

A concern about understimulation; a need for maximizing the opportunity to be occupied and to fill time; a need for distraction.

FREEDOM

A concern about circumscription of one's autonomy; a need for minimal restriction and for maximum opportunity to govern one's own conduct.

We coded our interviews (including scale anchors) with these dimensions and found that seven of them "fitted." One dimension (Social Stimulation) dropped out, but no new concept suggested itself as relevant. Chapters 2 through 7 describe and illustrate the seven remaining environmental concerns as they emerged for us in prisons. Chapter 8 shows statistical distributions of these concerns and describes group differences found through content analysis.

We next constructed a forced-choice, paired-comparison instrument based on the eight original dimensions. This instrument and its development and validation are described in Part III of the book, which discusses possible uses of the instrument in prisons and elsewhere.[9] Chapter 12 de-

[9] Excellent instruments that gauge "social climate" of prisons have been standardized and deployed (Moos). These instruments measure Murray's *beta press* (perceived climate), but often yield consensus, suggesting that *alpha press* (the "real" climate) is approximated. The instruments have been used to show that climate differences can produce behavior differences (violence, absconding, recidivism, etc.).

The work of Stern and his associates (Stern) systematically explores student–environment transactions in colleges and universities. Like Moos, Stern deals with consensually perceived (or "third-person"-described) environmental presses. Stern applied Murray's scheme somewhat more comprehensively than Moos. In his studies, he measured personal needs and environment dimensions. Stern maps *needs of different persons in the same environment*, and describes *environments that correspond, or fail to correspond, to the needs of those who inhabit them*.

If we rely on Murray, our instrument partly measures *pressive perception*, which Murray defines as "the process in the subject which recognizes what is being done to him" (Murray, p. 119). When our respondents endorse or reject an item, they tell us about presses that are *relevant* to them. Social Stimulation, for instance, represents the salience of Murray's *vAffiliation* (a friendly, sociable companion), and Freedom shows in *vDominance* (restraint, an imprisoning and prohibiting object).

The primary aim of the instrument, however, is to measure *sentiments*, which are positive or negative *reactions* to press. Our items are sometimes prosaic equivalents of Murray's own items. Our Privacy statements may come close to those designed by Murray to gauge *sentiments of rejection*—items such as "The world is full of people not worth speaking to," and "Society is a hospital of incurables" (Murray, p. 179). Our Freedom dimension could be illuminated with Murray's *sentiment of autonomy* items, which include "Society everywhere is in conspiracy

tails the design of our survey, and Chapter 13 reports the results of our work using the questionnaire.

Part II of this book deals specifically with stress. It describes groups of vulnerable inmates and formal and informal ameliorative settings. It deals with self-initiated and environment-initiated transactions designed to reduce suffering and to prevent breakdowns.

In its totality, this book is a book about prisons, but I hope it is more than that. Each of us, inmate and noninmate alike, is to some extent a prisoner of his environment. Many of the concerns of inmates may be shared by persons who are imprisoned—by choice or otherwise—in other settings. This book may suggest ways in which the generic human condition, irrespective of setting, may be better understood and explores some means whereby it can be ameliorated.

---

against the manhood of every one of its members," "A member of an institution is no more or less than a slave," and "To accept a benefit is to sell one's freedom" (*ibid*. pp. 158–159). Where we deal with stress, we traffic with Murray's *negative sentiments*, with feelings "of aversion or antipathy, of disliking, not wanting, not valuing, not enjoying, hating, scorning, being disgusted, annoyed, or bored by, dreading, or wishing to escape from" (Murray and Morgan).

I

TRANSACTIONS WITH
PRISON ENVIRONMENTS

Introductory Note

The chapters in this section portray the perspectives, or nuances of perspective, of inmates who rank "high" on the environmental concerns we have located in prisons. The inmates we shall refer to are men who strongly prize one of these attributes of environment, meaning that the absence of that commodity creates discomfort for them and that its presence tangibly enhances feelings of well-being and facilitates adjustment.

The orientations we shall delineate are collages of individual testimonials, and they are less neat than one would like them to be for definitional purposes. That is a price we may pay whenever the connotational flesh that we add to conceptual bones is drawn from real life. This price is doubly paid where we deal with strong motives, because these are rarely unidimensional, and are frequently overdetermined. A person who vaguely prefers solitude is thus more simply described than one who fiercely pursues it, and a man who takes superiors with a grain of salt has needs that probably are less contaminated than those of his vociforously alienated peer.

A third problem is that environmental concerns come in packages, while we discuss them one by one. Later, when we discuss *profiles* of concerns, we can accommodate persons who (like most of us) make multiple demands on the world, or must sacrifice some ends to attain others. Where we read those descriptions that follow, we must keep in mind that in real life we are apt to meet several of our subjects under different headings.

What we have tried to provide for our readers is a sense of how a given environment—the prison—can be viewed by persons who make systematically different demands on life generally and on this environment—the prison world—in particular. Later in the book, we shall show how some systematic differences in concern translate into different relationships between men and settings. We can then trace some practical implications of our findings for inmates and for those who imprison and keep them.

2

Too Little or Too Much:
Activity and Privacy

ONE WAY IN WHICH THE EXISTENTIALISTS HAVE CONTRIBUTED to the study of man is by stressing the importance of experiential highlights or *events*. Existentialists have told us that man is not a passive receptacle of experience, that he can *create* events by acting on his environment and by making it react to his actions (Sartre).

We are aware of existential facts from daily experience. Each of us relieves boredom by creating nonroutine experiences through actions. While the wealthy take trips to Europe, some slum-dwelling teenagers steals hubcaps or cars. Housewives may have love affairs, and children can throw tantrums. Such acts modify our environments by broadening the range of our experiences and by reducing the redundancy of our routines. There is also a benefit in sensing one's role as a modifier of environment and through the use of energy that can produce tension if it is allowed to accumulate.

There are many environments that are redundant and eventless. Among these environments are places in which most of us spend most of our time, such as factory assembly lines, schoolrooms, and street corners. There are also places and occasions in which enforced passivity is extreme, such as waiting rooms and static trench warfare (Remarque). Prison cells fall within the range of institutional milieus in which redundancy and routine can be extreme.

William James tells us that during periods that are devoid of highlights our time clock slows down, but that in memory such periods of time seem to speed up. Both facts work against prison inmates. If time in prison is psychologically longer than the chronological sentence of the inmate, his punishment exceeds its prescription. And if time in prison seems short in retrospect, the deterrent effect of imprisonment is reduced.

It is clear that the management of time, the "doing" of "time" is the dominant challenge to the inmate. Individual differences in the way inmates approach time utilization tell us much about the coping styles and coping skills of different types of men.

Activity

Inmates differ in their approach to time through the importance they assign to being distracted, entertained, or actively occupied. Some inmates feel that continuous activity is crucial to their survival. Such inmates rate prison environments in terms of the opportunity that is furnished for them to keep busy.

Activity can serve a number of purposes in coping with the environment beyond those of ameliorating redundancy. It can be a release for feelings, can distract attention from pain or anesthetize, and can keep the mind from being concerned with unpleasant thoughts or memories. Transcending survival needs, activity can provide goals, fulfillment, or scope for creativity.

Activity and Stimulus Deprivation

The eventlessness of prison life over served time is a general stressor for inmates, but it acquires more salience for some inmates than for others. The discomfort of eventlessness includes retrospects of dreariness, feelings of boredom, and a future perspective of redundancy and emptiness:

Cox S 9: What you look forward to is you hear a bell, you wake up, you get ready to go to the job, and you go to school or wherever you're going to go—to school, shop, or line up to go to lunch, go back to the school or shop, what have you, then go back to your cell. And you never have nothing to look forward to as something in the future.

• • •

GHN 15: But it's that confinement, being in one place day after day after day, and nothing new to look at, and knowing that it's going to be the same thing day after day. . . . It gets me very uptight. I'm confined to the same area day after day, and I'm doing twelve years. And just to know that I'm going to see the same thing, see the same faces and be in the same place every day, there's nothing to look forward to.

In addition to noting the redundancy of their experience, men complain about its constricted range, and about the lack of relevant social or human stimulation:

Att R P: Life is going on outside, but there ain't nothing happening inside, if you can make sense out of that. It's like another world. If they took that radio away and didn't let us have any magazines or newspapers, we wouldn't know there was anything out there. Where I'm at, situated in the institution, I can't even see over the wall. I haven't seen a car in I don't know how long.

Such conditions are not only unpleasant on their own account but may have even more unpleasant corrollaries. With restricted stimulation, suppressed ideas and feelings from the preconscious break through, and one's consciousness is apt to be invaded by material that is otherwise out of bounds because it can be disturbing or painful:

Cox S 8: They ain't got no program on Saturdays and Sundays . . . like sitting in that cell on Saturday and Sunday is when I do my most thinking. Laying in the cell, you be thinking about the streets, and there ain't nobody there to rap to until you come out of your cell. They're about the worst days I have in here. But during that week, the week goes this way to me. When it comes to Saturday and Sunday, it takes its time going by.

● ● ●

Att R 26: If I sat in my cell in that little cube it was worse because your mind starts to wander and it will wander from one extreme to the other— you know, from understanding to hate to jealousy to compassion or whatever you want to get into. You just—you just don't know where to go. You want to sit and talk to somebody. You want to sit and cry even, but you can't because nobody is going to listen to you, plus you can't show emotion. It is impossible to show emotion in this place. So what do you do? You go and you walk around the yard and you freeze your ass off—right? Or you go and get involved—anything to keep your mind occupied, right?

There are two related options for dealing with runaway thoughts or feelings. One is to retreat from the immediate environment into fantasy, sleep, or psychosis. The alternate option is to engage in frantic or consuming activity, which occupies the senses with self-produced stimulation.

Activity not only compensates for external stimulus deprivation; it also interferes with internal stimuli by demanding attention for the immediate business at hand, the content of which may be optional or irrelevant:

GH R GG: I don't have that much idle time—if I am not reading books I am practicing my guitar, so I don't waste my time. . . . Times when I don't have anything to do I am very edgy and I get depressed.

GH R P: You can't stop thinking about it. . . . You got to keep busy. I started to make nails. I got a plastic pen and razor and make a nail out of it, and it will take me two hours and then some exercise or something to distract me, and then I am tired, and then I will lay down and I try to go to sleep, and then I find myself waking up, and there ain't no way to get around it, unless you are stone drunk all night.

• • •

GH R A: I couldn't sleep at night and things like that. You know, all kinds of things were going through my mind, you know. . . . The Attica riot would be there, still fresh in my mind, you know. Me seeing people getting killed and like that. Thinking of my brother's death and things, you know. It seemed like about the first six months up there, you know, there was a constant torture coming to me every night, you know. . . . I had to switch it around to the night. Like sleep during the day, you know.

ACTIVITY AS RELEASE

Being busy releases energy. It stabilizes the economy of the body and the mind by discharging tension, modulating moods, and providing point and focus to restlessness. Whereas in a free setting this sort of function is served casually in the ordinary course of work or play, restricted options may create a need for consciously self-arranged regimes that ultimately allow for relaxation and peace of mind:

GH R V: I'm on the go all day long. I don't stop for one minute. I don't stop to relax for a minute. I could never relax. In fact, when it's time to sleep I don't relax and I can never go to sleep.

• • •

GH N 15: I know inmates who just sit and watch TV all day long and all night long, and they could do their whole bit that way. I can't do that. I would prefer to be working all day, and then at night I can relax and watch TV, play cards or write letters. But if I didn't work, if I just sat by the TV all day, I could never do it.

Where stress produces tension, the need for mood modulation is sharper and more urgent. Activity becomes the valve for self-release, self-stabilization, and self-control.

Activity serves this end for feelings that are nonspecific and hard to label, and for concrete reactions to concrete frustrations, such as resentment, anger, and feelings of guilt or self-hate:

GH N 4: See, I got this hobby, glass painting, painting on glass and stuff, and this is my safety valve. It takes time and patience, and it's like a safety valve, it's like an outlet. Where usually a guy will be striking out, you put me here.

Cox S 1: If we want to fight we wait until after everyone is done cutting hair, and about a half an hour before we leave there he locks the door and we fight. . . . It's better than getting into a fight in population: You fight for—what?—maybe half a minute, and then the guards break it up and you get locked up for it. I mean, what good's that do you?

In this context, activity is the constructive equivalent of destructive or self-destructive behavior.

Task Involvement, Ego Involvement, and Self-actualization

Activity can be functional for its own sake—for energy and attention it consumes, for feelings it channels, for distracting or anesthetizing effects. For such purposes, the nature or content of the activity is almost irrelevant, except for the degree to which it expresses feeling, facilitates energy discharge, occupies attention, etc. One prefers the exercise that tires over the one that does not, or the more engrossing of two books. But the basic goal of activity remains that of coping with stress.

Different criteria come into play where activity becomes a tool of the person's "higher" needs—where activity serves the ego as a source of pride or self-esteem by supplying a purpose to the person's (immediate) life, or by helping him to discover, to express himself, to create.

It is not necessarily true that a prison setting must be totally and unredeemably stressful. Meaningful and engrossing activities can be oases of psychological nurturance; they may become dominant, positive features of an otherwise negative experience:

Au R Q: Now, in all the years that I've been in jail, and all the jobs I had, I can honestly say the only—I'm honestly enjoying myself in the job I have now. It's a type of job where the man gives me credit for knowing what I know, he assigns me a job and leaves me alone. This is the type atmosphere that I like even in the street.

• • •

GH R V: I'm taking a course in marketing, and I got interested. So I'll put an hour a night aside and I'll get into the textbook. And I'm enjoying it. Really enjoying it. I never wanted to go to school, school and me just didn't get along. . . . But now I'm taking this college course and it's without any pressure. In other words I'm not forced to do something, get so many credits. Just something I fell into, something I really liked. . . . I'll tell you, I really like it. In fact, next semester I'm going to take two or three. It's going to keep my nights active. I'm going to do a little studying, I'm going to go to school three nights a week. . . . At one time I just figured, what do I need education for? Number one, I got to do this bit,

I'm going to be an old man when I get out. And number two, I did very well without an education. Education didn't hinder me in any way from being successful. But I fell on this thing and I'm enjoying it.

• • •

GH N 4: And as I said, in the last four years, having this job down here, I've been happier than in any other institution no matter if it was outside a wall. Because there's no fulfillment.

At this level, the person may select or reject activities in terms of their ego-enhancing or self-actualizing capacity. He may condemn a status-conferring, lucrative assignment, for example, because it gives insufficient scope for self-expression or is devoid of purpose:

GH R 1: Working in an environment that has no meaning—for instance in the library, which could be considered a good job, and I was working there, and I had to type up numbers on books and put them in a file and do another card, and we didn't even know if the book was there, and it was like I couldn't understand it at all. It appeared to be work for the sake of work, and it didn't have any meaning behind it, and it was inventory time, and it was all mixed up. I thought that the work was meaningless, and I said that I cannot involve my life energies with something that is meaningless, you know.

• • •

GH N 12: This guys comes in and tells me he wants me to write him a writ because they wouldn't give him his sneakers. And I told the guy, "I'm not interested in your sneakers." I said, "If I did write something, you'd be out there playing basketball. First of all, I think it's frivolous anyway, you don't have no leg to stand on, much less sneakers to put on them." You know, this I have to deal with. So he went outside to the officer and he complained to the officer. So the officer comes in and tells me, and I tell the officer I'm not doing it, point blank. I said I'm not out here to serve everybody's needs. I said I've got work to do on my own, I got people that do have a legal beef, they do have a legal question, they do have something serious or something to be worked on. I can't handle all that frivolous stuff.

By the same token an assignment that is objectively menial may prove attractive because it provides a sense of achievement and a feeling of accomplishment:[1]

Au R Q: Industrial body shop, which this is actually the only type of work that I have ever found that I really enjoy doing. It's a form of creating.

---

[1] A superlative illustration is provided by the story *The Bridge on the River Kwai*, involving a British army engineering unit in Japanese captivity that worked enthusiastically on a bridge construction project for the Japanese.

Well, maybe I'm wrong in saying creating. It's working with my hands, which I like to do, and it's taking something, a wreck, and making something usable out of it.

• • •

EI S 8: Every time that you get up in the morning you feel that you're going to work and you don't feel tired and you feel like you're going to work and it's a good feeling. . . . Because I can see a job that I do. See this place, how it is? If you ask me to do it, sure I could scrape it clean and fix it up, and then I could come in and paint it, and that is me. That is my job. And I know that and that is beautiful and I do it right. . . . It's like when—bring up a flower or something, you know that it is there, and you see it growing, and you're proud of it. There is a thing in here that you can say, "Yeah, this is beautiful."

Like other environmental commodities, Activity fills a need for some persons but is a matter of relative indifference to others; and like other environmental offerings, Activity serves the most basic—and the highest—needs of men.

Privacy

Before we discuss our second dimension, Privacy, it may be well to reiterate that (1) even a person who is strongly oriented to one aspect of his environment (such as privacy) reacts positively or negatively to other aspects of the environment; and (2) the multi-dimensionality of environments frequently requires a person to "trade off" a dimension he may prize for another that he also needs. In the words of an inmate,

Au R Q: Well, as far as—see, you got a different type of situation in every prison. Now, maybe one would have the type of peace and quiet that I'm looking for, they might not have the type of work program that I'm looking for.

In a sense, privacy can be thought of as the opposite of activity. Where activity is a means of enriching experience through self-stimulation, privacy involves *reducing* external stimuli to streamline experience and to make purposive adjustment a simpler task. The incentive to privacy is the threat of overstimulation. This threat is "transactional," in the sense that some persons are more annoyed and endangered by stimulus "overload" than others. The need for privacy is related to introspection, for instance, in that a complex inner life demands protection from interference. A young inmate describes this equation by complaining,

Elm N 19: It would all happen at one time. Just too much at one time. And everyone is limited in their brain capacity, in what they can think of at one time.

The desire for privacy is the desire for obtaining freedom from noxious stimuli. Though noxious stimuli can take different forms for different people, the dominant physical form is noise, which the brain has a limited capacity to shut out.[2] In the social sphere, noxious stimuli are apt to involve other persons whose behavior intrudes into our psychological or physical activity, or who demand responses that are alien to us.

The need for privacy as an enduring trait involves rationed and modulated social interaction. The intensely private person lives at peace with himself when he is left to himself. He feels harassed when others demand attention, response, or social contact from him. The picture is that of a precarious equilibrium that becomes psychologically tenable in a self-created sanctuary, where it is possible to control one's thoughts and feelings:

El S 16: I don't open myself up to anyone. I open myself up to a point. Only so far, regardless of who it is. My wife—that is the only person. And besides that, the little bit that I do open up, I give them just something to understand my decision. Don't pamper me. I stopped letting people pamper me now when they know I'm down. All of my personal problems, now I don't say anything. . . . Me personally, when I am in my cell I am at peace; I don't have anyone following me and bothering me. Except when I am in population and I have the officers harassing me and inmates harassing me, and that is the part I don't like. When I am in my shop I don't talk to anyone but myself, only when I have to help someone with work or someone is going to help me with my job. That is when I talk.

● ● ●

Au R G2: Just I don't like to talk unless there is something to talk about and it is something that makes sense; what is the sense in talking about the same old stuff every day . . . and there is nothing to talk about, so why talk? . . . I guess it more or less goes back to the same thing—like, I more or less don't like hanging with just anybody. . . . I never liked hanging in crowds. . . . I was like kind of a loner, and I talked to people and I don't ever mingle . . . like, I don't like to meet a lot of new people. . . . I don't like to categorize myself or anything, but I'm probably pretty low-key.

Paradoxically, there are thus men in prison who imprison themselves beyond the point called for by prison routine, who prize the isolation af-

---

[2] Dr. Donald Kenefick has reminded us of the documentation for this point that is provided by schizophrenic reactions to aversive stimulation, which largely involve sound.

forded by cells, and who seek opportunities for a solitary life or a life involving minimal contact with others. Even where insulation affords opportunity for study or reading, the main benefit often seems to be of "peace" (freedom from excess stimulation) and "relaxation" (modulated feelings and thoughts):

Cox N 15: I am running all over the place, because they keep sending me out in the yard with all those kids that are playing basketball and handball. I am trying to write a report, and the basketball is on my head and people keep tripping over me. It is impossible, and the only time I get to study is three hours from eight to eleven when we lock in at night. . . . I have talked to a lot of guys in here since I have been here, and they all agree that a lot of times they would rather go outside than stay in their cells. The brass always seems to be fresh air freaks or something and don't remember you got the air when you were a child. . . . If you didn't want to do something, you know, like, if it wasn't required, like going to the yard or say skip a meal—if not—that would be kind of nice. Or not attend a program and wanted to relax and stay in your cell and read a book, that would be nice. . . . I don't mind the lockup. I mean, the only thing I would rather spend my time in my cell doing this college program. I would rather do my time in the cell. Like, the way the institution is set up, if the division goes to the yard, everybody goes—you can't stay in your cell. Like, you can't stay there and study. . . . Even when you get locked up, you take your whole cell—all your property, your food—you take your headphones and you listen to the radio and everything. There has been times when I have wanted to get into a fight just to get up there, because this population is so bad . . . just to get away from people.

• • •

Au R G2: I have been here almost two years, and I think that I have only been to night rec only twice. I lock in every night, and I read and I listen to the radio. I got a lot of books, and that is fine, because being a truck driver in the street I was always out at night, and if I wasn't driving I was out monkeying around.

• • •

Cox N 8: I just read a lot of books—get into this masonry thing and this thing at school—that is all I have to do. I don't even have to go to the yard. You know, sometimes I think to myself—all I have to do is go in my cell and stay locked up and read the books that I want to read, and when it comes time to lock out—go to the masonry shop and get this trade together and go to school, and that is it, and I can do that my whole bit.

Specific assignments or features of routine can be prized because they restrict the complexity of the physical and social environment. Such situations, which we shall discuss in Chapter 10, offer havens of privacy or opportunities to regroup or recover from the stimulus overload of the larger environment:

GH R PP: It is very good, because you can insulate yourself for those eight or ten hours from the rest of the institution you know, and plus the fact that I enjoy the work and everything. But when you come back it is a different story. In five or ten minutes you have to readjust and condition yourself to listen to this noise and that noise.

• • •

GH N 13: So there were jobs where you could get away from it. But that would be your aim, to get into that sort of a position and keep it. And they sort of just disappeared. You would have a small group of friends like yourself. And your aim would be to collect a small group of acquaintances and stay with them for as long as you possibly could. Because, you know, you have to face maybe fifteen or twenty or thirty years before you could possibly be released.

CROWDING

A hundred years ago, Thoreau worried about the incursion of civilization on Walden's Pond. Today, the ecology or environmentalist movement deplores the increased density of cities. We talk about the impact of "crowding" and about the need for human "territoriality."

Proshansky *et al.* note that, "given the population explosion and the urban crisis, discussions of the crowded city, home, ghetto, school, highway, hospital, mental institution, and subway have become commonplace" (p. 40). Prisons are more frequently described as "crowded" than other institutions, and crowding is seen as a cause of mental illness, violence, riots, and recidivism.

What does "crowding" mean? Proshansky *et al.* (1972) sensibly point out that

. . . crowding . . . is only indirectly related to mere numbers or density of people. It is possible to feel crowded in the presence of few people, or not crowded in the presence of many. The significant element appears to be frustration in the achievement of some purpose because of the presence of others [p. 42].

This statement is useful for two reasons: (1) It highlights individual differences in sensitivity to crowding, and (2) it links these differences to motives or aims of the experiencing person.

Though men live very close to each other in prison, human proximity *as such* is only rarely mentioned as a concern by inmates. It may be true that men who are *extremely* undercontrolled react—in some social contexts—to intrusions into their "buffer zones" (Kinzel), but the average person has little difficulty adjusting to the physical aspects of close cohabitation.

Where objections arise, they highlight esthetic qualities or social amenities, rather than physical density as such. The issue centers on offenses to the senses, rather than on invasion of space:

Att R 26: Like, for three years I haven't sat without an elbow on each side of me. I never have been able to put my elbows up to the table in three years. It is just a simple thing—you just—you sit down and when you are done eating you get up and you leave or if you want to, you know, after you are done with your meal and sit back with a cigarette, you have a cigarette—which you can't do here. You may be done eating and have to sit there and push together, bodies real close and smell everybody together for twenty minutes before you can get up to move.

• • •

Au R Z: You can just be sitting there, and you know you're not alone. Where I'm at I've got twenty-five guys on the gallery I'm on. So I've got like guys laying there, guys defecating, guys coughing, and it's close quarters. . . . You got guys that don't take showers, and you're around them.

Another crowding concern is with intrusion into what Proshansky *et al.* call "anonymity." One objects to being constantly exposed to the senses of others—to the difficulty of escaping perennial observation. The person here feels invaded, because there are no opportunities for the unobserved discharge of activities defined as intimate, personal, or "private," particularly of activities that are status-degrading, not part of the public image a man wishes to convey:

GH R 1: Well, there is a lack of privacy, and I just came from the county jail and the front of the cell is closed—I put a blanket up there so it afforded me some type of privacy, and privacy is important. And it is strange living in a room with three walls and an open front. It is absolutely no privacy.

• • •

Att R P: These cells with the bars, two or three cells down they can look in and see what you're doing. You got guys that get off watching other guys bathe themselves or use the toilet. I just don't like it.

• • •

Au N B: How'd you like to sit there taking a crap and have five men walking around watching you take a shit?

A third problem with crowding is *noise,* which is an uninvited invasion by others of awareness or consciousness. The concern here is with the fact that (1) one is unavoidably exposed to sensory input selected by others, (2) one is not free to reduce sensory input to achieve quiescence, and (3) one cannot attend to stimulation that matches one's own mood or emotional requirements:

GH R PP: Before, boom—the doors shut and that was the end of the day. Now they are out and running around at nine-thirty and ten at night. . . . The doors shut at four, and that was it. There wasn't all that rapping with the hacks—and the majority of the people, they just did their bits and that is it. I am all for advancing and all that, but this is okay for only the majority of the guys. But what about the guy that just wants to sit down there and doesn't like music or doesn't want to hear all that noise? What about that guy?

PUBLIC ACTIVITY AND PRIVATE ACTIVITY

The point of the discussion so far is that the impact of crowding is on *psychological* territoriality, not only in that the concern is with the invasion of one's senses rather than of one's physical space, but also in that the invasion originates in the purposive behavior of others rather than in their physical presence or occupancy of space.

The prototypical interaction is one in which the invader of privacy satisfies his coping needs and achieves his purposes through *public activity,* which, as a corollary, produces noise. (The noise may even be the object of the activity, as in self-entertainment with music.) The offended individual is one whose coping needs are for *private activity* that does not produce noise, and entails concentration or freedom from incidental stimulation. The social matrix is one in which (1) two sets of personal objectives cannot be conjointly achieved, but (2) the conflict is nonreciprocal, in that only one party can interfere with the other.

The environment is not only the social environment (which consists of persons engaged in public activity), but also the regulatory system that places public and private activity into juxtaposition, or allows for public activity in the subenvironments of high-privacy individuals. This point is made in very eloquent pleas by several inmates:

GH R M: They have dudes going to work during the night and going to school during the day, housing on the same gallery. . . . If you try to study within that time there's too much noise on the gallery. So you can't accomplish anything there. During the day there's so much traffic within the institution that you don't have the time to sit down and follow a train of thought, you can't concentrate for any period of time, because of the interruptions that you receive. And because of that, you can't study. . . . They have rules that after about nine o'clock, everybody ceases talking. But you have individuals that have their own personality that are trying to maintain their own sanity, will go beyond that. And you can't tell a man how to maintain his sanity, especially when you have no idea what he's doing. I don't know what his social problem is, I don't know what his personal problem is, I don't know what his familial problem is, but all that comes into play. And trying to get into a situation where you get away from that, so you can apply yourself to whatever it is at hand: The environments here are not designed for that . . . I used to come into the cell, I used to take toilet paper, right? Put it in my ears, take the towel and tie it around my head to filter out the noise. And as a result of that, I was able to study.

• • •

Au R Q: I might be working on my legal work or something. And you sit there trying to do legal work with some clown moaning and humming or singing in falsetto, it can drive you up a tree. And especially when it's unnecessary, it's just nonsense. I mean, they ring quiet down here, because they ring it for the purpose of giving people a time to do these things. . . . When they rang the bell, they [used to mean] shut up, and that's the way it was. You didn't have any guys whispering and singing and humming and all that. They knew better, they knew damn well that if they didn't shut up they'd be under disciplinary action. . . . It's annoying when you're trying to read to hear the clack, clack, clack of a typewriter. But now there are guys doing leatherwork, pounding. And that can really get on your nerves. So I asked this guard about it, "What's the scoop on the leatherwork?" He says, "Them guys are not supposed to be pounding after the seven o'clock bell." I says, "It's a funny thing, them guys are locking right near this front, and you don't hear them."

The issue arises not only in living areas but also in programs. Even though staff purposes call for a milieu conducive to concentration, these aims may be frustrated by the need of some for emotional discharge or playfulness. In such contexts, it takes inordinate self-insulation for purposive activity—such as learning—to take place.

GH R A: I see that a lot of young dudes, you know, is in Green Haven now, and the majority, all they got on their mind is drugs, you know, talking about pimping, and things like this. This has a psychological effect on a person. You know, he's trying to study at nights, you know. So, the program that I set up for myself as an individual, like, what I did is when I lock in . . . you know, we lock in at five . . . I stay up and listen to the six o'clock news, after the news goes off I sleep until eight or nine o'clock. That's when the quiet bell rings and I wake up and I study until about two or three o'clock in the morning, you know.

• • •

GH R PP: I would love to get involved in the educational or the vocational but there are 30 individuals down there and only two are interested in learning and the other 28 want to jerk off and play around.

• • •

EL S 16: When I was in school, we had a couple of clowns in my class, but the teacher would get all upset and start raising his voice, and it would make it hard for me, because I wanted to learn. I would not let people start raising their voice, because it got me all upset, and I can't stand noise. It makes my time hard. They don't want to continue in school, and they don't want to learn. They just want to clown around. It makes it hard for the teacher. He starts teaching and he does not have to be so upset if they don't have the clowns.

High-privacy persons have need of social environments composed of High-privacy persons. They need to be surrounded by individuals who have "settled down," in the sense of being free of "play," of joyful socializing, self-entertainment, energy discharge, purposeless activity, and rehearsal of skills. Where psychological homogeneity of this kind is not available, there is apt to be a generational conflict centered on varying maturity levels and stages of social development. Such conflicts are inequitable, because the behavior patterns of low-maturity individuals are inviolate, while those of High-privacy persons are disrupted:

Au R Q: Now you got a bunch of kids coming in here, and they got that hurray-for-me and to-hell-with-you type of attitude, and it makes it miserable for everybody.

• • •

Cox S 8: You can do a bit with some guys that know a little bit about jail, not them young kids that they got in here. You can't do no bit around them, because they're motivated, they always want to do something, being in the street for so long, they constantly want to play. That's little kids for you, they always want to be on the move, doing something.

• • •

GH R PP: Generally speaking, you got men coming in and out, and they have nothing on their mind, so to speak. They come in, and all they want to do is go out and horse around, and the guys that are doing something more constructive, it is like they impose on you. . . . They have a few months to max out, and the administration can't do anything to them. They can do what they want to do. Make noise and do this and create havoc. But for the guy that is doing time, he has to put up with this.

• • •

El S 16: This ain't no place for us adults to do time. You know, I am twenty-three years old and I don't even feel that I should be here. They have a lot of young kids here, and you have men that act like young kids.

The impact of heterogeneous social environments drives High-privacy individuals into patterns of adjustment that further increase their retreat into privacy. Such patterns call for personal and social insulation that reduces undesired stimulation. And where High-privacy persons associate with others, they select peers who are similarly oriented and can respect each others' need for low-stimulus havens:

Au R Q: We hang out together, get a group of tables, we hang out together. We don't mix too much with all these crazy kids. . . . The older guys tend to be more clannish, because either you've got to stay away from these guys, otherwise they'll drive you nuts. . . . If I let myself be annoyed by these guys, I'd be angry all the time. So I try to avoid them as much as possible. I find they play excessively—horseplay once in a while, fine, that's all right. There's nobody going to walk around with a long face all the time, that's ridiculous.

c • •

Cox N 15: I just try to fill my time with books and I have had a couple of friends here but they are mostly people like me—just trying to do their time and get the heck out.

PROTECTING PSYCHOLOGICAL INTEGRITY

Incursions by the social environment are not confined to the impact of one man's Activity on the Privacy (or private activity) of another. Heterogeneity poses threats to self-image or self-esteem that is tied to group memberships, or to interactions with nonchosen peers. A person can feel his integrity violated—and be driven to self-insulation—where affiliative links that are available to him are incompatible with his social requirements:

GH R V: Really, I look at these people, I'm living with them, and I manage with them. But had I been on the outside, I'd say half these guys are scum, they're beneath me. Put a gun in their hand, stick up an old lady, you know. I frown on this. I feel like I'm part of society sometimes, and I say, well, a lot of these guys belong here. And putting me in here, or putting a guy like this in here, you can imagine what they go through. Putting them in with all that garbage. . . . Like, I wouldn't hang out with a guy that went out mugging. I would hang out with the more sophisticated type of criminal. Somebody involved in organized crime maybe, or somebody involved with embezzlement. I don't bother with the others. That's how I class my type of people in here. . . . The hardest thing to me here is that I have to cope with some people only because I'm here, it's forced on me.

• • •

GH N 21: Like I say, Green Haven, they seem to throw the garbage, the shit from all the other prisons, they seem to throw right here in this cesspool. . . . In Clinton it's different. You got, like, your own little section, your own little court, your own little spot where you can get away from people and do your time. Here is the only place where I've ever seen that, like I say, you're thrown so close together, everybody wants to do everybody else's time.

Another incursion of the environment is where it contains stimuli that threaten a person's psychological equilibrium. The presence of more privileged persons (especially those who are conspicuous or self-advertising) may reinforce stress by reminding the individual of his hopelessness or low status, or by exemplifying a world he does not own.[3] Visible inequity of status and opportunities is thus a subterraneously stressful feature of social environments:

GH N 4: It all depends on how this guy with three years carries himself. If he's not constantly "Oh, I'm going home tomorrow, I'm seeing the board, I'm going out on furlough," not a constant reminder to you that there is a street out there, and this guy is going out there. . . . Oh, everybody's doing one day, today. You got to do today. So if I've got life and a friend is doing three years, we're still doing today. It's how the individual handles today and his surroundings that affects the life of the long-timer.

Still another incursion of the environment involves seduction or temptation. Tenous self-control is imperiled where emotional discharge or need expression by others reminds one of the brittleness of one's ego or causes stirrings of feeling:

El S 16: I don't smoke and I don't curse, and other people know that. I will be around other people, and they will be talking about evil things, and that will bother me, you know. . . . When they use profanity I don't say anything—I just deal with it knowing that that is the way that we are brought up. The majority of the people when they do speak to me, they know me, they don't curse in front of me or joke.

• • •

Att R 28: Like, I don't ever want to hear a guy talk about a woman, calling her bitch or call her whore or something like this here. I don't like to see people scheming on one another. I don't like to see people beat on one another, or something like this here. I don't like to see a white guy and a black guy calling each other names. I don't like to see a white guy calling a brother nigger, and I don't like to see a brother calling a white guy cracker, this bothers me.

The problem is particularly serious for men with tenuous control of their aggressive or hostile feelings. For such men, social interaction carries the seed of conflict, and physical isolation is the formula for self-control:

---

[3] This feature of "social privacy" has been observed by Glaser, who notes that, where inmates have "high diversity of prospects for release," this drives some inmates to insulate themselves in doing their time (p. 97).

GH N 15: There's going to be trouble or static [when] everybody gets together. I don't want to be bothered with this. I feel I'm over this gang-busting age, you know, I'm not looking to break a head, get in trouble in any institution. And I'm very happy to be by myself.

• • •

Au R G2: I control my temper anyway. I realize guys are doing their jobs even though some of them are a little cocky. So why get on them, as long as they don't physically touch me. . . . That's why I got in trouble and got in here.

• • •

Cox N 8: They play too many games, and that is why I don't want to do my time here, because I will wind up maxing out here because of the inmates, and I got two homies and I don't think I can do a bit with the homies. Like, they are always playing around and this and that and getting a ticket now and then, and I will probably wind up maxing out here.

The problem is compounded by outreach efforts in the social environment. Non-privacy-oriented persons not only encroach by being who they are but also by a propensity to spread their adjustment mode through recruitment. Coping styles conflict where one man protects his integrity by reducing undesired stimulation, while another seeks to cope with understimulation by maximizing information flow and by creating convivial partnerships and social networks:

GH R PP: You see, down here everybody wants to get familiar with you, and like, myself, I want to just be left alone and do my bit—let the administration leave me alone and in general by the population. I got my little game with my jewelry now, and I get my frustrations off with my active sports, and I just want to be left alone, but it is getting to a point now where you can't even play solitaire by yourself. Guys are always bullshitting and hanging around in and around your cell. . . . And these are the type of guys that when you are taking a crap or something they want to talk to you and they want to know everything you are doing.

3

Violence from Without and Within: Safety

OUR DISCUSSION SO FAR HAS SHOWN that what people need around them often depends on what goes on inside them. We prize conditions that help us to control our feelings, to govern our thoughts, and to achieve our aims. Requisites for our external environment relate to pressures in our internal environment.

The search for Safety is, in some respects, the extreme version of the pursuit of Privacy. In both cases, the person's equilibrium hinges on finding sanctuary from others. With the High-privacy person the issue is overstimulation, and the stimulus content is crowding. The issue with Safety is violence.

The content of the Safety concern is that of danger and fear. The aim of High-safety persons is to escape conflict. Their external threat is violence from others, and their internal press is violence from within.

The threat to safety is external danger and the impact it makes on the person who experiences it. The danger and its impact are both sources of discomfort. The combined source is sometimes referred to as "tension" of the environment:

GH N 5: It's the general atmosphere in here. It's like an explosive atmosphere, you know what I mean? It seems like everybody is at everybody else's throat, and it's not easy to live with. You walk up and down the hall, and everybody's shooting daggers at everybody. It's hard to hold a civil conversation with anybody. . . . It's more visible here, it's more visible here than in another institution that I've been in. . . . Tense at all times. And you don't know how to make your next move. If you should make it.

Att R P: Sure, there's always tension. You can walk down the corridor and see static electricity in the hall from the tension. It's only a figure of speech, but you know what I mean.

• • •

Att R 15: There is also a lot of tension there, not only between the officers and the inmates, but also among the inmates too. There is a lot of static jumping off down there. And a lot of the things that they did that I saw there got me emotionally involved, things that are terrible.

Tension must be controlled or discharged; if it is not monitored it accumulates and explodes. High-safety persons tend to see environments as not having enough checks on explosiveness and violence. Inmates in widely different prisons thus often make the point that their respective institutions are excessively "loose" or "lax":

Au N B: You take a young kid coming in a penitentiary, as loose as Auburn is here, he's pretty certain to be taken off pretty fast. Because these kind of people, they'll take you off in a minute. . . . There are animals running around this place. This is not one of these seminaries where you got a highly educated bunch of people. You got a bunch of animals in here. And it's too lax.

• • •

GH N 14: This was a cream puff. Everybody wanted to come in here. . . . Things just got too lax, too loose. You couldn't—like, even now, I've been down five and a half years, and I'm walking down the corridor. If I hear running, I have a tendency to check it out. Because the only time a man is running in the hallways, when I say a man I don't mean these jitter-bugging kids that are fucking around playing tag or something like that. I'm talking about when a man is running he's either chasing somebody or somebody's chasing him. There's got to be something to it.

• • •

Cox S 1: They have a lot more liberty and they can go around carrying shivs and if someone don't like you that's all there is to it.

Where lack of control is not a pervasive feature, it is seen as a feature of particular people within the environment. In this view, there are groups of people whose self-control is manifestly negligible or weak. Such people are feared because they are apt to explode promiscuously. They may attack or victimize upon slight and unpredictable provocation. They may be mentally ill or emotionally unbalanced:

Att R 37: I'll tell you the truth, this is the only institution that I've seen in my life, how people that they are sick mentally, walking around with other people that are in the right state of mind. They have these people over here that they's sick, I mean they're supposed to be in the hospital, not in an institution like this. . . . They've got them walking around here. You can see, like, let's say lifting weights, right? You got to be watching your back. You don't know when this man might break out and you got three hundred or some pounds on top of you, and he might kick your head off or throw something. You got to be looking for these people, looking out for these people.

• • •

Att R 38: You can understand, they get in here, and they get locked up and they get depressed, they get depressed. They get violent. . . . I say, everybody in here is sick to a certain extent. Everybody in this institution is sick. Even I'm sick, I know I'm sick. . . . I know that I was like this, so when I see a guy like this here, I just say, well, I was like that too. You try to stay away from them, but you can't. There's so many here like them.

• • •

GH R H: I had to get off the tier because a guy that sets fire to a book for nothing, there must be something wrong, and I can't figure out what's in his mind, so I had to get off. . . . I said, "Captain, this was where I was before, and I had trouble here, you know, and I wanted to go to another jail, man, because this other guy, he must think it's a joke to him to burn things." Guy comes down and sets everything on fire, and everybody starts laughing, and stuff like that. So I told him, "I got to get off here, man." . . . I told another shift that I didn't like this tier either, because I don't like it . . . it was a homicide tier, you know what I mean?

Emotional disequilibrium or loss of control in others may sometimes be ascribed to stress. In this model, the environment acts on dangerous people, and it subjects them to pressure that makes them dangerous:

GH R P: Well, the lifers make it difficult, because you can never tell when they are going to be tired of doing their time, and they don't go nowhere, because this institution keeps them here. . . . They either escape as you see they have done before, or they turn against another inmate.

• • •

GH R P: See, but something may jump off, and your wife may die, and you may not receive the letter, and you will turn on me, and I wouldn't understand that. You would be grouchy one day, and I feel good, and why should you be grouchy? Or we are both in grouchy moods, then you may have static.

A double control issue is posed where the environment contains controllers who may (as the fearful person sees it) run out of control themselves. A prison or hospital inmate can begin to see his keepers as potential sources of violence. This view is harrowing, because it (1) removes the most prominent source of institutional stability and control, (2) makes for an environment that has a person totally at its mercy, and (3) places danger at the doors of men who are potentially effective threats:

GH N 7: You always have the impression that any time of the night they might hit your cell for some reason, and something might happen to you. You never know. That makes you very uncomfortable also. That existed in Comstock and it existed in Clinton. You never know when they're going to hit your door and for what.

• • •

GH N 21: I left there in 'sixty-seven. They never have to worry about me coming back to a mental institution. Because I had never knew that stuff like that could ever exist. I used to hear about it, and I used to say, "Well, these guys have got to be lying for what they're saying," but when I seen it there, forget about it. It's the only place I've seen where a person gets sick and they try to kill you. I couldn't believe it. I saw things, like I tell you, they don't have to worry about me, because every day when I was in the bughouse, I went to work just to get off the hall. They had no problems out of me. . . . The officers are mean. I was doing pushups one day, and the officer says, "What, are you getting ready for me?" I couldn't do no more pushups. . . . I was scared to death over there. And, like I say, I've never seen nothing like it before in my life. I seen guys, one old man about sixty-five years old, I seen four young hacks put this guy in a strait jacket and beat the living hell out of this guy, and then throw him down the stairs. And I tell you, when I saw that, every time they came up to me it was, "Yes, sir" and "No, sir" and "Do you want to go off the hall to work?" Yeah, man, every day.

• • •

Att R P: There was a guy in a cell with blood all over the place. They took him out of his cell and put him in the hospital, and when he got out of the hospital they put him in the box. And they had the audacity to say that he had done it to himself. There aren't too many inmates that'll take a razor blade to their face.

Total institutions pose another threat in the control that they can exercise—and can fail to exercise—over life-preserving or life-sustaining functions. From a fear-ridden perspective, malevolent neglect by staff or peers can place an inmate's physical existence at risk:

Att R 38: The doctors they got here, right? They tell me that in the last six months or something, ten guys have died. . . . If a guy's dying and a doctor could save him, he won't get saved.

• • •

Cox S 8: And that mess hall, I was back there one day, and these guys back there, they're the type of guys, if you don't know what they're doing back there, you could wind up eating something that you're not supposed to eat. I seen guys back there, they be cleaning the food, they're only halfway cleaning that food. They just throw it in, cook it up some old way, drop it right on in there, and take it and give it out to somebody.

• • •

GH R P: Us inmates are worried that they are going to lock this place up, because the food is getting so short in this prison, and they are worried about they might lock this goddamned place up for that.

The Impact of Perceived Threat

The High-safety person lives in a world of low trust, high vigilance, uncertainty, and discomfort. Danger occupies his mind, circumscribes his actions, and governs his awareness. The anticipation of cues to danger makes the environment a map of open areas one must traverse between precarious and very temporary sanctuaries. It makes life a matter of being tensely and continuously on guard against dangers one cannot hope to locate, to anticipate, or to guard against:

Cox S 2: Here if you go in your cell, you got to think about the next day, how's it going to go? If you go in a shop, is some guy going to be waiting for you with a pipe, is something going to happen? When you come back to your cell, is your stuff going to be in your cell?

• • •

Au R DD: In a place like this you don't know who to trust. The main thing is you don't know who to trust, and with the small population you know everybody, you get to know everybody, and you know who to stay away from, but every day I see faces that I never seen before, and I have been here for two months.

With accumulating tension the link between external and internal violence may become explicit or manifest. The individual finds himself harboring violent thoughts and feelings or may sense himself nearing an explosion point. He may feel a need to seek protection from himself or may become concerned about harm he might do:

El R BB: This is when all the tension just builds up in you over the months, and one day you feel tense, and you put the earphones on, and bam, too late though, you break down, and bam, you beat on the wall. It be all that tension, you know. . . . Well, it's just tension. The tension builds. You know, if too much tension builds up in you, and you get tired of beating your walls, and it still don't come out, then sometimes you might get that urge to do something evilish then. To relieve that tension, regardless of what it is. So you might get in that keep lock, so you don't get in no trouble. That's the safe way. When it comes down you're ready to do something, you say, "Give me a keep lock." And relax.

Att R 38: Just like the riot, that's what messed me up. When I got out on the street I started having nightmares from when I seen the dudes get killed and stuff like that, and I started drinking. I tried to avoid drinking, but, see, when I drink I forget about the problems. . . . Take a guy here, you come here—right?—when you're young. You come here, and there's older people here. He listens, and he don't never hear nothing good. He only hears that they killed somebody, they're going to rob this here, they're going to do this here, they call a woman a bitch. And a guy, subconsciously, he inherits all of this in his mind. And he starts acting like this too. Not that he wants to, but he be around day and night, around people like this here, and he start acting like this too. Acting like an uncivilized people. And when he gets out, the impression that he had built up in here, and when he gets out it explodes. Especially if he drinks, and all the problems that was in here, whether people knows it or not, all the problems that a dude gets in here, when they get in the streets, see, they freak.

Sometimes a frustration–aggression mechanism is at work, where the person feels retaliatory urges (particularly against controlling agents in the environment), which threaten to break through messily or violently:

GH N 19: I've been talking to the doctor, and, like I told him, just like I told you, life can get to a point where I'm not going to be able to control myself. And, like, if I do anything in here, I'm not going to be held responsible for it.

I: Would this be like violence against other people, or against yourself?

GH N 19: Against either. Because, you know, I keep thinking, like, man, they accuse me of assaulting an officer, which I didn't do. They accuse me of assaulting a doctor, which I didn't do. Maybe I should do it. Get a payback or something.

● ● ●

GH R R: If you just keep a man confined, so much pressure builds up on him, and the least little thing happens, he's like a time bomb, he blows up. He holds it in, he keeps holding it in. He's responding to a negative thought coming from a correctional guard. It's one of them things like, if you hit him now, they're going to take you off the count. So what you do, you just hold your head, be cool. And you just wait. But some guys can't hold it down too long.

A more immediate issue is posed by the option of responding or not responding with violence to violence. We shall see in Chapter 9 that Safety is very often seen in fight–flight terms. Fight, however, may entail (1) the threat of retaliation from one's victim, (2) a potential loss of self-control, and (3) a response of the larger environment, with a loss of status or safety:

GH N 21: The man has never really threatened me, but to avoid a problem for him and I—see, that's why I did ten years before, a lot of problems like hitting guys. I knew if the man approached me it would be a serious thing. I'm not running out of fear from him. I'm just running, I'm afraid if he does approach me somebody's going to be hurt very bad, in this crowd or the crowd that I'm in. Put it like this, I don't want to do anything because I still have eight and a half years to be in jail. . . . See, my brother, he's with organized crime, I'll put it to you that way. . . . You're not by yourself. So I know if I go out there it's going to be a war. And I know, whether I get hurt or not, it's going to jam me up bad, where I'm going to wind up CR, and I'm trying to avoid this.

Exercising the Flight Option

Despite its perceived liabilities, the flight option may be exercised by the High-safety inmate. He may seek physical sanctuary in a subenvironment (should it exist) in which he is protected, or where the peer group is low-pressure and nonthreatening:

GH N 15: I wouldn't leave this place if they offered me a thousand dollars, or a million dollars. It wouldn't pay to leave. Because there is a sense of security here.

• • •

EI N 1: I'm away from the population and I have peace of mind. I'm not always looking over my shoulder. In here you never know what is going to happen next.

I: So you feel that your job assignment is beneficial?

EI N 1: Yes, very beneficial.

Another flight option is to withdraw from social intercourse or to restrict contact to a subgroup who is nondangerous:

Au R AA: Just mind my business, man. . . . You know, avoid unnecessary static. . . . If you mind your own business and don't fuck with nobody, you won't have no trouble. . . . Me, personally, I don't have no trouble.

• • •

EI R BB: If you're stupid enough to get involved with it, and knowing that you can get in trouble doing this and doing that there. If you're that dumb enough to go ahead and do it, then you deserve—if you stick your hand in the fire that's hot, you're going to get burned.

A third retreat option is psychological and involves restricting the range or intimacy of communication. While maintaining himself in physical circulation, a man may insist on superficiality and reserve in all of his contacts with others:

Au R DD: I am out in the streets, and the people that I hang around with, I trust them. I am not used to this, you know—like wanting to know who you talk to, you know, and all that. I have to change now, and I have to be careful what I tell someone, and most things I can't even tell to people, because I might be in a spot, you know.

Any retreat option has two liabilities. One is that a person may find it hard to reconcile a flight strategy with a self-image of autonomy or potency. The second liability revolves around the person's public image.

A person with High-safety concerns may be stigmatized to begin with, because victimization tends to go hand in hand with a reputation for weakness, cowardice, or explosiveness. In this connection, flight can ameliorate physical danger, but it can also exacerbate a man's stigma. Where a sanctuary protects, it also poses the question of how a man is to view himself when he leaves or when he rejoins the outside world:

GH N 21: I've always had a good name for myself, what they consider in jails and everything. And it's hard. . . . Maybe my mistake was the way I was brought up, with so-called wise guys. And I always got stuck in prison with them. Maybe if I got stuck with the so-called creeps, who I think are the best guys, maybe I would have never come back to jail again. . . . Well, what they consider like a creep is a guy that's not with the so-called guinea mob, a guy that's not pushing dope or who thinks like that. A guy that just came in for a jive crime, he ain't with nobody in the street, so he's supposed to be a creep. . . . It's hard, because, when you come to protection, right away everybody puts you down you're a stool pigeon. And it's uncomfortable, and you really can't talk when people know—it's hard to explain, it's just that you get a name. "I don't know why he's up in protection, but I think he's a stool pigeon, he ratted on somebody." It's not easy, especially when, like I said, you been a good guy all your life, with the so-called good people. People start saying "I can't believe Denny—" . . . They'll make you feel it, because a lot of times you'll walk into a room or something, and guys will be talking in a corner, and right away everybody will stop. And right away you feel like a weasel. If you feel, like I said, like me, I'm right from the old school, where I say it was tough. If a guy was a rat, he was hurt.

The Safety Cycle

We shall discuss the problem of prison victimization in Chapter 9, but a review of one individual case may help us better to understand the Safety concern of the obsessed inmate. The case is relevant here, because it highlights the relationship of environmental "threats" to individual "concerns" and environmental "solutions."

Our victim is a twenty-year-old white property offender serving a four-year sentence at Auburn prison. He is a parole violator with a juvenile record whose institutional experience includes three years in an orphanage. He is tall (6 feet), of normal build (153 pounds), with some education and normal intelligence.

Auburn is an institution with a substantial client age range, and it can make a young inmate conscious of his youth. "Here I am, like, younger than everybody out there," our man tells us, "and I just got to watch myself more, you know. I just can't slip. I just can't say the wrong thing."

Constant vigilance reaps its perceptual result in the shape of repeated "evidence" of danger:

Well, see, the first day I came in here—I walked in the reception area, and I was standing down there, and I seen this guy, you know. This black guy just staring at me—just staring at me from about 6 feet away. And he started smiling. And I knew—I have been around, you know, and I have been through all of this before. And he started smiling, and I see him go away and talk to somebody else, and he was whispering, and I knew right off what was going on.

• • •

No one actually approached me, but I heard things running around, like so and so would say something, and they would come back and tell me, but a few instances like that—nothing that I would really worry about, but I had to watch out for it.

• • •

Like my hair was long and everything, and I looked about sixteen years old, so I used to go to the mess hall and everybody would stare at me. I don't have no complex, but, gee—when everybody is staring at you— how can you miss it, you know? So I figured that the best thing would be to do was to cut my hair, so the next morning I got up and cut it. . . . It eased up after a while, and I realized that there are certain people that stare at you all the time. . . .

You try to be calm if you can, but you can't, because it really bothers you. Like, I will see some people out there talking, and they look my way, and right away—they are talking about me, and I don't know what to think.

As fear builds up, the young man has thoughts of trying to escape into a segregation setting, possibly permanently. He holds this gambit in reserve, but rejects it as an immediate option. His reasoning here follows lines similar to those we have already discussed:

When I first came, I wanted to go to protection, and then I started to think, and I found that if I do that, you know, once they transfer you out it will be on your record that you were in protection . . . and then you have a bad name, and they make you look like a punk or something, so I figured that I had just better stick it out. So that is why I didn't go to protection. . . .

Like, I have been taking chances all my life—like going out there and steal and petty stuff, you know, and I am in jail—just by taking chances. So that I am taking a chance being in the population, you know. And, like, if I hear today—if my friend comes up and tells me that he heard that they are going to jump on me—I will go and lock right in. I won't come out. Why take a chance, you know? I have been taking chances all my life.

To be sure, there are some saving factors in the picture. For one, the presence of guards is reassuring because it reduces the chances of a physical attack. There is also the fear-reducing counsel of friends, who raise questions about the seriousness of actual danger:

Like, I will go and call up my friend, and I will go and tell him, and he will say, "Don't worry about it—they ain't going to bother you." I guess that I am paranoid. I tell everybody that I am not, but I guess that I am, you know.

On the other hand, the help one gets is not all equally helpful. There are those who increase one's distrust by raising questions about the credibility of other men. And there are those (both among staff and peers) who stipulate the inevitability of violence, and who advocate a "fight-fire-with-fire" approach to the problem:

Like, this one guy that I was talking to out there, he seemed like he was all right. He was an Italian dude like me. A little bit older, but we are both Italians and we should look out for each other. So he looked out for me. And then I had this other guy come up and say, "What is happening? Don't turn your back on him, because he might do something to you, you know." I don't know what to think, because here this guy is going and being nice to me, and this guy is telling me to watch out for him. Like, I don't know what to think. . . .

I: So you have had an opportunity to discuss this with one of the officers? And he understands the problems?

Yes. He told me—I told him that, like, when I came I had a knife and all that, and he told me that I had better put it up or better use it. "Just don't pull it out, you know, because if you pull it out and scare somebody—it will make them leave, but the next time they come up on you they will have something, and you might not have yours, and that is that. So if you are going to pull it out—use it." . . .

And then, like, I met this one guy from New York and he was a nice guy. He was about twenty-four—not much older than me—and I found out that I could trust him, you know. And he had apparently the same kind of problem, but not as bad as me. And we would talk and talk, and he would say, "Don't worry about it. If anything comes of it—just jump on the guy who bothers you, you know."

Both types of advice dovetail with one's concerns. They reinforce the sense of one's impotence and add to the disquieting feeling of being out-manned and outgunned. They increase one's awareness of the violence and malevolence of others, compared to one's babe-in-the-woods innocence.

One here buys the assumption that violence is the only way of counter-ing or preventing the violence of others. If one is unsure of one's fighting prowess one can at least appear capable of violence by acting circumspectly, by behaving seriously, and talking tough:

I would say that it is making me act a lot more older, act more mature and everything. Like, really, on the streets I am immature, but in here I don't do those things like fooling around and stuff like that, because the first wrong move that I make it costs me, you know. . . .

Like, I don't fool around. I don't say nothing. If you just walk up and don't say nothing, they won't bother you, because they won't know what to expect. You know, like karate or black belt or something like that. But if you are always fooling around and playing around, they know that you are nothing but a talker and, you know, you are always trying to make people think you are a tough guy, but when they know what you are they will try to put it over on you. But if you keep quiet and don't say nothing, they don't know what to expect, and they don't bother with you. So that is mainly what I am trying to do. . . .

Like, I will be standing in line like so. I will stand up straight and put my chest out a little bit to give them like a good impression that I am not a little kid and all that stuff, you know. I make sure that my hair is straight up and everything, and I am always thinking. Every time that I walk by the mess hall I say, "I wonder how many are looking at me, and I don't want them to see me then like this." I say this to my friends—when one of them is fooling around I literally punch them back, because there are always people there to see that.

This pose is carefully thought out but has two serious defects: (1) It deviates from a self-image of carefree playfulness, suppresses urges, and causes strain; also (2) how can one convince others with a performance about whose credibility one has one's own serious doubts?

In here you have got to perform. I am not myself in here. If everybody just left, I would be out there fooling around and playing basketball, but now I just walk around and keep my mouth shut. . . .

Here I consider myself a phony, you know. If I am in camp, I run around and have a good time, and here I just walk around with my head down, and I don't hardly say anything to anybody.

The strain of such a pose exceeds its benefits. To secure relief, one must resort to the seeking of staff help. To reduce the implication of dependence this entails, one claims that violence includes one's advertised potential for lethal retaliation:

I went to him to see if he could call someone—the service unit, because I had been dropping slips, and nobody was talking to me or nothing. And I had to talk to somebody, you know, because I was afraid that something was going to happen, but this way—like, if I hurt somebody bad I had some type of reflex. I could tell the guard to say—come to the adjustment committee, and, "I told him what would happen if you did not get me a transfer"—and, "I told you what would happen and now you can't blame me for it."

A staff member receives a plea for help. When we talk to him later, he remembers his solution, which consists of removing the inmate from population and placing him in a succession of "niches" (cf. Chapter 10):

He had been approached by unknown individuals, if he would be interested in homosexual activity. The way it occurred is, when he came into the program committee, I don't know—a feeling or sixth sense just said to me, you know—"This is a weak one, and I think, you know, that he can have problems." So on a direct question he had admitted to me that he had a problem, and he wanted to—he didn't want protective custody—he didn't want to have the population think that he was coming back out of the situation, but he just wanted to be put off to the side someplace. So at his request we marked him in idle for about two weeks, and then I called back for the program committee, and he was assigned to the storehouse butcher, which is one of these isolated sections. And after about a week he came back to me, and he said, "Well, I think I have got it under control, and I would like to now go to another area," so he is presently up in the silk screen shop learning the silk screen process.

In considering environmental options, the advantages (in this case, safety) must be balanced against the liabilities, such as stigmatization. Ultimately, some compromise can be achieved of the two:

And (Idle Company) is kind of good, you know. You know, really, I wanted to stay there, but I figured that I wouldn't ever get a chance to get transferred if I stayed in Idle. It looks bad, you know.

I: It looks like you are a fuckup?

Yeah. It goes on your work record. So I got out of there, and they offered me another good job in the butcher shop, and I turned it down, you know. So I went back and I went and told my friend of the offer, and he said, "What, are you crazy? That is a good job that he offered you," so I went back, and they gave it to me. . . .

You know, it is not too bad in the utility room. It is all white people, and it is pretty good.

I: So when you are working, do you feel relatively relaxed about this?

Uh, yeah, because, like, I work in the utility room, and I know that nobody is going to run up on me. And, like, there is always something to grab around there if I have to protect myself. I feel safer up there. I have been up there about three weeks, and there has been no problems.

The solution that is achieved for this inmate includes not only freedom from external danger, but also congruence of self. The inmate speaks to us of an environment in which "you can be yourself and you can talk to people and you can trust people."

Admittedly, the cards in this case are somewhat stacked, because the situation is much less extreme than are others we could review. On the one hand, the "objective" danger is less than that encountered by inmates who are subjected to overt threats (Chapter 9). On the other hand, there is less struggle with violent impulses, less of a Freedom issue, and more openness to Support than in other case histories.

The dynamics of the situation, however, are reasonably representative. A man is presensitized to violence and scans the world for cues to danger. He feels powerless, fears the unpredictability of other men, and withdraws. He also feels tension and must struggle with feelings about himself. Violence and its control become the main theme of the inner and outer environment. The man–environment match that must be achieved includes not only physical safety but the facilitation of an adjustment mode that permits self-modulation, relaxed impulse control, and trust.

4

A Concern with Positive Feelings: Emotional Feedback

THERE ARE MANY REASONS WHY "Man is not an island unto himself." He is dependent on others as a child, and he requires sexual partners with the onset of puberty. Group memberships provide him with identity, and organizations supply him with a role. He must exchange goods and services with others or lead a life devoid of amenities.

Of such links, the bond of mother and infant shows (1) the strongest need for intimacy and positive feeling, and (2) the heaviest component of unilateral dependency. Beyond this stage, persons vary greatly in the extent to which they are emotionally involved with others and in their admission of a nonreciprocal need for personal links.

Intimacy and dependence tend to be interrelated wherever they occur. Where we are emotionally tied to someone, we are always dependent on their emotional support, and we admit our lack of self-sufficiency in the area of feelings. We also place ourselves at the mercy of our intimates, who can affect us by breaking the vital bonds that link us to them.

Psychoanalysis has shown that, where we are most closely and intimately linked to others, the types of bonds we form are infused with our earliest experiences. We tend to "replay" positive links of our childhood, while we create problems for ourselves and others through the re-creation of childhood traumas.

It is also probable that those of us who are most oriented toward intimacy carry the strongest investments or the heaviest burdens from our infancies. We continue to need nurturance, and we feel inadequate ("lonely") in isolation. To live our emotional lives, we need emotional feedback in the shape of positive affect or through recognition of, and response to, our feelings.

51

Persons concerned with Emotional Feedback see their ideal environment as "warm," responsive to moods and feelings, supportive of psychological change, or interested in the individual's happiness or personal adjustment. Crucial to this orientation is the availability of truly significant others, of human beings who care. A person "high" on Feedback prizes his links with other persons, particularly the links that are intensive, intimate and nurturing.

In total institutions the immediate environment may not only be a perceived source of emotional feedback, but also a mediator of feedback from the "outside." A High-feedback inmate may look to his family as an important, sustaining source of love. If he has this perspective, his physical environment—the prison—becomes the key link in a feedback chain and acquires importance for its gatekeeping to the outside.

The Environment as a Mediator of Feedback

Goffman has defined the "total" institution as one that furnishes a "barrier to social intercourse with the outside" (Goffman, p. 4). Prisons clearly furnish such barriers. Though many prisons have gradually increased their permeability by lifting censorship restrictions and by liberalizing visiting rules, an inmate's contacts with outsiders is usually rationed and relatively sparse. The degree to which this fact remains salient for inmates and the extent to which it impinges on their adjustment vary greatly from inmate to inmate. With some Feedback-oriented men, writing and receiving letters not only is the most significant feature of their routine but becomes the weathervane to their mood, disposition, or ability to cope. Outside communication is an impinging force to which the remainder of life can be inextricably subservient.

The absence of contact can create a psychological vacuum; its presence can be a mood modulator or safety valve:

Att R 26: Writing a letter to me would be a—it takes a lot of pressure off. It seems like you are talking. . . . It feels like you are actually transmitting through the words, and it seems to take the place of somebody that you don't have to talk to—you have nobody to talk to.

• • •

GH R U: They calm me down at night; we get letters here at night. . . . If I don't get a letter that night, I'm unbearable to live with all the next day.

I: What do you do when you don't get a letter?

GH R U: I'm moody, I don't even rap to people. Fortunately, I got one last night, so I'm all right.

GH R U: The thing I want from them is that communication. In their letters I want to know everything that they do, everything that they experience. If they go to concerts or anything, I want to know it, because this is youth that I've missed. And they give me this youth. Actually I'm them, even though they're broads.

I: And this makes you less angry?

GH R U: Yeah.

Visits can also acquire complex subjective connotations, and the environment's accessibility or its facilities for visiting can emerge as its key features:

GH R M: A word exchange, a caress, a stroke, the verbal reinforcement, and the verbal assurance that they can get on a one-to-one physical basis, would be more beneficial and more instrumental in dealing with the problem than to try and sit down and deal with it in terms of a letter. Because a letter doesn't convey no emotions, no direct emotions, anyway. To sit down and see an expression in the face or see emotion building, to see the inhibitors actually at play. To see not being able to get out a word because the emotion is so powerful that it has me nonplussed. Those things are very essential. You can deal with that basically on a personal level much better.

● ● ●

Att R 26: There is human contact, and it doesn't have to be sexual—it is just to be with someone that you—just to hug someone. Your children or your wife or your girlfriend—just to touch somebody.

Where Feedback is a core concern (with the outside world as its focus), breaks in communication act as disequilibrating forces. Interruptions of contact are crisis promoting, and even short lapses of contact can lead to depression, worry, confusion, or obsessive concern:

Att R 26: It takes three days to get a letter from here to Buffalo, you know. You know what can happen in three days?

● ● ●

GH R V: There was a number of things on my mind, the last month, we'll say. My children aren't writing to me. They were writing once a week, corresponding regularly, and then all of a sudden they dropped out, stopped writing.

● ● ●

GH R P: If you don't get the visit or the mail or the phone call, then you are damned. I ain't got no mail in three weeks, and then, boom, there is nine letters, and I looked at the officer and I laughed.

Feedback Ruptures: Threats to the Feedback Loop

Feedback issues in links to the outside arise for inmates to whom these links are the perceived requisites for survival, with the ever-present risk of loss or abandonment. Physical separation means not knowing how people feel about you and not being able to do anything about it. Time connotes an irreversible increase in social distance, a loosening of links whose restoration may prove impossible to achieve:

Au R 29: Right. Well, see, by her not seeing me, by my not being around at all, the relationship starts to go further and further apart. And our relationship is way apart now, and I'm trying desperately to hold on. It's the only family I have, my wife and kids, and they're having it very rough out there.

• • •

Au R 29: Now, he's gone from the arm to one and a half. And he doesn't know his father. I feel if I was closer to the city, which I'm trying to do now, that possibly I could hold my family together a little more. There's this thing, I've been away in jail so long that my wife feels that, I can tell she feels that she's capable of handling herself more better, she's become self-sufficient. This might cause a little static between us when I get out. And the kids, my oldest son, he knows me, but there's so many things that he's missed, I've missed. I've lost some of the important parts of my younger son's life. And my older son, he was three and he's almost six, in May.

Married inmates may have to struggle with a sense of vulnerability of their marital bond. They may oscillate between efforts at self-reassurance and periods of depression, jealousy, or of nagging feelings of helplessness:

GH R P: Did she leave me, and is she fucking with this other man? And any guy that tell you that he don't think that his wife is having sex is full of shit, you understand, but then you walk in them doors and you think—well, soap and water cleans everything. That is a Spanish saying, and you go back, and it will be all over. There is not problem. . . . Uptight is the word.

• • •

El R 2: I feel like my wife is away from me, and she might leave me.

I: So do you get ideas that she is running around in the street?

El R 2: I get that idea, and I write her a letter, and she says no, and I get all kinds of ideas, like if something happen to my mother, and I am not there and not around.

I: And sometimes you feel like hanging up?

El R 2: Yeah.

The most tangible prison crises (the ones most familiar to staff) are those where marital or quasi-marital bonds are in fact ruptured and where the tenuous equilibrium supplied by mail or visits breaks down. Feedback concerns may become dominant even among nonfeedback inmates if being abandoned by someone draws their attention to the vulnerability of their support systems:

GH R V: Oh, I was in bad shape as it was then, but I tell you, I came out of that visiting room—well, I knew, I seen it coming, because we weren't getting along before I came in. And I knew the first opportunity that this was, I sort of felt it. But I was in bad shape. A few nice guys talked to me and tried to cheer me up a little bit. The only reason I didn't hang up—because I tell you I was ready to hang up, I had definitely made up my mind, in fact if I knew that I would be in prison three and a half years already, I would have hung up then. But now I take it a day at a time.

• • •

Cox S 8: That's when I cut my wrists, on Saturday morning. I was thinking, I let my mind go. Before I knew it, it was this . . . I was thinking about this girl. I had got some news from this girl. Like, she didn't send it to me, she sent it to her brother, and her brother's here. She didn't want to tell me, she told her brother to tell me. So he showed me the letter, and I kind of let that get me upset.

• • •

Au R 22: It was hurt that made me do it. And my ex-wife, I was living with her at the time, and we had problems constantly—well, anyway, we broke up. And I was hurt by that. Hurt to be away from my children and my family, just like losing my whole life. And that's when I started working on my mind.

Feedback is by definition two-way, and being unloved may imply one's failure to earn love. Conversely, unearned love raises questions about one's continued entitlement to love. This issue arises particularly for inmates whose significant others face problems of their own:

Att R 26: My wife had come to see me Thanksgiving Day, and she sat in the visiting room for two hours and just started to cry. You know the pressures of raising the kids—trying to raise them right, you know, and she doesn't get out to go anyplace. She just—it wasn't like she was missing sex or anything—it was just that she wanted somebody to lean onto, and so she sat there for two hours crying, you know. And you figure that, any time you see anybody cry for two hours, you figure, you know, they are ready to snap.

• • •

GH R M: My problem was my inability to be useful in terms of my family. In terms of kids that I left in the streets. Not being able to give them some of the things that I felt that they need. Especially like material, psychological support, emotional support. Not being able to give them that. Not knowing what was happening to them every moment of every hour of the day, not being able to read beyond the things that I received in letters that said the kids are all right, I'm all right, the family's all right. Not being able to see the problems that they was going through, the changes, the emotional strains that they were going through, and not being able to deal with that.

The issue of one's potency also arises for inmates whose free-world sense of identity and worth is tied to their role as providers, nurturers, or influential family members. A twenty-eight-year-old New York City property offender serving a twelve-year maximum sentence at Auburn prison is a case in point:

Au R 29: For Christmas, I couldn't send my family nothing. Easter Sunday, I couldn't get my kids nothing. My son's birthday is the fourth of May, he ain't getting nothing. What can I send him, a dollar and a quarter? That's barely enough for me to get cigarettes and stuff, to last for the next two weeks till I go to the store again. So as far as my home, "Daddy" is just a word that doesn't exist. "Husband" is just a word that doesn't exist. There's no meaning or no function there. . . .

See now, I'm less than a man, if you really get down to it, I'm nobody. To my older son I'm Daddy, because it's a name he's used to calling me. To my other son, I'm nobody. He came to visit me—he didn't know me from anybody else. So you know, that's an emotional thing there. . . . It's bad enough doing time, but it's even more of a strain when you're wondering about where your family is and how they are, and you can't help them. It's like being in a glass here. You know this is existing outside, you know they're suffering, but there's nothing you can do.

Self-diagnosed Vulnerability or Feedback Need

Feedback concerns are linked with self-definitions of feedback targets that make them worthy or plausible recipients of love, concern, or human services. The minimal import of self-portraits that highlight feelings is the need for emergency intervention to reduce one's suffering and to ameliorate one's despair. More long-term needs can be implied by self-characterizations featuring serious or chronic psychological deficits. The case may be made with vignettes of one's past transgressions or with complaints about the redundancy, chronicity, obsessiveness, or compulsivity of one's evil-doings:

GH N 4: Years ago I used to be rough, no doubt about it. I was in a box and strip hole, idles and keep locks and all this other. Couldn't find a worse knucklehead than me. Every time you turn around I was in a strip cell.

• • •

Au N B: I had one problem. I went out and got drunk one night, and kicked the fucking door in and took $125. I turned it into my company the next morning, I turned myself into the State Police. . . . I turned myself in. I turned in $1,926 from my company. I could have kept that. That's the first time I've ever been honest in my life about something like that, and that scared me to death. And I've been thinking about that, you know. But the same problem, I got drunk and I just didn't give a shit. I stole money that we didn't need.

• • •

Au N A: It was twenty years ago, and I'm still doing the same thing. I mean, I want to live a little. . . . I feel age is catching up to me, and I want to stay out in the streets. . . . This is really hindering me, because I'm just going through the same cycle as before.

There is a plea for help in such self-portraits. There is also, sometimes, a nuance of blackmail, because of the tacit implication that, in the absence of intervention, continued destructive behavior is virtually inevitable:

Cox S 21: I told him one thing—I know that I go out there, and I figure that I am going to hurt somebody and get hurt, because there is so much evilness inside of me that I know that it has got to come out one day, and I just hope that the person that it comes out is not my family.

• • •

GH R U: Like me, I've never been familiarized with society. I was born in a reservation, from a reservation I went to a children's center, from a children's center I went to a reformatory, and from a reformatory I went to prison. And when I go on the streets and meet people, I don't know how to act towards them. First thing, I go up and say "motherfucker," because this is the language that I'm accustomed to using. And I'm accustomed to hurting people, to survive. So the minute somebody gets out at me, at least I think they get out at me on the streets, I hurt them. Because I'm not familiarized with people, from a normal environment. Whereas when people come in here, even you, I can familiarize myself more with people, that they're not all dogs. That they're not going to bust my head open.

The Prison as a Source of Feedback

Some inmates are explicit about their demand for help and regeneration. They offer case histories as testimonials to their needs and complain about the inability or the refusal of prison to concern itself with intervention. An example is a statement by a thirty-eight-year-old alcoholic who is reproachful of failures to rehabilitate him. He argues that he should at least experience some concern for his problem in the shape of individualized assessment:

Au N B: I used to fight a lot, because I used to get drunk, I didn't give a shit. Big shot tonight. And I found myself really going downhill with this. And when I come to the penitentiary, I walk in, they weigh me, take my clothes off, took my weight, my height, my fingerprints and asked me if I've ever used drugs before. And that was my aptitude test in New York State penitentiary. Now I feel this is very wrong. What happens to the inmate now, he don't know what the hell he's doing, and he don't know who to go to. These people have to go to the inmate too, you know. They get paid to do this, the inmate don't. They get paid to go to the inmate, to go to the inmate and help him. But they don't. Not once have I been called and asked if I was Catholic or Protestant, not once have I been called and told you've got a hell of a drinking problem, or you got a hell of a family problem. Not once have I been asked by these people. And they're rehabilitating me. I've been going through this now for twenty years, and I've got the same problem today that I had when I got this sentence. . . . But there's nothing in here to help you. I mean really help you. Sure, I can go to school, be a good guy and go to school five days a week and read and knowledge myself, right? But it doesn't solve my problems, personal problems by doing that stuff. Why, I can go out there and have four shots of whisky or half a quart of Jack Daniels and just don't give a shit. There's got to be something to this when a person don't give a shit about his life. . . . Every time I turn around I'm back in this position. But not once has the administration ever come to me and said, "Tex, I'd like to talk to you about this problem. Maybe I can find something here to help you." See, they solved my problem, because there's no liquor stores in here, there's no bars in here, unless you buy homemade hootch. . . . But what's going to happen to me when I go out there drinking, and I'm setting in one of them bars, is it's going to happen to me again. But there's not one of these, I have to call them turds in the administration here that gives a damn that this will happen to me again. All I am is a number. . . . I've been in the institution two and a half years. And never once has a sociologist, psychiatrist, psychologist, or any of these guys called me for an interview. Saying "I've been looking through your folder and you've got quite a record here, what seems to be your problem?" . . . I'm considered what you call a pretty hardened criminal, I've been in jail ever since I was a kid. I was kicked out of the army when I was seventeen, eighteen years old, and I've been in a penitentiary ever since. I've probably been in the streets about six years since 1956. . . . I'll probably spend the rest of my life in one of these damn places. . . . They don't say, "You've got this certain problem, so we're going to put you in group therapy programs, maybe we can hash this out and see what's what; you've probably got a problem and you don't even know it." . . . I have never taken an aptitude test, to see what my aptitude was. I've never had an IQ test since I was in here. . . . In other words, they don't give a shit.

While some inmates call for outreach by the environment, others show initiative in approaching staff for help. "Help," here, means Feedback. Where staff members respond formally to request for services, they risk being seen as cold, uncaring, or disinterested. The avoidance of intimacy frustrates Feedback-oriented clients, even where staff are friendly:

Att R 26: The man was a copout. He was not a priest. He was not here to help the men. He was here to get his paycheck and pacify as many as he could so that they would say that he was all right. . . . The man showed no concern for the men.

● ● ●

I: Well, has the psychiatrist in here helped you at all?

Att R 38: No, I talked to him, I seen him two times. The only thing he talked to me about is medication.

● ● ●

Cox S 21: The instructor is like the big brother type—you can joke and laugh with him, and then I started to let him know my problems and started talking about things that he didn't want to deal with, so . . .

● ● ●

Au N A: They just won't go into anything with you that's personal or anything like that.

Similar issues arise in peer-centered programs. Fellow participants are seen as "superficial" or "unhelpful" if their participation doesn't emphasize exploring feelings or creating intimacy:

Att R 38: Like rap programs. Like they have them here, but most of the guys here, they're not sincere.

● ● ●

Au R 22: Well, I'll be truthful. In the program I haven't found anyone who is willing to give of themselves. In other words, to be open, to be free, to just say the truth.

● ● ●

GH R GG: They want you to get into these programs like, for instance, group counseling, which is really a waste of money because you have got maybe fifteen guys in the same group that are all there for the same purpose, and the one that wants to learn or get something out of it, he can't do it, because everybody is just trying to put on the act. I know, because I put on the same thing. I beat the state when I was in Coxsackie. I went to the psychiatrist and that guy and this guy, and they let me go, so who did I beat? So I wasted all that time, because I was here for two years and I wasted every day of it.

Curbs on Feedback

A number of considerations inhibit the expression of Feedback concerns in institutional environments. One set of issues revolves around feedback-processing or feedback-management routines, which create risks for the honest client. Such routines may demand the inclusion of diagnostic data in files, the exploration of self-incriminating details, the invocation of mental health channels, or the use of preventive detention in extreme cases:

Att R 26: Now, if I go there—right?—and . . . this guy classifies me as a very nearly neurotic, right, this goes on my record. And when I go to the parole board . . . and this is the thing, that I am not sure—I can't say what goes into our folders, but this is what we believe. This is why we stay away from them, because if you have a problem that you might want to get solved but you can't go to them, because it is that confidential and it can be used by another agency which would be detrimental to you, because when you go to the parole board you have to have a psychiatric evaluation. So it can be either for you or against you, but I guess we most always are looking at what is going to work against us.

• • •

Att R 38: I seen some psychiatrists, they called me criminally insane, because I had a drinking problem. And the psychiatrist told me that if I told that I committed this crime it would help me . . . he should try to want to help me. No matter if I know I committed the crime, or if I did. That's not his job; his job is to help me if I'm sick, that's the way I look at it. But he didn't help me. All he was looking for is, did I do the crime? People don't want to help you, that's the way it is, I don't care who it is. They don't want to help.

• • •

I: You have never mentioned it to the counselor, the psychologists, or anything like that?

EI R 2: I don't think that they will understand. They just then will think that you are crazy and send you to a crazy place. They will send you to a nuthouse upstate.

I: So you really don't have anyone that you can express these feelings to?

EI R 2: No, you don't. Because when you talk to your counselor, all he does is write up a report and say that this guy is thinking about hanging himself, and right away they classify you as you're crazy, and they want to send you up to Matteawan or a place up in Clinton. There is a nuthouse up there. So to avoid this, I keep my feelings to myself, because I believe there is nobody here that you can talk to that can understand your problems. Even if they do understand, I don't think that they want to help you anyways.

Another issue relates to social distance. Where staff backgrounds differ from those of clients, there is often a presumption that (1) differences in experience are unbridgeable, or (2) incentives for empathy, based on shared experience, are lacking:

Cox S 8: I see a lot of old officers here. You can't really get down and rap to these guys, because they don't know what it's like, going on down in the younger generation, you know. . . . I feel that I could relate to a younger guy that kind of knows what I'm talking about.

• • •

El S 16: Let's put it that way. It is hard for a person, you know, for a high person to relate to a low person, because they don't know what it is like to be far down there. It is hard for that person to know. Like, the type of changes I have been through. My minister, he really knows me. Mr. Johnson, he knows me, but he don't know nothing about me. My personal or my mental.

• • •

Au N B: I can't accept it when a person that doesn't drink or smoke is trying to tell me what goes into it.

• • •

Att R 38: Get guys that have been through this before. Maybe a guy from the institution, that he's sincere about helping people. He can really help them more, because they know that he's from the same environment that they're from. Just like a guy, a wealthy man, right? He's always had everything that he's wanted, right? He'd never know how I feel, being poor. He don't know how I feel.

A third context is cultural or subcultural. Feedback needs may exist side by side with antifeedback norms. A man may strongly desire contact, while subscribing to the prevalent working-class assumption that such contact is unmanly or incautious:

Att R 38: Like, when this problem comes you can talk to a friend, and he'll help you. But, like, where I come from, in the ghetto, we don't have no friends. Everybody's just trying to beat one another. You can't just go to someone and say, "I need your help," or something like that.

• • •

GH N 12: The only ones you really answer to are the clique you hang out with. You don't care about nobody else. Most inmates know their place as far as bringing something up in front of another inmate. Because naturally there is that commitment you have by being in this type of environment, you know, to save face. Something on that order. And the people you hang around with, you got to respect them by saving face for yourself. You don't answer to nobody but the people you know.

• • •

El S 16: I use an example. Like a month and a half ago I received a letter from my wife that she wanted a divorce, and it got to me, and the next thing I knew my shop teacher knew about it already, and my minister, he knew about it already too. And this guy, he spoke to me—he wanted to lift me up. When I went out to the yard he started to speak to me and I started to express myself and told how I felt, and it made me feel better, at least better than before. It didn't do me that much help, but there was a lot of things that I did not want to say.

The Rationality Premise

Individuals who are high on Feedback are usually very conscious or aware of their feelings. On the other hand, such persons also may subscribe to the model of the rational man, which speaks to the necessary subservience of feelings to the dictates of reason. This model—where it is patently not an accurate self-description, may take the form of a pious, self-renewing resolve:

Cox S 9: I'm a human being. And at times we all get emotional. I feel that when a man can think his problem out, before getting all emotionally upset to where he cannot reason, just sit back and think before acting, he would come out on the better end. So what I do regardless of, I might get uptight or what have you, but I think about it first. And then I go from there, after I've thought it out. Because I know that in jail your emotions will give you trouble.

• • •

Au R 22: I myself, as a man, I try to be a man. Rather than constantly fooling around, which I find myself doing sometimes.

The person may also see himself as an exploiter of other people's feelings, who, except for occasional lapses, is a Dispassionate Seeker of Psychological Truth who profits from the emotionality that surrounds him, or from the lessons of history:

El N 19: Especially things that relate to kids and family situations and married situations and things like that, because I'm irrational at times. And I try to read to see what somebody else does. And I guess I'm a seeker. Anything I think is going to benefit me, I try to get it. . . . And I can go and talk to my counselor, and sometimes I would be in a bad mood, and I can show him my bad mood on purpose, and I can show it to him. And I can take it out on him. And he knows this. And then he talks me out of the bad mood. And then I listen to what he says, because if he can talk me out of it, then I can talk myself out of it. . . . My boss, too. Some of the officers. It all depends on how I feel at that time as to what I say to them. And sometimes I say that I feel like a piece of cheese on a trap, and I bait them and see what they can come back with.

• • •

GH R M: It think it came more or less from my own strength. Things that I read, things that I've been exposed to in trying to see my problem as a little different than the problems I've encountered in other people. Being able to capitalize not only off of my experiences but off the experiences of people that I encounter.

I: So, once again, reading and education helped you out in this problem?

GH R M: Yes.

Where help is sought, it may still be seen as subserving rationality. The individual may be convinced—or half convinced—that "insight" or "understanding" of a fatal flaw leads to regeneration of feelings, motives and values:

Att R 38: I want to know from my childhood what made me be like I am. Like, I don't want to get into trouble, but I always do. I want to know what makes me get in trouble. It's some kind of problem that I got that makes me get in trouble. It's something that happened to me in life, right? That it bothers me. You ever sit down and get nervous for no reason? Well, that's the way I feel, I get nervous for no reason. I try to think—right?—but I can't think. . . . I get confused. And when you get confused, you can't cope with what you're doing, you go drink.

• • •

Cox S 21: Like, we could sit down and talk about the things that you had did in the past, so the counselor can see where you are coming from, and the rest of the inmates, and they can try to understand you better. And that way you could understand the problems more.

Self-study

Since man is a social animal, it is not surprising that the weight of Feedback is on one's relationship to others, nor that social support in times of stress is a dominant Feedback theme.

Since man also sees himself as rational, it is similarly understandable that a sense of his irrationality may lead him to reassert the role of reason as a dominant or governing force in his life.

But the emphasis on human links and on rationalizations yields comfort at the expense of change. If a man wallows in dependency, abrogates autonomy, suppresses feelings, or seeks logical formulas for regeneration, he may gain relief but prevent a personal reevaluation.

Change, in the shape of new approaches and goal changes, is sparked by discomfort, by active self-inquiry. We have mentioned before that

> ... only by pausing in one's track does one open the possibility of changing course. Why pause? The most obvious reason would be a hitch or obstacle that prevented one from proceeding. As Dewey put it, "only a signal flag of distress recalls consciousness to the task of carrying on." Obstacles, however, have to be recognized. Some of us hoist "signal flags" more readily than others. A question of individual threshold arises [Toch and Cantril, 1957, p. 146].

The "threshold" we refer to marks the difference between seeking reprieve from stress and embarking on the road to self-reform. It marks the difference between a demand for crisis intervention and a search for new solutions.

Prison creates stress, and our Feedback inmates are characterized by the fact that they are conscious of their feelings. A significant number of these inmates take the difficult step of capitalizing on their awareness and of seeking long-term solutions (rather than short-term relief) for their discomfort.

Though critical self-inquiry does not ensure rehabilitation, it does create the potential and lay a foundation for it. And periods of self-inquiry are seen as rehabilitating by a number of our inmates:

Au R 22: And the tension might have helped me at that time, come to think about it. I spent most of my free time lying in the bed staring at the ceiling, like some kind of a nut, a mummy or whatever. Zombie. . . . There were people who were watching me, waiting to see, waiting for me to crack up and whatnot. But I didn't care, because I knew I was working for a worthwhile cause. . . . I feel that for an individual to probe into his own mind and determine what got him into trouble, what the circumstances were, things like this here, would be more beneficial than anything else.

• • •

El N 1: A person has to, if he doesn't want to return to prison, he has to have a certain amount of time each day that he can reflect upon himself. Do a little meditation and look into himself and see where he is going and where he has come from and what he is doing now. The biggest rehabilitation that goes on is in one's mind. And at Attica I had a lot of time to do necessary meditation. And I searched myself.

GH R 1: I was writing this woman, and it all seemed to pour from within about everything, and I looked up, and I saw that there was clouds and sun and a butterfly, and it was a lot more in the environment than I had ever seen before. And from then on there was a lot of changes in my own evolution, and because it was a matter of the change in perception and the viewpoint on everything.

On a more short-term basis, self-inquiry is sometimes used to improve a man's social dealings—particularly where they had tended in the past to degenerate into conflicts:

El N 19: I don't like to have them treating me like an animal. And the way I act, the way I present myself, if I act like an animal, I should be treated like an animal, and I find myself going back into that same old fuck-everybody bag. . . . I can sit there and have a little bit of solitude to myself and contemplate on everything that I do. If I go out in the hall and give the officer one of these, then I can go back to the shop and analyze why I did it. And after I analyze why I did it, then I can reach a solution as to how to avoid it. . . . There is a lot of officers that I would never talk to before, and I didn't care who they were. I wouldn't say anything unless it was some derogatory remarks. And now I find myself talking to them. And they are talking to me. Not in a bad sense—trying to help me and telling me what I should do.

• • •

Cox S 9: Some people are mistaking harassment, they get negative meanings and stuff, see? Before I can call or say someone is harassing me, I look at myself first whether I'm in the wrong or whether I'm in the right, you see? Now, the inmates feel that regardless of whether they're wrong or right if they are yelled at or privileges taken away they feel they are harassed. But they don't look at whether they was wrong or right.

• • •

El N 19: You're always thinking that he wants something from you. Why is he talking to you? And when I got out I changed that. I was prejudiced, and I changed that too. After a while I started talking to people, and all of that changed. It all changed as a group. When I was out, everybody that wasn't in my group were outsiders. I realized that everybody was an individual, not a group. . . . And I'm still learning. And I'm not afraid to ask questions anymore. I'm not afraid to learn.

A number of inmates even reported conversion experiences or junctures in their institutional careers that produced qualitative changes in their approaches to life. In each case, an environmental impingement within the prison was felt to be of sufficient magnitude to lead to self-reexamination and to the evolution of a new outlook:

GH R A: I was still wise, and I still had a lot of street things in me, you know, like, as far as the programs that were going on in the institution, I wasn't involved in them. Like the progressive young brothers, we used to hang out with each other and just walk around the penitentiary, like . . . it was very easy for you to be wise, get drugs and anything like that right here in the penitentiary, and this was what I was involved in. And they got homosexuals and whatnot running around the institution, so like, this is what I was participating in, you know. Like, there wasn't nobody forcing me to go to school, wasn't anybody forcing me to work anything like this right here, so I figured what I would do is just wait and do my bit. But now, um, 1971, I was in Attica and now, you know, I don't have nothing to hide, and I'm one of those indicted Attica brothers, you know. And they have indictments arising out from the Attica riots. It affected me in a hell of a way. . . . Like, I might not have had access to, you know, a female, but here were homosexuals, and actually I had more experience with persons who did crimes like pimps, hustlers, things like that. And this is where I was getting my education from, you know. So like, after the rebellion, you know, like, it changed my whole ideology, you know.

• • •

Att R H: Well, when I was at Riker's Island, you never have good thoughts. "Well," you think, "when I go back I'm going to do this, I'm going to do that." But you never have in mind to do nothing right. But once you accept Islam, even if you just heard it once, you're going to remember some of the things that you heard, and if you keep coming it will change your whole attitude and your ways.

• • •

El N 19: I was in institutions since I was about eleven—in and out of California jails. And I never lost my attitude, and I always went in one way and came out another way. . . . And I was crazy, and I didn't care. And when I came out in '69 I came here, and I got married here. And everything changed. I began to get into people. I began to realize what people were all about.

Social Learning

Maxwell Jones classifies environments as "therapeutic" when they provide opportunities for persons to profit from their own feelings and experiences, and from the feelings and experiences of others—particularly from personal crises. This type of social learning is enhanced when there is open communication and diminished social distance (Jones).

Though prison is not a therapeutic community, circumstances favoring social learning sometimes arise for inmates. A case in point is that of a Green Haven inmate assigned to a psychological assessment clinic:

GH N 4: I figure it this way. I screwed up half my life. . . . I had it all. Now, to look back on this and to brood on it is what I used to do. Now I come out and see other people and other people's sufferings. I say, "Damn, these kids here haven't got nothing. I ain't too bad." . . .

I look at myself where—a lot of people don't know how to do a very long time. If some people can look at me and see me laughing and joking and I walk around with my finger stuck up my nose, and they're doing five years or ten years, they say, "Gee, why should I cry?"

Of more ambiguous import are situations in which interventions by fellow inmates are perceived as beneficial by their targets. Such interventions may range from advice and reassurances to mood-modulating moves:

GH R V: Like I said, I had a few good friends. They would cheer me up, you know, make me feel a little bit better. In fact, one guy really snapped me out of it a lot of times. I'd be ready to blow, like charging down the corridors. . . . Like sometimes I'd be in the mess hall, and all of a sudden my mind would drift off, and I'd be looking up, and this friend would say, "Cool yourself," and we'd start talking, get in conversation.

• • •

Att R H: See, like, a lot of the brothers got problems. And so they're trying to teach the brothers, like, if you have a problem, bring it out. Instead of holding it in, like a lot of us hold everything in and then explode. So they're trying to make us understand that, if something's bothering you, you have to tell it to somebody whether it's an individual or group.

• • •

EI S 16: We have a [Moslem] minister who does the teaching, and, when you feel down and you have problems, he is there to advise you, and it makes you feel better. Like, he has more understanding and more wisdom.

Therapeutic communities emphasize the constructive role of all staff, including persons who have no formal authority or mental health training. Prison offers instances in which nontherapeutic staff members do intervene and provide feedback experiences to the inmates with whom they deal: [1]

Cox R V: We have a little chat session every night after lock-in. He stops by my cell, "hi, how you doing." And we start from there, you know. "Did you get a letter from your wife today?" Because he passes out the mail, he just asks as a joke type thing, you know. And I say "yeah, I got one." "What'd she have to say?" And I tell him this and this, and I won't hold nothing back. If she writes in there that she's having problems with the landlord or something like this, I'll tell it to him. He'll come up with either a suggestion or relate a story that happened to him and his wife,

[1] Glaser's parole interviews are relevant to this point, because they show that an appreciable number of inmates trace their rehabilitation to a relationship with a prison work supervisor or a chaplain.

that would possibly help me out in my situation . . . it helps people, I don't know how, but when somebody's concerned about you, you've got the natural instinct to give them something back, whether it's affection or concern. You know, you've got to give them something back. And when you've got a contact like this, when you're concerned about somebody and he's concerned about you back, you've got a relationship going there that brings you above your environment. Brings you to be what you want to be. If you want to be back out in the world, you can put yourself to the point to remember when you were there. And how good it's going to be when you get back out there, not how long it's going to be, you know?

High-feedback inmates are disproportionately oriented toward dealings with staff who function in a feedback or human service role. Even though the inmates may be tied to the norms of their peer groups, they are amenable to reduced distance with concerned staff, and they are apt to be disillusioned by the trend in today's prison that deemphasizes the therapeutic function of staff:

GH R 1: The best possible prison would be when you walk into reception someone would come up and say, "Listen, you had a bad trip out there, and we want to see if we can take a look at what happened and get on with becoming a member of society."

• • •

Au N B: I'm not talking about a guy that goes out here and knows how to, goes to schools to teach him how to stop riots or how to kick ass or how to make an inmate feel like he's an animal. I'm talking about qualified people. . . . You evaluate personalities and stuff like that. Put people like that into jobs. People that are really interested.

• • •

Cox S 21: Oh, man, I was souped up—souped up to the tee, and I gave the dime. . . . I was really souped up. The way the counselors was saying, if you have any problems come and see us, and the chaplain and everybody is so much there to help you, I was super souped up to the tee, but . . .

Feedback inmates are also apt to welcome the intervention of "outside" programs and community volunteers. They are potentially hospitable clients for an open systems approach to prison programming, an approach that provides social learning in institutional settings through Feedback opportunities from without:

Au N B: You got a human being here, he's not a toy. Some people think he's a statistic. Then you've got these people that really give a damn, that's not getting no money for this, and they show more interest in this inmate, by coming in in their own spare time, like I said before, than a guy getting fifteen or sixteen grand a year. And he doesn't give a shit, as long as he makes that annual monthly report. I can relate to people like this, because maybe they've been down the road themselves and they've had their problems. . . . They're giving up their time to come in, talk to the inmates. In other words, they're not listening to people bull-shit. Now, these people who give up their time, they could be with their families. They've got a hell of a lot more to do out in that world than get to visit a bunch of damn inmates. Now I have more respect for these people, because they've showed me that they can come there, because they're not getting any money for it. They're not getting paid. As a matter of fact, some of them take off from work to do it. Now, these people are the people I admire.

●   ●   ●

GH R U: Like kids have Big Brothers in the streets. We should have things in prison, where people from the streets, even college kids, where they can introduce themselves, and be a big brother. Maybe even a little brother, because I'm a little bit older. But to familiarize people more with inmates, with the real environment out there.

●   ●   ●

Au N A: See, me talking to you today will help me for about two or three weeks. Because I unloaded a lot of things that I can't normally talk to another inmate, you understand? So up there, if you got help every day, and they go in to you, it's a big difference when somebody takes an interest in you, not just because of the job, that it's a personal interest that they really feel for you, that they want to help you. . . . And that means a lot to me, because I feel that somebody really in my life is taking an interest, and they want to help you to stay out there.

5

Opportunity for Achievement: Support

THE HUMAN ANIMAL IS PRESUMED TO BE DIFFERENT from other animals not only in having speech but in being goal-oriented. However man defines success, he incrementally pursues some version of it. We scan our environments for opportunities they afford us to improve our lots, to gain the rewards life offers in terms of status, material goods, and recognition. True, individuals differ in their ambitiousness, and environments do not all promote goal-directed behavior. The very young are presumed to enjoy life for its own sake, and a sandbox or playroom is not a place to advance a career. But even in play there may be opportunity for the rehearsal and development of skills, for the "educational" impact of experience. And in the most grim and hidebound work environments, some sort of movement—however minute or improbable—may be anticipated.

Prisons are environments designed for those who pursue the wrong goals, or the right goals in the wrong way. Prisons are self-consciously intended (1) to remind inmates of the wages of sin by being uncomfortable (to serve as punishment and deterrence), (2) to help inmates to "shape up" by providing opportunities for self-examination (to rehabilitate), and (3) to increase an inmate's chances for negotiating future life opportunities by supplying him with marketable skills (reintegration).[1] These goals of prison intersect with differences among inmates in the avidity with which they are responded to. That holds just as true for the

---

[1] For most inmates, incarceration interrupts some sort of pro-social career, although the latter may be sporadic and evanescent.

reintegrative tools that prison provides as it does for its efforts to motivate inmates to pursue pro-social careers.

Men who hearken to career support that is offered by a reintegrative environment are those who see themselves having a future and a social role, and can thus relate environmental opportunities to ends that they prize. They can regard the work involved in reintegration as making sense to them (rather than to support-givers), as being responsive to their own version of advancement, and as having a valued payoff in a personally meaningful life:

Cox R J: I'm only seventeen years old, you understand? I think of myself as a man grown up already with full responsibilities, you understand? Because that's the way I see myself. I say to myself, you know, seventeen years old, why should I be out there playing games like a kid? You know what I mean? Now it's time to sit down and do something for myself, you know what I mean? . . . If I sit down here and wait, wait and do my bit and do nothing for myself, you know, it ain't going to get me nowhere when I get out there, because I ain't got nothing to give me a start in, you understand? Because this is what you call a little booster here. When you get out there, that's when you start, you know, reactivating, you know.

• • •

Cox R M: I can take advantage of, you know, various trades and whatnot, and I could put my time, you know, to use instead of just laying back, because if I was in another institution they may not have all these trades. And instead of, you know, going to different trades, you know, and different shops and whatnot, you know, you just lay in your cell most of the day and just, you know, go crazy. But I feel myself, personally, in here, you know, I put my time to use, because they have good trades and good schooling.

Support is particularly welcomed by those who see themselves as handicapped in the past by deficiencies in skill or knowledge. The environment is seen by such men as helping them to remedy or supplement their tangible deficits through the training and experience it provides. This means that past failures are not only acknowledged but are also attributed to defects of past support systems rather than to predestination:

Cox N 8: I know it is kind of awful for a person to say that I am glad I'm here, but, like—me myself, when I was out there and I got sentenced, in a way I was kind of glad. I wasn't happy about coming here, but out there there was just nothing.

• • •

Att R H: A whole lot of us didn't have a chance to get much schooling. We don't have no trade. So I guess that's why so many of us keep returning to prison, you know? . . . My English is real bad, and I'm in the

English program, trying to tighten up on that. And my math. Like, when I first came here, I didn't know fractions. But now I'm coming along fine. I'm trying to get through decimals right now. Like a lot of the guys in here, none of them can read or write, but they don't want nobody to know. And, like, they set up a program, individual, you can have a one-on-one group. Because we was made into a people that was so proud that we don't want nobody to know our ignorance, you know? But that's the only way you can be helped, is by your ignorance being known.

• • •

GH R M: People coming out of my social milieu—right?—they doesn't have the cognitive skills, let's say, reading, writing, and math. Which are things that we are deficient in. And we need those things in order to live in this technological society. An individual that doesn't have the ability to handle abstract concepts, or isn't able to gain some degree of control in spatial relationships, is an individual that is designed to fail.

Support can intersect with pre-existing interests to uncover options or possibilities for unsuspected long-term involvement. This holds where a person discovers that a new career can mean a chance of doing something that he finds pleasurable or rewarding, rather than as the price he must pay for wages or other rewards:

Cox S 8: Like, when I was in the streets I always wanted to build things, you know? Bricks, cement, stuff like that there; so I didn't know what you had to be a mason, so I told the man I wanted to be a construction worker. So he said, "We got a nice mason shop." So I said, "What's that?" He said, "Doing bricks." He explained it to me. So I said, "Yeah, I think I want to do that." So he put me in here, and about the first week I didn't dig it. But then I started getting into it, and that's when I figured I wanted to stay. . . .

That has always been on my mind, has been being a mason, and every time I would go somewhere, and I would see construction workers. I always dug it. I say, yeah, it's all right, and you don't have to work too hard. I always dug it, and I wanted it to be my occupation. . . . After I complete the trade and get my equivalency paper, then I can go to camp and learn a little about forestry, you know? You know, no matter which institution I ever went to I could make use of that trade. But, like masonry, I really dug it.

A man may also take a more open-ended view of life and seek skills from which new perspectives and goals must emerge. The new support system may be a rehearsal for change; it can mark a hoped-for turning point from a non-goal-directed past to a goal-directed future.

Cox R M: The highest in my mind is education, because, once you have that, everything else is going to come right on top of it. When I have an education, when I get to learn more about society and the way the world is made around me, I'll be able to see where I fit in my world and try to work out my problems that are going to come along. . . . I got to get down on the books, you know, and find myself while I'm in here, you know, because, you know, in my own mind, you know, I try not to look at it as just, you know, doing time, you know, but I look at it as trying to get myself ready for the unknown. So, when I get out I'll be able to say I'm here—right?—and I'll find out what I left when I was here before. So now that I know where I left, I can do something about it. . . . I want to see something that would be, you know, helpful for myself. Some place I would be able to go into and hopefully get something out of, so I wouldn't have to return, you know?

At the opposite extreme are men who take a fundamentalist or pragmatic view of supports. They see environmental programs as vehicles to short-term improvements or benefits, or as a way of showing good faith so as to impress key persons into making decisions that favor their immediate interests:

GH R M: The guys really don't want to participate, but they realize that, if they don't participate, then their chances of getting furloughs, their chances of getting study release, their chances of getting work release, is minimized. And as a result they have to do this, so they participate.

• • •

Cox S 9: The mason shop, that is pretty good, you know? It is something to look forward to if you ever need any money, you know. But the laundry, I do that for a reason, you know? And you can't learn, oh, nothing there, but you can stay pressed. Otherwise, you will be walking around with wrinkles.

• • •

GH N 19: The thing, like I say, with therapists or psychologists, social workers, psychiatrists, all of these people—right?—these people just being in here, and the people in the community knowing that they're in here helping these inmates, straightening them out, whatever it is, whatever they're going to do to them, would make the community accept them more when they get out. Instead of not accepting them, the way they do. You see what I'm saying? It would make employers give him the job, knowing that he got all this treatment.

The Intersection of Support Orientations

Problems can arise through the commingling of persons who are oriented differently from each other toward available supports. The most serious problems arise for Support clients when they must live among persons who are dedicated to making hay while the sun is shining.

The short-term view of Support can be troublesome for those who take the long-term view. A career-oriented person is likely to resent it when programs are prostituted or preempted by persons who have no serious or legitimate claim to them. He may also feel that pragmatic, selfish individuals can destroy the integrity of a program by affecting its orientation or by impugning the motives of other participants:

GH R M: It is a plus that they bring the college programs in here, and they give the inmates an opportunity to get in. But it's a negative to the extent that no one really is interested in education as a means of trying to rectify the past, trying to modify behavior patterns. It's just some program that you get into in order to try and get paroled. . . . They got this thing they call scribe roles, then you got achiever roles. Everything in Green Haven was a scribe role; I didn't see anybody that was really achieving anything. For example, they have several organizations in here, and you have an individual that's sitting on all of those various organizations. In terms of key positions, if it's not chairmanship, it's secretary, if it's not secretary it's vice-president, if it's not vice-president it's president. Now I'm looking at this, and I'm saying hey, man . . . this guy's playing a game, and his game is out, right? And as a result of this he's stepping on the other guys that could make the program work for the inmates. In other words, Green Haven says, "Here you are, you got some time, take advantage of this time. We got this type of program, get involved in this program. Do your time, participate in the program, I'm not interested in whether you accomplish anything while you're in the program, and then we just might let you out."

● ● ●

GH R GG: Well, I decided that when I came here this time that I was going to do what they wanted me to and play the game and get out, and I was going to stay out. And I can't do both. If I play the game and act out, I'm not going to be sincere to myself, and I am not going to get any help, and I am going to waste my time here, so I am going to waste five years here and then go out and then expect things to be as they were in 1970, but I sacrificed that by not getting my education and things that will help me. . . . If they change the programs, I would assume that the inmates would have to change, and if they didn't make it so rewarding to get into such programs, then they might not get them in at all, and the ones that were getting into them got into them because they were sincere about them. . . . They are taking up, say, space for someone that could get some help from them.

The presence of people who are completely non-support-oriented can be most deeply disturbing. The presence of such persons raises questions about the value of a philosophy that prizes goal-directed behavior. It also creates a subcultural pull by highlighting the dichotomy between a self-denying ("mature") stance and the pleasurable pursuits ("irresponsibility") of others:

Cox N R: A lot of inmates in here say, "Well, damn, I'm going to do a bit of four years now. I'm just going to sit back and wait until I get out there, so I can start all over again."

• • •

Au R Q: You can feel their attitude or irresponsibility. They have no respect for anyone, they don't even respect themselves.

• • •

GH N 14: These young guys who are coming in with their zip-threes and zip-fours, you always get the idea that they're on vacation, they're going to go out in a year, big deal. Back here on the next bit they may have a few more years, now they'll start smartening up and realize that they're going to be doing time.

• • •

Au R 22: They don't seem to care about the future. Of course, they want to get out, but their reasons for getting out to me are senseless. They want to get out to get a bottle of whiskey or a woman—any woman—and things like this just don't add up.

The presence of non-support-oriented persons can also contaminate the climate within which support is offered. The learner needs a learning environment, which can be destroyed if it is consistently or vociforously challenged:

GH R M: Green Haven doesn't have that type of environment. She has the programs, but she doesn't have the inmate population that's really interested in those types of programs. You get bogged down in a whole lot of political rhetoric about the administration, etcetera.

• • •

Cox N 15: The tools in here, they are here, and a person just has to use them. Like, I think that most of the people in here, they don't use them. Like, they just all want to prove that they are a gangster and prove "I am it" and all that. . . . If you want to work, the teachers will be glad to work with you. But when I am watching the classes and all that, I can't understand how they last a week. . . . If I was a teacher and the dudes were giving me that shit, I would just go get a gun and shoot them.

Motives and Incentives

One reason why Support clients are disturbed about nonconsumers of supports is that disinterest in goals is related to high impulsivity. The Support client is a man who prizes his own superego. He prizes it not only because it keeps his nose to the grindstone but because it promises later success. This leads to the emphasis by Support clients on the need to be strongly and persistently motivated. It leads to the proposition that neither water nor thirst produces a drinking horse—that the key ingredient is the desire to pull a wagon:

Au R Q: As I said, they've got good vocational training. You've got to go get it, it's not going to come to you. A man's got to have some gumption. You can't just lean back doing nothing and expect that it's just going to happen. It's not like that, I don't care where it is.

• • •

GH R M: I saw an individual that was practically functionally illiterate sit down and take a problem, he was in industry. He took the money that he earned from the industry, sent it outside to his family, to help his family. And then I'm analyzing this in terms of guys that are running around in the so-called prison elitism. And I'm saying, "Hey, man, this guy has more desire, he has more of a grip on life, he knows what life is about." But the most important thing, he has a thing that plugs him into his family, which is a key factor. And I didn't see that prevalent in the other guys, although they get $1.15 or $.85 for participating in these various programs. I have yet to see them take that money down and say, "Hey, my wife needs this, the kids need this, I don't need this, because within the institution I have security, food, clothing and shelter, I have that." That is another thing that turned me off in terms of Green Haven. . . . There would have to be certain sacrifices, certain reconciliations. I have to be persistent. I have to know what I want. I have to find goals, and I have to find them realistically in light of what is actually happening around me. And I would have to pursue that vigorously.

Providers of Support are assessed in terms of the honesty of their commitment to the ethic of Support. The inmate presumes that the environment respects a strong superego, or even the verbal manifestations of it. To be "supported" means to be met halfway. This means being provided not only with the tools to success but also with an expression of human interest. Where the manifestation of one's desire to achieve meets no reciprocity, the environment is perceived as hypocritical. While it pays lip service to achievement, it shows—through its actions—a lack of real concern:

El R 7: They will put a book in front of you and write something up on the board and tell you to read the book and find out what is wrong with it, but how can you find out what is wrong with it if you don't know what the hell you're doing? You know, you don't know what you are looking for. And I just got to the school about three weeks ago and already they told me that I have to take achievement tests . . . and I don't know what the text is about, and the teacher just gives me a book and sits at his desk and tells me to go over the book, and I don't know what I am supposed to go over.

• • •

GH R A: Then, when you do go to school, it only be for an hour a day, you know? Like, they weren't teaching you nothing. Like, you go into the classroom and the teacher give you a book, right? They say, "Read this right here," and the other inmates, they'd be talking and so forth, you know, like a lot of talking going on, you know, nothing educational or anything like that.

• • •

GH R R: I asked them to give me something that's containing air-conditioning and refrigeration. You know what they gave me? The broom. Corridor porter. And there's a hell of a lot of psychological impact when it's like, "okay, I want to learn and I can learn," yet they don't want you to learn. And yet they tell you, "you have to get a high school diploma" and all this here. And this is what your counselor says or may tell you before you go to the parole board. But yet they don't give you nothing. You know, it's like you're in the middle on a parallel line, here's one guy on the right telling you something and one guy on the left telling you something. So what you do, you just walk the line, you say, "the hell with both of them."

A superego, when it is young, requires nurturing. This presupposes an environment with a value system that stresses the importance of self-denial and dedication, and one that provides encouragement, help, and rewards.

"Support" includes *human* support in the shape of persons who grease the wheels or who smooth the road when the going gets rocky. It means persons who understand the difficulties of what one is trying to achieve. It means gentle coaxing or firm urging if one's motivation temporarily flags:

Cox R R: One of the teachers here, he went out of his way to help me to try to get me into college, you know . . . when I go to the board, you know? And they done a lot for me, you know? But they don't try to push a rap on you, you know, like, "I can tell you what to do, so you got to do what I say." That's why I like a lot of them.

• • •

Cox R Z: They have some programs here, and they make people make clothes and things, and they teach you things, and you learn pretty quick. And if you're messed up, you can get to it, and then, if you don't do too much, then you're going to get an officer on your back, and they keep after the inmates to keep doing it right, and they stay on your back. They make you do right.

Support also means *social* support in the shape of peers who are strongly inclined toward achievement, who can provide mutual assistance and who can help strengthen one's resolves. Social support includes task-oriented interactions such as tutorials, joint activity, and problem-solving groups:

Att R H: Like, when you do it in groups, they push you more, you get more out of it than when you do it by yourself. When you exercise by yourself, you're only going to do so much, and that's it. But, like, when you go in a group, they say, "Let's do more than that." And then, "Let's do another one." But when you're exercising by yourself, you do ten and then stop. But you sometimes get in the spirit when it's more than one, you enjoy it more.

• • •

GH R M: Auburn, as far as I was concerned, was one of the institutions within the whole penal complex that was extremely academically oriented. . . . You could come in the yard, and you found out that guys that couldn't read or write had guys in the structure teaching them how to read and write. They had a cat that was proficient in math, he held a math class in the yard, English, etcetera. So the whole environment was geared towards academics. And that was based on the caliber of cats that was here. Like, the old timers that had all the time prior to the penal reforms the legislature enacted, they realized they was going to be there for some time. And as a result of this they tried everything possible to try to utilize that time the best that they could.

• • •

GH R A: It's a lot different here. Like, they have outside teachers that come in and teach you, plus they have, like, older inmates here that teach classes too. These days it's more or less like black culture classes. And, you know, now people is trying to get into these classes, and so when they go get in these classes they show the inmate teachers the same respect they show the outside teachers.

Congruence of the Opportunity Structure

Where the environment is a vehicle of change, it is a dictum that one must meet the person at his current state of development, that one must "start where he's at." Such support implies classification of support candidates and the desire to match programs accurately with clients and their capabilities. It means having to have a range of supports, starting with remedial work or building blocks, and including programs for men who seek to deploy well-developed skills:

Cox R J: School, also: Like, they should start out, you know, where they think it's best for them, you know? Like, you have places in this institution now which I think I said is very good, because they can give you the opportunity of starting from the first grade if you want to and go all the way into college, because they got college programs here at night. Understand? And that's how I would want it, too.

• • •

GH N 24: Whereas in here, I might be the only one with a college education, and yet they won't utilize me in a position where I can be beneficial. To them, too. I mean it's beneficial to me; as I say, I'm not looking to be completely altruistic. I'm looking to better myself.

And while programs of all kinds attend to developmental needs of their clients they must also assess the opportunity systems that exist for their graduates. This open-systems view comprises a number of different points. One is the question of matching skills or credentials with the opportunities or markets in the outside environment:

GH R A: Prepare you to go back into society? Well, how can they do that when nothing in the institution has anything to do with society? Like, none of the educational programs fit into the society . . . not what they're teaching you in here anyway. You know? The jobs that they teach you in here, you can't get none of them in the streets.

• • •

GH R U: The things that they teach you here, a barber, I can't get no license outside. Business administration, who's going to hire me? I got armed robbery, murder, I've got everything but sex crimes. I never committed none of them, but who's going to hire me? Give me auto mechanics, construction, these are the people that are going to hire me. There's no bank going to hire me.

• • •

GH R M: I found out that the type of training that I was getting wasn't the type of training that would allow me to function in the labor market out there in society. As a result of this, I was getting shortchanged.

The second area is level of proficiency. Supports can maintain internal congruence by making minimal demands on their clients, and thus reducing the strain on them. This strategy boomerangs as soon as the client reaches the outside world and discovers that he lacks the skill for carrying out necessary tasks:

GH R GG: I wasn't ready for college. I wasn't ready to get out. . . . So you haven't had time to grow or anything, you just went through the program, and they just pushed you through—push you right through.

• • •

Cox N 15: I kept getting A's and A's and A's. I got out of there, and I'm getting my back end stomped on.

• • •

GH N 7: They had one inmate, about a good eight or nine months ago, that left here with sixty credits, and in finding a job on the outside he couldn't find it, he just got to read eighth-grade level.

The third area is psychological, and it relates to the challenges and temptations of the outside world. The degree of ego and superego development that is necessary for dealing with protective supports is not commensurate with the psychological requisites for sustained involvement. A person who has harnessed himself to acquire skills may not be ready for the long-term pursuit of resistant goals in a world full of temptations, and of pressures to rehearse presupport life-styles. Widespread failures of men to pursue goals for which they have been trained (recidivism rates) point to the need for more explicit attention to real life work settings or for supplementary support systems, such as "halfway" experiences that bridge from protected environments to the world at large:

GH R M: And I found, like, when I was in Auburn, the academic environment was there. The dudes came out, like, with a change in values, a change in orientation. And the main factor that contributed to the fact that they wasn't as successful as they should have been was the fact that he goes back to the same environment. With new orientations, new ideas, new concept, new philosophy, cannot cope with that environment and those type of values. And as a result of this, the environmental forces over a period of time take all of that away. There's no way of reinforcing it, and as a result, they find themselves in the previous mode of behavior. . . . What happens is the programs seem to be an RX type of program, designed for behavior modification while you're within the prison setting. But it has nothing to do with relating to what you're going to do when you get out of here into society. Because a lot of guys acquire certain things in here that they can't apply in the street. . . . We try to feed him what we think is a realistic goal and realistic programs for him. In the absence of relating it to the environment that he's going to have to go back in. Like in terms of the ghettos—right?—you have had individuals in the ghettos all their lives that have never committed a crime. And they are functioning, they are law-abiding citizens, etcetera. Why don't they come to jail? Is the fact of the system as it is, with all its imperfections, or is it something else that lies beyond that? And that's what you try to plug in, you try to figure out what it is that allows those people to stay out there as opposed to coming into jail, and trying to find out if there's something in there that is valuable or concrete that you can take out and transfer to an individual that has so-called deviated from that particular norm, try to see if you can't plug him back into the same situation. . . . And in the meantime have some type of follow-through program, so that when he reached the community, that you have some means of reinforcing the things that he has acquired previously. Because without that reinforcement he's going to degenerate into a previous state of existence. And me, myself, I know for a fact that, if the situation warrants it, that I would have to follow the line of least resistance.

6

Stability of the Environment: Structure

IF WE WISH TO LIVE SANE LIVES, we must have environments that respond sensibly and predictably to what we do. We must know what to look for, what to expect, and when and where to expect it. Hadley Cantril has observed that "it is necessary for us to maintain some degree of stability and continuity in our assumptive world if any of our value judgments are to make sense; if any of our actions are to be effective" (1950, p. 91).

Though stability in the world is a general requirement, there are some people who are more dependent on order and predictability in their lives than are others. We can speak of people who are "tolerant of ambiguity," while we classify others as "rigid" or "compulsive." We know that some people live contentedly with disorder, while others punctiliously insist on precise arrangements.

Any environment provides Structure to the extent to which it furnishes reliable guides for action. The most structured environment is one that tells a person *exactly* what to expect if he does A, B, or C. It has built-in, or man-made, "rules" or laws that ensure specific reactions to given actions. A person who prizes Structure is a person who depends on such rules to orient himself.

Prisons have always told inmates exactly what they may do or not do in their daily routines, and precisely what the prison would do for or to the inmate in particular situations. Such information was traditionally found in a "rule book," to which the authorities rigidly adhered. Contemporary prisons often introduce rules almost apologetically and may stress the spirit of regulations at the expense of their letter. The *Resident's Handbook* of the Auburn prison, for example, tells its readers:

> Specific rules have been included so that you will know what conduct is expected of you. We hope you will keep in mind that the more cooperation is

81

received from you, the better and smoother this facility will operate for your benefit.

The *Handbook* also alerts readers:

> You will notice as you read this handbook that regimentation is held to a minimum in order to allow you to develop internal controls that will assist you when you re-enter society.

What "regimentation" may be to some, "Structure" is to others. High-structure inmates reject the notion that their environment is the place to "develop internal controls"—at least not by deemphasizing the external rules of the prison game.

The demand for adherence to "The Book" is independent of what "The Book" prescribes. For High-structure persons, undesirable contingencies are less noxious than the uncertainty about what to expect next:

GH R R: Any other joint that you go to, as soon as you come off the bus, they take your handcuffs off you, you go into reception. As soon as you go into reception, the moment you look into the block, like on the vertical line on the bar, you look straight down on all the doors, you see rule books, toilet paper, soap, things like this. And they'll tell you just like this, "If you get out of line we're going to bust your ass." . . . You know, the whole thing is, if there's no system where, as like you come into the institution, they don't give you no rule book saying "This is what you do in order to stay out of trouble," like there wouldn't be all this bullshit.

● ● ●

GH R M: Up there, the administration doesn't make any pretense about what its position is in terms of racism, etc. That you can deal with. You got rules, you got criteria, you got standards, you got something tangible that you can relate to. In here, it's not that tangible. It's covert but it exists, and as a result of this it's very difficult to deal with. And as a result this is impinging.

● ● ●

Au N K: It is hard, because I don't know—I can't adjust my program. See—man is a funny thing. He can adjust and adapt himself. He can adapt himself to just about any type of situation as long as he knows what is desired of him for him to have a certain amount of relaxation of the mind, right? If I know in the morning when I get up that I am going to have to get fifty lashes, I can face this. I might dislike this, but I can face it. I know that, when the fifty lashes is over, I am going to go and do something else. I know that, if I subject myself to this for a period of time, eventually I can move out of here and better myself— right?—and then if I get up in the morning, and the man tells me, "We don't give out lashes here," and then later on during the day I do what I think I'm supposed to do, and he reaches out and hits me with a whip —I mean, this is a hypothetical case—then I don't know what to expect.

The less Structure is available in an environment, the more discretion can be exercised by the persons who constitute key figures in the environment. Different individuals can exercise discretion differently in the same situation. This means that one cannot tell how any particular act will be responded to or whether it will be approved or disapproved. It also means that, where one depends on a given individual for guidelines, one may run into difficulties with the next man on the assembly line. This sometimes carries danger, and it always creates uncertainty about the appropriateness or desirability of one's conduct:

GH N 24: And you may do something one way for six months. And then all of a sudden you come by one morning, and you're doing the same thing, and there's a new guy on, and he's going right by the book, because he doesn't know better, he's a relief officer, and you get locked up. And to me that's a hassle. It's not that you're really doing anything wrong. You don't know what's right and what's wrong. There are certain things obviously that you're doing wrong regardless of who's on. But there are other things that it's a gray area, and I don't think they define it.

• • •

Au R AA: Knowing where you stand. See, you got to know where you stand with the police. . . . You wouldn't know how to act, if you tried to do what's right. And all the time you be going against a brick wall, because one dude tell you something, another dude tell you something else. That fucks you around, because you don't know how to react.

• • •

Cox S 24: Some CO will come and tell you one thing, another CO will tell you another. And one guy says, "If you don't do this, you get a ticket." So either way around you wind up getting a ticket. So you always wind up getting in trouble.

Securing information becomes difficult where there are no reliable information sources. In the absence of guidelines, personnel can express private views or—if they are honest—can confess total ignorance. In either case, the credibility or legitimacy of authority is reduced:

GH R U: They're all brand new guards. It's not their fault, they just don't know nothing. You ask one of them a question, he knows less than me. To me this ain't no prison, it's kindergarten.

• • •

GH N 5: You can't blame the officers that much, because they're kept in the dark as much as we are a lot of the times. And it changes from one day to the other, they don't know what's happening either. I heard one of them remark about the same thing a couple of days ago. He said it got to the point where he doesn't want to know what's happening any more . . . if he takes his time on anything, nine times out of ten he's got to guess, because there's no set rules to go by.

I: If he's wrong, people are going to come up in his face and say—

GH N 5: Right, that's the whole problem.

Stability over Time

Though redundancy can be boring (Chapter 2), it is also dependable. If tomorrow is a replica of today, tomorrow carries no real surprises. We are psychologically prepared for the future, and we need not be concerned about risk or disequilibrating experiences:

GH R R: You know, every morning when you wake up you're doing something different. It's like one day you go to school, and the next day if you go to school you got to go to the gym. You don't want to go to the gym, but they tell you to go to the gym anyway. And the joint, it's messed up.

• • •

GH N 5: Doing a short bit here is beautiful. If you're going to be here for any length of time, I'd recommend that you go to another penitentiary. . . . It has more or less of a street atmosphere. It's not regimented, let's put it that way, it's not regimented. And you more or less don't know what's going to happen the next day, from day to day. And in other penitentiaries, when you wake up in the morning you got a schedule, right? And you go through that schedule, so you don't have to worry about what you're going to do next.

I: Confusing?

GH N 5: Yeah, it is, it really is, because it changes from day to day. . . . In other words, when you come out in the morning, the rules that you went by yesterday may be null and void today. So if you start to do something, and you get reprimanded for it, you say "Well, yesterday—" Well, today's a different thing.

While minor instability carries minor risk, extreme instability can bring breakdowns of social control. Where sharp discrepancies occur between human expectations and environmental offerings, bitterness can lead to violence (Davies). Sharp environmental discontinuity can lead to prison riots:

Au N 5: If you give a man permission to do something and then turn around and try to lock him up for it, what would you think? That's what happened. They gave the men permission to talk. They got up and aired their views . . . this went on all day. Nobody was interested. Then they're saying they take them up and lock them up. Now they locked them up, the rest of them say, "Wait a minute, this isn't right, you told them they could do this." If they didn't want it done, they should have said no. "Let them out, let them out." "No we can't let them out." "Send the warden down, I want to talk to him." "No, we can't do that." "All right, if they're not out by morning—" That's how it happened—so simple.

• • •

Au R Q: He tried to tighten it down, quick. You can't do it, you just can't go from one extreme to the other without something happening, and that's exactly what happened. They went from one extreme to the other, and bam, the top blew off. And it stands to reason that, I don't care what you do or what type of situation you have, if you go from one extreme to the other you're going to have something go haywire.

Changed routine—however systematic—can be an affront to Structure. A transfer of environment—however well intended—can be stressful. Social engineering is risky, because it takes inadequate account of needs for stability, and particularly for the disproportionate requirement of some people for constancy of experience over time:

Att R G2: I am the type of guy that don't like switching around even on the street. Once I got a job I just stayed right there.

• • •

GH R U: See, I get adjusted to another prison, and then they move me here with no program. I'm adjusted to doing time in another place, and they just pick me up and change my whole program.

• • •

Au N 5: And you can't mess with that routine. All right, take your television up there, take your radio up there, at night when you go in, you want them stories, you want them particular stations. You see what I'm saying? You change that, and you got a conflict there. Because we've had it right here. They've petitioned to get it all back. You see what I'm saying?

Social Stability

Stability in the social environment entails predictability of other people's conduct as it impinges on one's own. It means not wanting to encounter behavior among others for which one is not prepared. Maximum stability exists where everyone in the environment seeks to reduce his interference with the experience and conduct of others:

GH R U: It's where you don't bother me and I won't bother you, you do your thing and I'll do my thing. Where in the old prisons, nobody was going to do nobody's things.

GH N 13: It would be a place where there's the very least possible interference from the personnel, the administration. And most of the upstate prisons, Clinton, Attica, particularly, Clinton has always been a prison that's been pretty exclusively composed of lifers or people with a great deal of time. And the administration has developed a program to meet their needs and to meet the needs of this population. Basically what it is is a noninterference policy. It worked very well there for most of the years that I was there. And this is exactly what it was. You leave us alone, we'll leave you alone. That's all there was to it.

• • •

Au N 5: And as I say, Clinton's strict now. They're strict, they got the rules and regulations. The majority of them like this, because I can't intrude on this man, he can't intrude on me. This is the way it should be, this is society. I don't want to be in his pocket, he don't want to be in mine. That's still the same way.

On the opposite extreme is social anarchy, a condition in which people's behavior intersects unpredictably, where individuals with diverse orientations try to carry out their purposes without regard to their impact on the environments of others:

GH R H: Disorganized . . . disorganized environment. Like . . . the social . . . they didn't sort us out correctly to our personalities . . . our personalities in regard to one another so that we can get along. That would be bad. You know what I mean? Disorganized environment, you know?

• • •

Au N 5: Look at your lifers right today. They're all hollering because these kids are coming in here with three or four years, five years, and having their own way. And they're tearing down the institution. When they came to the institution they were on a set pattern. Now here comes a group of young kids, they're going to make this change, or try to make this change. You're interrupting that man's bit.

• • •

GH R PP: If a guy likes a lot of commotion and he likes a lot of action, so to speak, then there is always something going on, and some guys like this, and some guys, the more they get involved with the less they think about their time. But the guy that has a lot of time, that is the last thing that he wants to do is get content here, and then he will forget about all the time that he is doing and that will deter him from all his legal work and his trying to get out of here. If you are pacified and content you fail to absorb that you are going to do this for twenty more years and so on.

Some stability can be achieved through classification and grouping. Segregation not only ensures social compatibility but can logically match the built-in features of each environment with the capabilities and behavior patterns of its inmates:

GH N 14: You can't have the mixed age differences, sentence differences, all of that conglomerated into just one population. It's wrong. This creates a lot of animosity. It's guys like, you hang out with your own kind, I'll hang out with my kind. This is a normal procedure anyways. . . . Like, you see a black man and you know that he's raped five women, or he was convicted of raping five women. He's probably raped twenty-five or more. And this is a black guy, he's been raping white broads. So automatically, you don't want nothing to do with this guy. You stand farther away from him, I don't bother you, you stay away from me. So, like I say, you got to classify, and if you start doing that, then you're discriminating.

• • •

GH N 4: They'll take the guy that's doing five years and they'll put him in Green Haven, next to the city. And the guy that's doing twenty years, send him up to Clinton. Now it's an impossibility for this man to have any kind of a rapport with his children. Whereas the guy with five years, he knows he's only got to be here two years. His family life is not going to be as impaired as this guy's. And yet they'll take all the long-timers and send them up north somewhere.

• • •

GH N 24: I think the only thing that was really bothering me was when they put me in shipping. They went through a whole thing, and you have to picture them telling me—I think it was three men on the panel for classification—and they went through a whole rigmarole, asking me everything. They pulled out my college background, my work, what I did at Sing Sing, my work on the street. And just said, "Okay, you're in shipping." You know, one of those things. It threw me a little bit. . . . And I'm not trying to sound conceited or pat myself on the back, because I'm no genius by any means. But I'm certainly well above the average educational-wise in here. And my business background. And one of the biggest gripes I could have with the institution—not just in my case, I've seen a number of cases in the institution—is when they do get somebody in here with qualifications for something, they don't use it. . . . In Sing Sing a guy came in that was a high school principal, and they gave him a porter's job. Now they were looking for inmate teachers, and they had some inmates teaching there who—alright, they might have had a little better education than the average inmate in there, but most of them didn't have any real, none of them had college degrees and so forth. Here was a principal, in high school, and they wouldn't utilize him in a teaching capacity. And in fact, he had been a principal in a ghetto area, mainly with Spanish kids, so he was familiar with teaching techniques to this type of element. And they wouldn't utilize him, and they were utilizing inmate teachers.

Social instability can occur if we create climates that dilute the definitions and the borders of formal roles. This occurs where staff roles are modified to promote democracy or to create a therapeutic milieu (Jones). This may satisfy High-feedback or High-freedom inmates, but for High-structure clients, such a move can be both stressful and threatening. It violates expectations of familiar staff–client interactions and makes staff uncomfortably unpredictable. By making staff roles ambiguous, one can also violate the integrity of the familiar client role:

GH R U: The hack [used to be] sincere, even though he was a dog. He did his job. These guys here don't even know what their jobs are. . . . I'm saying, if I got to do time, I would rather do it under the old system. . . . They're sincerely hacks. There is no fraternizing with them, they'll let you know ahead of time if you do something they'll break your head open. So you don't do nothing, you know? These guys here have got nine faces. "Hello, brother," and they stab you in your back. I don't play that. . . . I'm thirty-three years old, I've been in jail since I was actually 9, for a long time. I didn't fraternize.

• • •

GH N 13: I don't like fraternization with these guys. I can't get accustomed to it. If I try to leave here, they'll shoot me, they'll kill me. That's their job. So I don't want to be friendly with them. But this prison is run on that basis. Friendship, everybody ha-ha-ha. I can't understand that. Some people like it, I don't like it. I can't get used to it.

• • •

GH R PP: The only thing the officer would have to say is crack your door, and you know everything else, and the man doesn't have anything else to say to you. They are overemphasizing this "relate to the officer." . . . Don't profess to like me and in the back of your head you don't like me. I know you really don't like me. . . . There used to be principles, and you didn't rap with the hacks or anything with them, and you don't look in a man's cell unless he calls you, and now everything is reversed. And now they don't even know you and they rap with you, and they rap with the hacks and everything. There is no more principles. They fail to realize that you are still a man even though you are in jail and a convict.

High-structure inmates prize staff who play consistent, traditional roles. They may also prize disciplinarians who exercise control over their environment and ensure its stability. Inmates may see chaos in the untrammeled, out-of-control behavior of other inmates who surround them:

GH R R: Then they opened the joint, like open house. And then that got out of hand. It's one of them things, making a whole lot of wine and carrying on.

• • •

Cox N 15: There is just constant bullshit—you know?—like, go play cards and up yours and all this and, you know, be quiet, and there is no discipline, and that is something that I have written to the superintendent about a couple of times, you know? . . . get some discipline in this place and there is not. . . . This place is far too lax in my opinion. Okay, they say, walk to the mess hall two by two—it ain't two by four, it is four by twelve—people walk where they want to. And, "Be quiet, shut up"—nobody shuts up. They just keep on talking, and the guard will stand in their way, and there is no discipline.

• • •

GH N 14: There wasn't sufficient security from the officers. In other words, the inmates were running wild. They were running up and down the corridors, there was no uniformity or anything.

• • •

I: Now take the opposite side of the coin and describe a place where it would be difficult to do time, what would that be like?

Au R Q: Well, a place with no discipline whatsoever. Well, we had a sample of it here just prior to the riot in 1970. We had a warden here that was, he was completely lax. He was lax to the point where people would do what they wanted to, and the hell with anybody else. They didn't care. The individual just did what he felt like doing, and that was it.

I: So the place was really loose?

Au R Q: Oh, it was too loose. In fact, basically, when you get right down to it, in my opinion that was what caused the riot.

Organizational Stability

A third source of stability is provided by the smooth operation of administrative machinery and formal organizational process. Such organizational stability is important as a protection against arbitrariness. Where formal rules are not adhered to, tainted relationships govern the means to prized ends. Individual purposes are not achieved by following the rules; Structure is replaced by the corrupt exercise of arbitrary discretion and can be based on informal bargaining or friendship ties:

Au R BB: So, due to their fantastic system here, all you have to do is talk to a guard that likes you or something like that, and he can put you in another job, which they don't like to admit, because they say that they have got a list for everything.

• • •

GH N 14: You have to have connections in order to get into these programs. . . . They have the criteria, they're dealing from the criteria simply to satisfy their friends, or whatever have you.

EI N 1: The rule book is printed for a purpose. It wasn't printed to let one inmate overlook a certain regulation, and then another inmate has to abide by it or adhere by it. Here at Elmira, certain regulations in the rule book they turn their back, they overlook them for certain individuals. Other individuals are expected to adhere to them.

Even those High-structure inmates who negotiate the informal system successfully may come to feel that their integrity has been violated and may argue that their capacity for future dealings with an orderly world has been compromised:

GH N 13: And there's also the fact that people here manipulate you. They really destroy whatever, I don't know, whatever character you might learn from a prison, they're trying to take it away from you. They're trying to turn you into a sneaky person. The program, it's not written down where it says that you must be a sneak. But everything is set up so that you almost have to be in order to get ahead. . . . They try to make you sneaky, to compete with each other for things that you really shouldn't have to compete for. They try to make you operate in I suppose the same way they are. In other words, to get anywhere here you have to know someone. You have to have influence. You have to have a friend who's a lieutenant or—and this is the only way you get things done. Now, if someone knows someone who is a captain, well then you're out of luck. His influence is better than yours. You're encouraged to do this. . . . The job I have now, I [got] by going to an inmate that I knew that knows somebody in the administration, that's how I got it. I got moved out of segregation and went through three or four jobs before I got this one. But never once on my qualifications. . . . You got to do games on everybody else. It's meaningless.

• • •

GH R GG: They are enforcing rules when they want to. I mean, I can be told to get a shave when another guy is walking around with a beard. If I don't shave, then I will get locked up.

I: And this seems unfair to you?

GH R GG: Sure. I get advantages from it too, but it doesn't make it any less unfair.

A threat to organizational stability is created through abrogation of staff authority. As with social stability, democratization and diffusion of organizational roles reduce predictability. In the eyes of High-structure persons, democracy emasculates organizational functions, because individuals without credentials (and thus with dubious skills) are permitted to exercise responsibilities that should rest in more competent hands:

GH R M: You got programs that is being designed, operated by inmates.

And you find out that the inmates themselves don't have a realistic evaluation of what the inmate's about, or what his problem was, why he found himself in prison. And without that type of information available to them, then they cannot evaluate the individual, and then they cannot come up with the program that's designed to alleviate the problems or the condition that brought them here in the beginning.

• • •

GH R A: They had a couple of them, but inmates was teaching classes. Now inmates feel that if you're an inmate, I'm an inmate, me and you got the same kind of uniform, you know, what can you tell me, you know? So, really, there wasn't too much enthusiastic about, you know, going to school there, because inmates, you know, the majority of the inmates that was teaching classes in Attica were homosexuals, you know, so then nobody got no respect for them, man.

Diffused roles are also seen as corrupting: They bring about arbitrariness, and produce conflict and danger:

Au N B: Here it's closed groups. You got to wait in line to get into any kind of a group. You got to wait maybe five months before some inmate decides that he wants you in there . . . the same way with all the other programs, they let the inmate run it. Which is no good, because, once you have an inmate running it, you're going back to the old chain inmate who's got the inmate boss. And if he don't like you, you won't get in his group.

• • •

GH R R: They have college courses in here too, but you have to go through so much trial and triumph to get to them. Because you have guys cutting one another's throat, playing prison politics, and that's bad.

• • •

GH N 7: You go there for three or four years and never pass the equivalency exam, because on the exam it's totally irrelevant to what he had been taught. So they found out that it's more easy to get four cartons of cigarettes and buy you the program. But you can buy the program here, you can buy any kind of program you want, if you have cigarettes. . . . They even have a thing now where inmates can write up the evaluation reports on other inmates, and it goes in his parole file. . . . Now, if this inmate don't like you, you don't know whether he's writing your report up or not, because the officer has put his signature on it.

The desired model of administrative stability is a system in which everything runs smoothly, in accord with a logical design. A desirable environment is one that is organized for the coordinated, efficient use of resources. The gain is that, when one presses the right organizational button, one is assured of a prompt, predictable response:

GH N 5: This penitentiary could easily be converted into a meaningful place if it was run correctly. It has the facilities, as far as the programs are concerned. And I think it's all a matter of coming up with a workable system. That's the biggest problem, a workable system. . . . I'll tell you, it keeps bringing me back to the same thing. It depends on the system that is set up in any penitentiary. . . . This one is run inefficiently, and you can see the effects of it. Everywhere you go in the place you can see the effects of it.

• • •

GH N 13: This is a totally disorganized prison, the staff here. They're incredibly incompetent, some of the people here, it's unbelievable. There seems to be no organization or any type of institution, with hundreds of people here, or thousands. They should have some type of program, and they don't have it. Just on a daily basis. Things change from day to day, nothing is ever together, nothing is ever standardized or established. Everything is just in a flux. You have the staff changes here—you have some permanent staff members, but many of the hacks that you come in contact with on a daily basis are constantly changing.

• • •

GH R U: I'd rather see the old type of prisons than these here new ones. At least the old type prisons had a system. This place here, they got so many programs but they ain't got no system, to the programs or nothing.

Credibility: Stability in Communication

To achieve stability, we need not only rules but also assurance that the rules will be equitably and reliably applied. We need "metarules"— rules for how rules must be used. Such conventions are sometimes more important than the rules themselves. The degree of discipline in a home, for example, may have less impact than the consistency or inconsistency with which discipline is used. It is also pointless to punish a child if the child doesn't know what he or she is being punished for. Criteria of rule-application must therefore be clear, plausible, and reliable.

Men who have no quarrel with rules still need to be assured that rules will be lawfully and consistently invoked. Sloppy metarules have the same impact as no rules at all: They make it impossible to know what one may expect when one does A as opposed to B, C, or D:

GH N 14: I went to the board in January, they turned it down. So this was like five months of psychologically preparing myself for the street. Because I'm doing a nice bit, I figure, Jesus, how can they turn me down? Then, all of a sudden they turn me down by saying I'm too smart. So I wrote to the commissioner and I asked him, "I would like some suggestions and advice on how to appear for my board in May. Should I be dumb desperate, or should I be smart good, because I'm confused now." And he wrote back, "Bullshit." . . . All programs are based on whatever an ultimate goal is for prerelease or early release. If this is so, it's a privilege. Now, if it's a privilege, all inmates strive to attain this goal. Now, how can I take from this board appearance, how can I strive to gain this privilege, only when I get there to be told, "You're too smart, you should have been a dummy." The concept of the whole thing doesn't make any sense to me. Why the hell don't you just put this program and just keep it for your dumbbells?

• • •

Au R AA: So there's no way that you can really prepare yourself—they have no rationale, the parole board.

• • •

Au N K: We had an officer there, and he is still there, but there is one thing that I enjoy about him, he was consistent. If he told you no today, he was going to tell you no tomorrow. There was no favoritism at all, no hypocrisy, etcetera, etcetera. He was the same every day to everybody.

The issue of credibility arises in terms of whether what people say they will do tells you what they *will* do and therefore serves as a reliable guide to your own actions.

Persons concerned with Structure have a need to know. Since they use structure as a guide for action, they have no use for communications designed to cheer them up, to improve rapport, or to raise hopes. The Structure person must know where he stands; this knowledge tells him how the outside environment is arranged and what he must do to cope with it:

GH R U: Well, I know what's happening: Nothing happens. There's a lot of talk, that's what's happening. In the other joints you got doers, here you got talkers. The other joints offer less, but what they offer they're doing. This joint offers everything but it ain't doing nothing. . . . They're telling me they're going to do things, and they don't do them, and I hate that. I hate to be lied to. If you tell me you're going to kick my teeth in, kick them in. But don't lie to me, tell me you're going to brush my teeth and then kick them in. Because then I'm going to go for your mother, your goldfish, everybody. I'm one of those guys that don't forget, that's my problem. I don't forget nobody. This is a place that could turn a lot of kids to killing. Because they build their hopes up so much, and then these kids start believing in this, and then they let them down. . . . They're feeding you so many lines, that all they do in here, it's like nothing. There's no communication. There's nothing. That's worse than anything. See, before, I knew what I had to do. Now they're keeping me running down this yellow brick road here. With all these dreams. And I'm going for them in a way, because I want to believe them, that they're going to give me this and give me that. They're going to help me do this, and they ain't helping me do nothing, except get back. I sit here dreaming of killing these people regularly.

GH N 13: One of the things that was really outstanding at Clinton was—you think of words that don't really seem appropriate in discussing prison, but it's sort of an honor system you had among inmates themselves, it's very high. . . . And there's naturally a social order, a pecking order, that's adhered to very strictly. But the relationship between the staff and the inmate population also operates on an honor basis, you might call it an honor basis. The point I'm making is that, if you perhaps were in line for a job of some sort, anything at all—and a staff member, like somebody in a position to help you, like lieutenant or brass or whatever, told you, gave you his word, that you could get this at a certain time—a few years ago in places like Clinton, he would, like, give up his job rather than go back on his word to you. If he gave you his word he kept it. Exceptions to this rule were almost unheard-of. Now this is something that's very important. You might have the same guy tell you that you would never under any circumstances get this job, the same thing applies. You knew he meant what he said. He wouldn't go back on his word. Which is a very important thing in a situation like this. The worst possible prison is one where the opposite is true. And that's Green Haven. People lie to you, they never tell you the truth here. They feel that you can't face the truth, or they can't—they never say no. Under any circumstances they never say no. But they never mean it. This is very disturbing to anyone who is used to other types of facilities.

• • •

GH N 12: I mean, there've been good changes, but I prefer the old way. Because they tell you, "Yeah, we're going to do this for you," and they ain't going to do nothing. Where years ago it was either yes or no, and that was the end of it.

Structure and Self-control

Like other dimensions of environment, Structure helps persons to deal with themselves, to govern their actions, manage their feelings, husband their urges, and achieve peace of mind.

Structure helps the ego mediate reality by tracing the borders of the world more sharply. Structure also provides external control. It is a coping tool for those whose internal controls are relatively weak, whose super-egos do not provide strong moral imperatives. What the Structure person demands is not only insight into What Is, but clear Dos and Don'ts. He wants an environment that facilitates appropriate conduct, that modifies behavior. Unclear limits are threatening, because they constitute the sort of temptation to which one habitually succumbs:

Au R G2: I realize that I wouldn't be in here if I didn't break the law, so treatment—I don't expect that they have to bend over and kiss my ass. But I made a mistake, and so I don't expect them to thank me for anything. Just really treat me decent and that is all. . . . I don't want to be given a lot of stuff, because I am in here for a reason. . . . I was offered Walkill, and I guess that is minimum security, something like that, and I told them no, because that is kind of like out in the streets, and you are still in prison, and they give you a little bit of freedom and a little bit of this and that, and you go out in the street and work or whatever you do, but they still got a hold of you—and I trust myself, but I would rather do my time like this, because then you are not on the street, and you are not tempted to do this and that.

● ● ●

Au R BB: Like, if you give a guy a little bit of leeway, and automatically they expect more, which is just common, you know? And, like, you got a lot more leeway here than I had in Attica, but yet at the same time I am always looking at things, like—why can't they be different, you know? And I mean, like, in Attica, when I was there you never would have thought, like—say like you do here . . . you just did it. But here I have found with myself and since I have been here I find that, if something strikes me as not being all right, I am going to tell them so. And, like, it is just that there is moods that you get into, and I have been in moods where a guard will say something that is really stupid, I will, like, tell him, "Well, that is really dumb." . . . Like, I try to keep associating with myself in my mind that I am in prison, and so therefore the prison has to be what I think that prison is, and this is prison. I wouldn't want to be in a situation where there was a fence, for example, or there were rooms, because then you have—you are not in prison. . . . Pettiness is part of prison, and harassment is part of being in prison—everything. The silence, the whole thing, it is part of being in prison, and I think that it is in a way that it is kind of demonstrating. In a way I think that it helps keeping a guy from coming back.

● ● ●

GH R M: Where you had an administration that took a definite stand. And I have to comply with the definite stand. And there was more of the institution allocating responsibilities than an inmate taking responsibility for his own behavior. And I'm saying on the basis of what we have coming within the institution, I don't think that the inmate himself is ready for this type of responsibility to police themselves, to police their values.

Some Structure persons prize regimentation. For them, the environment doubles as an external superego, which is a benevolent (or at least a helpful) tyrant. Discipline is welcomed, because it is seen as ultimately building self-discipline:

Au R AA: Sometimes too much comfort and being too lax is bad for you. Like, say, jail is something bad, but if you don't learn from it, then you come back again.

Cox N 15: This place is changing. The only thing that they have to do is just to figure out some kind of discipline that can work while they are changing it. From what I have heard of the prisons five years gone by, they sounded a little bit too much, but I would just as soon done my time then as now, because I would have done it better, because I just follow the rules. . . . I must have been born jail-wise, because most of the guards will tell you to shut up, and if you shut up the first time you are fine, but—I always shut up. . . . You just have to have something where you tell them if you don't do this you're going to have to go over and shovel shit off of that roof over there or something. It has got to be something that the inmate don't like to do and don't want to do.

• • •

Au R 22: One year to life, or one year to twenty, or whatever—that type of a sentence I feel is good, because the man says, "Gee, one year to life or one year to twenty-five, that's the best years of my life." This is going to hurt the man in such a way that he's going to think, why? And you'll have your officers who are trained to help him here and there, and hopefully within a few years they will come out of that way of life. . . . With the officers' special training, they would be able to help these people. Rather than having them the way they are now. Just running around as if they're in the streets, practically. But to lessen the security and make things more lax, I think, would be wrong, because they would dislike it that much less. And the more they dislike it, the more they should try to help themselves.

Structure may also be prized as a curb to explosiveness, but the controlling impact of Structure is temporary and lasts only as long as Structure is available:

GH R U: In the first place, my crime is murder, so I know I need to be incarcerated. It's got to have a wall, because I will go. . . . I don't want a wall, but I mean it has to be. Till I get some kind of help where I'm not going to go out there and just hurt people. I'm liable to hurt somebody at any time, I know this.

• • •

I: Where do you think you were in better control of yourself, here or in Attica?

GH R U: Attica.

I: And why's that?

GH R U: Because I knew what I had to face—at all times, I realized what I was facing. There was no dreams there. . . . That's the whole thing. You got to know what the score is. Otherwise you'll flip right out.

7

Issues Related to Dependence
and Autonomy: Freedom

A MAN'S RELATIONSHIP TO HIS ENVIRONMENT carries tangible sediments of problems or difficulties he has had with his past environments and of the way in which these were resolved. The climate of a child's home governs his responses to school, and a worker's experiences with his family and school affect his reactions to his job. Persons who have had positive experiences with others approach new encounters with trust; men who have had to fight for survival are apt to gird their loins in anticipation of the next threat or challenge.

One of the themes that carry over most frequently in our reactions to new environments is that of autonomy, dependence, dominance, submission, or authority. This theme rehearses its role particularly in organizations, because formal hierarchies are a prominent feature of organizational environments. McGregor, who was a student of industrial settings, has pointed out:

> Psychologically the dependence of the subordinate upon his superiors is a fact of extraordinary significance, in part because of its emotional similarity to the dependence of another earlier relationship: that between the child and his parents. The similarity is more than an analogy. The adult subordinate's dependency upon his superiors actually reawakens certain emotions and attitudes which were part of his relationship with his parents, and which apparently have long since been outgrown [1944, p. 56].

Elsewhere, McGregor notes that

> . . . to be a subordinate in an organization is to be placed in a dependent relationship which has enough of the elements of the earlier one to be sensitive and, under certain conditions, explosive [1960, p. 27].

97

In working-class and middle-class families, the resolution of dependence bonds is the chief task of adolescence. During adolescence the connotations of one's childhood are rejected, and an adult identity (with a sense of its autonomy) is created. This developmental period not only is stormy but often does not complete the task set out for it. To the extent to which the adolescent mission is incomplete, strong feelings are awakened in the adult where authority issues arise. Such feelings include extrasensitivity to infringements of autonomy, resentment against anyone in charge, and concerns about the way power is exercised.

The progress of adolescence in the slums is often similar to that of adolescence elsewhere, but it is also sometimes different. A slum child may be pushed into the quasi-adult world of city street corners at a very early age, and he may never experience the support of adults in his intimate environment. It may be forced to play a manly or womanly role at age eight, with complete autonomy and with very little help from anyone other than peers. In entering the first organizational environment (the school), such a child may conceive of itself as entitled to the prerogatives of adulthood, like the personal respect of others, and complete freedom. This self-image raises a live issue where teachers seek to exercise control over their classrooms by circumscribing the spontaneous acts of students. Carl Wertham notes that the slum child carries its "posture of premature autonomy . . . directly into the schools. . . . As early as the first and second grade, his teachers find him wild, distracted, and utterly oblivious to their presumed authority" (p. 162). Wertham describes a determined battle, waged by miniature men and women, against what they perceive as "disrespect." The weapons in this battle include the testing of limits, the challenging of orders, and a stance of consistent insolence. The same battle is waged against police officers on the street (Wertham and Piliavin) and, later, against staff of penal institutions.

The Abuse of Prison Authority

The history of penal settings includes the most arbitrary and sadistic, the most bestial abuses of power of which men—in the guise of debased authority—are capable. The outlandish range of living nightmares designed as imprisonment includes concentration camps, debtors' gaols, and tropical or arctic settings in which the cruelty of nature combined with the inhumanity of man to make survival impossible.

In American prisons that exist in our living memory forced labor, lock step, silent rules, beatings, shackling, and long-term segregation were features of an unremittingly harsh routine. Today's American prisons have advanced unevenly but very dramatically. Drastic innovations such as grievance machinery and inmate participation in governance are widespread. There is almost universal stress on custody training and monitoring, and on circumscription of the penalties and restrictions that may be imposed on inmates beyond imprisonment itself.

Harassment

It is significant that rankling abuses of authority cited by today's inmates often revolve around "petty" or minor circumscriptions of their daily lives. Such restrictions are not necessarily seen by inmates as discrete incidents but they may be regarded as demonstrations of a propensity by authority for unwarranted interferences with inalienable rights:

El R 10: They have got a big sign out there, "No pressing of the pants in the tailor shop" . . . nobody wants to walk around with their clothes all wrinkled, not really, you know. A dude has pressed clothes on the outside and he wants it to stay that way. And they don't want you to press your clothes—like they are trying to dehumanize you.

• • •

GH R 1: It was rough doing time, and there was a lot of petty rules, and if the rules all said you can't have your shirttail out, then you would get busted for that, and you would get written up and go to court, and as far as I am concerned this is insanity, and there is no sense to it.

• • •

Cox T 1–1: The officer wouldn't let me go to the shower. And that's how they start a riot. And those are the little things that come out to be big things. So I was getting locked up for calling the officer a motherfucking guard because he wouldn't let me use the shower.

There is also a recurrent inmate concern with inequity, which raises the suspicion of arbitrariness wherever decision making is not completely standardized:

Au N A: They came out with a rule last month where your hair has to be up over the top of your collar, your sideburns here, your mustache here. Now you got the blacks, they got Afros like that, nobody says nothing. As soon as a white guy comes around with long hair, "You better go and get a haircut!"

• • •

GH R F: But over here, they have little things like you can't braid your hair. You know, which over there you can. You know, where one doesn't have, the other does. But it all comes out to the same thing. You might be missing something over there, you come here and you're missing something else.

• • •

Att R 37: Like, if you are in a place where the officer tells you to put your cigarette out, and then you are in a place where there is no sign saying "no smoking," but this particular officer wants to pick on you just to see how your reactions are—right?—and he tells you to put out the cigarette, and you tell him, "What about the other guys?" and "There is no signs," and he keeps quiet, and then you go to your cell, and he will tell you that you are locked up for smoking, and then when you go out there is fifteen days for simple things like that.

Encroaching rules or decisions can be defined as "harassment," a term carrying dictionary connotations of "persistant interference and annoyance." Inmates who define themselves as harassed tend to think in terms of (1) malevolence of authority, and (2) core behavior with which authority interferes. The motive of authority (malevolence) is inferred from its impact, which one assumes is designed to compromise one's dignity, and to tamper with the achievement of one's needs:

GH R F: For everything that they give, they put a bounty on. Like you go to your visits and you're having a very good time, you know, your mom's coming up, and there's this man sitting there looking at you. Now, as soon as your visit is over you're going to get stripped. This man is going to look in your asshole. He sees you right there. It is impossible for you to put anything there, but yet he is going to tell you to strip, bend over, and spread your cheeks. Now, that kills the visit. I don't care how nice the man is, no man is going to look up my ass. This is just another way of harassing you. What is he telling you, you know? He's getting some kind of pleasure out of something, you know? That he sees my thing, that he wants to do this constantly. And then, if you're in the box, they not only do it there but when you go up here, they do it again. So they don't give you nothing, without causing you . . . without those boundaries on you, man, you know? They don't give you nothing. They're always looking for a time to harass. They think they can rule.

• • •

Att R 26: They have locked up guys in the place for felonious kissing in the visiting room. If a guy kisses his wife six times it is felonious kissing, and they lock him up for it, you know?—and it is his own wife, you know?

Even where interferences with one's affairs are acknowledged to be trivial, the aim is seen as to injure seriously. The victim feels that authority uses every opportunity (particularly those that are trivial) in order to assert itself, to remind the rest of us of its omnipotence and of our own helplessness.

The Demand for "Respect"

Some men approach environments with a strong interest in the way authority is exercised, with the expectation that authority will be abused. This perspective not only makes circumscriptions salient but also lowers one's threshold for reacting to circumscriptions:

GH N 12: The general appearance that struck me was the authority itself. It wasn't the appearance that they had nice clean floors or clean bars or all that. . . . I go by administration policies and how they operate or run an institution. Like, they were very authoritative when I first came here, everything was regimentation.

• • •

GH R P: I was born in Harlem, and I take everything. To you it may not be nothing, but we take abuse every day, and we see it every day, and when we come to jail we see abuse all day.

• • •

Cox S 17: A lot of the other guys, they sit back, mind their own business, read their books, come out of their gates and talk. So of course they have an easier bit. You don't bother them, they don't bother you. But me, I've always raised hell all my life, so that's why it's tough for me in another division. I don't take no shit from anybody.

A person with this kind of perspective may explicitly broach themes of adolescence, in the sense that he sees himself relegated to a child role that for him is degrading, unacceptable, and demeaning:

Cox S 21: Like the constant marching and the constant, you got to stand up and can't talk and can't this and that, and you can't talk to them like you are a man, so you have to talk to them like—you're not a woman, but you have to talk to them like you are a child, and, like, it isn't no prime communication there.

• • •

Cox S 13: You feel like an adolescent, and it blows your mind. It is a bad feeling.

• • •

GH R 1: There was a terrible sense of being treated like a mindless child . . . you do this and that, and there was no choice. It amounted to, like, being dead.

• • •

Cox T 1–1: You know, I took my medication—right?—but I was angry for them trying to use me like a kid, and the nurse was going to snap at me, because she knows that I can't touch her. If I do I get broke up. So then the nurse told me to open my mouth so they could check to see if my medication went down, and I said no. So they had me locked up.

Orders given by others can be painful, because they are (1) clearly efforts by someone to impose his will on yours, (2) ways of emphasizing that you are lower in status, and (3) means of ensuring that you have less say over your affairs. To a person who has exercised complete autonomy on the streets, each of these aims may be unfamiliar, and may be seen as an attack on one's personal integrity.

Cox S 24: Well, see, I was raised up in the ghettos where I wasn't used to being told what to do. . . . So I get tickets. They feel that by locking you up you'll correspond to them a little bit better the next time. But by locking a person up, more things come out, breaking them down to a lower form, making him worse than he really is.

• • •

Cox T 1–1: The police said, "Yeah, get ready for chow," and then, what do you do if you don't want chow? So why should you have to go to mess hall? So he says, "If you going, you better be ready on time." If you're not, then you get a ticket or get locked up or whatever. So you get ready for chow and you don't feel like going down and you don't want to, but you have to do it anyway, because you're forced to do it. That's one thing to start off the morning with! And it's petty, man.

• • •

Au R BB: Little things, little harassments with the guards, the haircut trip. Just like they know where they're at, and they like us to be lower. Just little things. I mean stuff that they would not even dare write up a report on, because they're so stupid.

There is also the issue of "respect," the discovery that one is not dealt with as a person of worth, while one is expected to treat others as worthy. The working assumption of "do unto me as I do unto you" (and vice versa) may call into question not only the legitimacy of hierarchies but anything that smacks of status differences or privileges of rank. Where there is no equality or reciprocity of interactions, there is no "respect," no recognition of personal integrity, of "manliness":

GH R A: Some people, like, you go to the dermatologist and get a permit you can wear a beard, and, like, in Attica you couldn't do this, you know? They say the reason was for the identification purpose, you know, but you got officers running around with big Afros, you know, beards and long hair. Now, how can you identify them? You know, it's the same thing. We can't wear it, because if we attack an officer, he can't identify us. Now, one of the officers attacked us, how would we identify him? It's the same thing. . . . Things like this that people look forward to. Like, I'm a man, you're a man. I might even be older than you, and you telling me to shave it and that. Things like that.

• • •

Au N B: Here I am a thirty-six-year-old fucking man, and an officer is twenty-two years old, twenty-three years old, and because he's got a badge on and he don't like to hear nobody talking, I can't talk. I can't talk, after seven o'clock at night.

• • •

Cox N 20: And I know myself I can't communicate with the officers, because they say that I'm pushing their authority. But if I'm around a person, and they are constantly asking questions, then I have to be able to ask them questions. That is my affair. So if I start asking them questions, then they say that I'm a rebellious person. And I don't agree with that.

In posing authority issues, age is a significant variable, both developmentally and chronologically. Norms about modes of control are tied to distinctions between the maturity and immaturity of (1) persons generally, (2) oneself, and (3) others. In heterogeneous settings, the self-defined adult may feel inappropriately dealt with, because the climate is defined by the requirements of the less mature. If one stipulates the validity of the person's self-image, the syllogism has merit, because control systems do respond to those needing higher levels of control. Persons who in theory could be unsupervised are caught between the impact of the immature behavior (which needs control) and the impact of the environmental reactions to immaturity:

Cox S 5: It's more rough here to do a bit, because the average inmate in here is real young. And with these dudes, these young dudes, the police have to be strict on them. And by them being strict on them, they get used to being strict on them, and it makes it more difficult for the older inmates. . . . Like a young dude, he can take it. But I can't take that. Like a kid, the officer might say something to him, and then he'll look at me and say the same thing to me. Whereas he won't say nothing, I'm the one that'll tell him how I feel about it. So I get into even more difficulty.

• • •

Au R Q: Now, with all these young kids, you never know from one minute to the next when one of these guys is going to start to hassle here. So they got to watch everybody closely. And by them watching everybody closely, you get this more confined feeling.

• • •

Cox S 8: Them guys will get in the classroom, when the teacher ain't looking, like, if the teacher's writing something down, you'll see a book come flying. And the teacher turns around, nobody knows nothing, you dig? It hit the teacher in the head. . . . Well, the teacher'll say he didn't see who threw it, he'll pick somebody here, and he'll get locked up. A guy goes to class and gets locked up for nothing. It don't even make no sense.

Husbanding Resentment

Where a controlling environment impinges on previously uncontrolled individuals, it invites resentment and helpless rage. These feelings stem from the fact that "infantilizing" or external control makes the person feel unfairly circumscribed. There is also the fact that internal controls (which usually mediate environmental demands) may be a scarce commodity, as a result of which the person feels that, however he reacts, he is dancing to the tune of his keepers:

Att R 37: They take advantage of another man, they treat him like a kid. And when the man reacts to his manhood, they try to bring him back down. And this is what makes you hate them more. Anything you can see that looks like them, you want to hate, you want to get to them. You know, a person that can't relate to you, what you try to do, you try to destroy him. So, since you can't destroy him, you have all this hate in your heart.

• • •

Cox S 21: I understand why there is riots all of the time, because they treat us like babies, and anything that you do is wrong. . . . it makes you angry inside, so when you go back out in society you commit another crime, and they say you didn't learn anything.

• • •

Cox T 1–1: If you are very strong—right?—and they constantly are pushing you—right?—then you have to go along with the game but do all of the things that you say that you dislike for yourself and for your fellow inmates. Then you take all these things in, you suppress them. But when you get out in the world—right?—all this oppression, then you have to let it back out. It's going to be released. What they call racist, revolutionary, or whatever turns you against them. That's what they make you.

A key factor is rage at not being able to express rage, plus the humiliating knowledge that one is actually *afraid* to act. Persons who usually translate their frustrations into violence experience the cumulation of hostile feelings and fantasize retaliation or promiscuous destructiveness:

Cox T 1–1: I was angry and wanted to retaliate. When you check out that nature provided you with certain things to protect yourself, and then when you can't implement what nature has given to you to use as your protection, then you're defeated, and then you become less than a man. So you feel that you just want to strike out more time, that's all. To get something off, you know, retaliate. And you will end up getting the worst part of the deal. . . . You begin to fantasize that you're hitting the police. And then you're going to strike out. But once that you strike out, you're going to get in trouble, and then, if you keep at it, then you're going to get beat up. . . . And that's why the majority of times the dude goes back in the cell, and they begin to think over things, and they get so angry with what's happening in the institution, and they can't do anything, so they try to take it out in their cells. They get angry at the people—right?—for no reason. So all things start coming down all at one time. And that's why sometimes an inmate might be sitting there, and an officer might be coming down, and he might say something, and you might be so angry and under pressure that you might say something wrong and incorrect, and then they lock him up, and they don't have any justice.

• • •

Att R 15: I'm thinking of maybe just letting a little of the frustration out, banging on the wall. I might just think about getting some of the frustrations out this way. Or I might sometimes be thinking about hitting one of the officers here, because they just push me so far.

• • •

GH R U: I see myself as doing it in the streets of this town, hurting a lot of people. Not innocent people. I have delusions that I'll be the first man in the State of New York to leave these prisons and ice about half these fools that have been promising everything but giving us nothing. I don't want to hurt nobody in a candy store, I want to hurt these people that have been keeping me in this dream world, and then letting me down.

The handling of retaliatory urges or the management of resentment can be a consuming enterprise for some persons. These persons may oscillate between periods of seething rage and desperate, heroic measures of self-control:

GH R F: I have to deal with it, you know? It's hard. It's real hard. Especially when you're locked in the cell. . . . I just want to come out and knock one of them on their ass, you understand, and I'll have to go to the box. . . . I talk to myself. I say, "Cool it, man. Things aren't that bad." you know? . . . I get uptight but I control myself, you know? . . . They might say something I don't like, and I don't commit myself, because, if I do, I might go overboard so they have to stop me.

• • •

Cox S 13: There is somebody hollering at me constantly, and the bosses are always saying "Shut up," you know, and in that sharp tone of voice. That—I can't take that. . . . I am feeling inside that I am hurting and on the other hand I know that if I hurt him I will get hurt, so I just try to ride with it, and that is about it. Somehow I survive.

• • •

Att R 15: I've tried to condition myself over the years not to feel anything—to condition myself not to get emotionally involved with a whole lot of things. . . . I just relax myself a little bit. Because I know that I'm behind all this concrete, and I can't do nothing. . . . I sit back, and I try to tell myself to keep cool, but sometimes you just have to let it all out.

A person may also try to control his physical behavior so as to reduce the chances of conflict. He may try to disguise his rage and resentment, to avoid dangerous repercussions and loss of control:

Att R 37: I missed my shower, and he says, "Well, fuck you and your shower." This is the hall captain in the shower. And I say, "What?" and I know I would like to hit him, but if I do they will put another charge on me—right?—so I just go ahead and walk away, you know? . . . I analyze these people, so I stay away from them, as far as I can. And then, when they tell me anything wrong out of their face, I'm already prepared, because I seen what they do to the other person. So I say yes or no, and I keep walking. I don't even look at them at their face too much. If he's standing right in front of me, I turn my face the other way. And so, when they tell me to walk, I just walk over here. Somewhere else. Because, if you look at him too hard, he might think that you're looking at him, you know, something in your mind. So what you do, you just turn your back on him and keep walking. . . . Like, I talk to some of them guys, and I say, "Look here, man, it don't make no sense for you talking back to them officers when they tell you, even though you know they're wrong. All you got to do is turn around and walk away from them; you let them know that you have more sense than they do. You have more understanding." See, a fool just stands there and keeps arguing and keeps arguing, when you know all you got to do is just walk away from the man. Don't keep arguing with him, because, if he knows that you're right, his pride ain't going to let him say, "Well, you're right." This is what's wrong with these people, his pride ain't going to let him say, "You're right." They don't know how to say that. . . . I've been locked up four years. Since '71, and all I got is one report, for not taking a shave, that's the only thing.

● ● ●

Cox T 1–1: If you try to become something that is equal to the officer, you're going to be looked at as a leader, and the first time that something jumps off you're going to be seeing most of the retaliation. . . . Don't let them know your chain of thought. Keep them thinking on the train of thought that you will coincide with the institution.

● ● ●

Cox S 9: If I don't put myself in that position, I will not be harassed; although you have some officers that are just waiting for me, you know, to put myself in that position, and this is why I know I must be careful. . . . I will speak to them in a civilized tone, because I know that the second word is the one that starts the quarrel.

Compromise resolutions can involve expressions of hostility that are (1) thinly disguised, (2) indirect, and (3) hard for the target to document. Such conduct (which can get embroidered in the telling) amounts to a kind of "playing the dozens." The object is to make authority figures lose their cool without justifications that they can point to:

Cox N 20: The officer, he came at me and called me a black nigger or something, and I laughed at him, and he didn't agree with the way that I laughed. I was supposed to get upset with him. And then he came back and called me something else. So I asked the other inmate if he was hearing voices or if there was another clown running round here trying to impress somebody. So he got mad and came up in my face, and I called him a dog or something, and he got mad. So then he told me that I was going to lock up, and he came down with the sticks at me.

* * *

Au R AA: Some of these police, they say "blah, blah," and I say "I was wrong." That fucks them up, because they want you to react violently, and that just throws them right off.

* * *

GH R R: You see, I was trying to finish painting these murals, these big paintings. And the individual correction officer of the administration, they were harassing me. And I didn't respond violently, but what I did, I took out all my anger on the canvas. So what I did, I painted me in the picture with them, but yet with me the authority. And with them on the galleries. And that even brung more pressure. So it seemed to be one of them things where they see that my will and my determination is stronger than theirs. And, like, they still harass me now, every now and then, but not as much. . . . It's the only way I can fight back. You know, I can fight back legally.

A variation of the strategy is to calmly question authority by asking it to justify itself. This gambit challenges the legitimacy of authority and expresses hostility in an unimpeachably legalistic context. The gambit has the added advantage of hoisting authorities by their own ideology (Mathiesen):

Cox T 1–1: We asked him if he could present us with a copy of the rules. Because people were breaking the rules without even knowing they were breaking them. So the lieutenant, he got angry. . . . They're going against the rules. And you say then, "What's the rules, man?" "Look in your little green book." And you look in the book, but that's not in there. You don't see it, because the officers make up the rules as they go along. . . . One time a sergeant came in the mess hall and he said, "Move on down the table." So I asked him in a normal respectful tone—right?—I knew I was going to get locked up if I said anything to the guy, I said, "Sergeant, excuse me, but you know that you don't have to holler at me like this and curse at us." So he said, "Get over there by the fucking coat rack, you're going to get locked up," right? So I got locked up, right? And on the ticket it stated that I was disrespectful to a sergeant. So you can get locked up for anything. Sometimes you just get so angry that you say "fuck it" to everything. So I refused to get locked up for that. But I got locked up anyway.

GH R F: It's supposed to be a written statement any time you're in a service unit like this is. A copy must be written to the Commissioner; he must sanction every movement they make, and he must send back a written copy, which they're supposed to show you at your request. If I asked for it, I want to see this, understand?

• • •

Att R 26: The man tells me—you know?—there is not enough reason for a furlough—you know?—you might lose your wife or you might lose your kids. . . . So then I filed another set of furlough papers, and it was denied again. The same short answer—instant offenses. So I turned around, and I started court action in '75, to show cause of action. I had in my possession a list of inmates—big time, twenty years, fifteens, twenties, twenty-fives—who had got furloughs.

• • •

EI R 7: It was so hot that I can't stand to sit down, and he told me to sit down, and I didn't feel like sitting down, and I wanted to stand by the window and feel the air, and he told me, "No, you got to sit down," and so I asked him if there is a sign that says you have to sit down, because I know that there is none, and so I got locked up for thirty days because I don't want to sit down.

Reluctant Compliance

Milgram points out that "for many people obedience may be a deeply ingrained behavior tendency, indeed a prepotent impulse overriding training in ethics, sympathy, and moral conduct" (p. 1). There are also people who are prone to disobedience; in fact, we see that there are men to whom resisting authority may be the "deeply ingrained behavior tendency" or "prepotent impulse."

No matter how a person reacts, he often does what those in authority ask of him. He conforms to orders or demands because he is convinced of their reasonableness or usefulness (internalization), because he has personal loyalties (identification), or because he wants to be rewarded or avoid being punished (compliance) (Kelman). Most "obedient" persons may respond with ease, but the rebel conforms (or at least goes through the motions of conforming) under what he identifies as duress.

When a man who sees himself as free finds himself acting nonautonomously, he has a problem with the congruity or consistency of his feelings and acts. The compliance model becomes attractive, because it at least excludes the identification and internalization models. It is face-saving to be overrun rather than to betray friends or principle, or to discover oneself giving the devil (authority) his due. A prisoner of war may be a hero, but to be a collaborator is despicable.

Compliance is unthinkable where power is absent. To comply minimally means that you act as long as someone stands over you—preferably with a gun. If you exceed this norm, you must ask yourself why you are exceeding it. The most attractive explanation is that of reluctant, half-hearted, surface compliance, or—as in Korean POW camps—the presumption of hidden enemy power or "brainwashing." An ideal formula may combine these two themes:

Cox T 1–1: I started going with the program. It's not that I liked the program, it's just that they forced me to act in a particular way, so they can feel that they're rehabilitating you. They think they're rehabilitative, but actually it's not rehabilitative. I have an idea myself not to go along with them.

I: You're just playing the game to get out of here?

Cox T 1–1: Right. To get out. . . . They try to make people act other than themselves. That's the hardest bit right there. If you don't act the way the officer wants you to act, then that's your hardest bit right there. You have to go over the psychological things. . . . All the things that I was saying were psychological. Like, for instance, when they talk to you. You don't like to be disrespected. And manhood is one of those things that—like, if he starts talking to you like you're an animal and dirty—dig it?—and you can't say anything to him, or the first time that you say something to him, you get locked up. And, like, that's where your manhood is taken. . . . That was maybe it. I couldn't see myself being a man, right? All the other inmates in here are not being men—right?—except that it's called in Attica psychological repression, right? They realize that if they begin to try to do something to better their way in here that they're going to get in trouble. Get beat or more time, so they act childish so that they can do their time easier. And I don't want to submit to this, right? So everything starts psychological.

Extending the definition of "brainwashing" can make all authority malevolent and threatening. Conciliatory moves or extensions of benefit are never assessed at face value. They are hypocritical palliatives or fiendish gambits in a behavior modification strategy:

GH N 7: If I was looking at it from an individual point of view, certainly I would say, okay, the joint is nice now. Because they're giving me back all the privileges that I had, institutional pass, living in the honor block, which only consisted of a TV. All these devices that they have is just another means, I say, of behavior modification, or trying to control a guy so they have a guy in a position where they can look at him and see whether they approve or they disapprove.

• • •

Att R 15: I feel so, even though they do have a lot of inmates that are not aware, that don't know what's happening in this institution. And they get programmed, basketball, and they come out of their cells just like robots, you know, programmed. That's the whole truth.

• • •

GH N 12: I have a feeling it's a purpose for them, almost a devious purpose. They're planning on enlarging the cells down there, or they're planning on putting washing machines in. Yeah, this stuff is nice, but what is it doing? What is it doing for the prison, the inmate? . . . Passive, passive. You see what they do, a couple of years back they started saying we could have *Penthouse* and *Playboy* and all that other stuff. These were contraband before. So we figured out they probably knocked out at least twenty-five show causes. They let in tape cassettes, this knocked out fifty 440-10s. A guy gets something serious now, they send him right outside, to an outside hospital. They just knocked down fifty civil rights complaints, 1983s. So it's a scheme, it's almost like a pyramidic scheme, in which they organize these things for a passive overthrow of the inmate. . . . See, this is what I have against, not only the administration, but what I have against a lot of these inmates. That they follow, you give them all you can give to help them stay happy. You keep feeding them these things, they have really no place in society, they have no place even in here. As a matter of fact, this is going to turn into their home, they have to eventually kick guys out of here.

Such views cement perceptions of personal consistency and build a favorable self-image. Where others are duped by handouts and surface gestures, the rebel, who can "see through" authoritarian benevolence, stands as a tower of insight, sophistication, and principle.

Self-styled Militance

A rebel must fight against self-doubt when others around him conform, and where he himself sometimes conforms. He may also have to cope with feelings of futility in the face of obdurate, inviolate circumstance. To deal with impotence, it helps the rebel to see himself as a Feared and Respected Opponent rather than as an insignificant source of nuisance value. Incidents of rebelliousness are summated, and a revolutionary pattern emerges. This pattern is presumed to appear in one's "looking-glass self," or one's reputation with authorities:

Cox N 20: I do seem to have a reputation, because I disagreed with some things. And then I've talked to a lot of the officers that don't even know me, and just by the name they say, "Don't trouble me." They all tell me I'm a troublemaker.

• • •

Cox T 1–1: Then I went to the hospital. And when I was up there, I don't know, I guess they must have tried to diagnose me . . . and they came up with that I was a black racist. One of the wild ones. And I wasn't going to submit for nothing. And I stayed the way I was when I came. I am not going to change for them.

• • •

GH R A: I got a good understanding of the Attica indictments, you know, and why I was the one who was indicted myself you know, and why the other people that's indicted now, why they was indicted, you know? Like, it wasn't for crimes that was committed during the . . . during the night. Like, we were indicted for our past history inside the institution, you know, like, as far as speaking back to the officers, you know, and like holding classes in the yard, you know, things like that.

Fortunately *and unfortunately,* authorities often subscribe to stereotypes of militance. They may also be oversensitive to challenge, overconcerned with noncompliance, and eager to see patterned threats in isolated events. Authorities may engage in undignified, intemperate, and inappropriate reactions, which play into rebel hands. Such reactions may also create stress, both for the rebel and for the opposition:

GH R U: There was forty-two of us that came from Attica because we were the worst radicals of Attica. And they wanted to close this joint down, they were protesting us coming here. So when we went to supper there was about twelve hacks with us. When the other companies went to supper there was one hack with them. Right then and there I knew what was happening . . . It was misleading on both sides, actually. On our side and their side. Because they did think that they were going to have a little trouble.

• • •

Cox T 1–1: So then when you go upstairs, I met officers that never even knew me, they never met me in my life, but they know the other officer that I gave a hard time to one time. So you know, he raps to his buddy and he'll say, "Oh, yeah, I got this division." And the other officer knows that I'm in this division, so he'll say, "Yeah, this might be an all right division, but do you know that you've got this person up there, and he's a ball buster, and this and that." When that officer comes up and starts looking at me objectively, then he's got a one-sided view. And he's not going to look at my point of view, he's going to look at his buddy's view and his. And the first thing that I do, he's going to holler or lock me up.

There's no way that you can get around it, unless you be a child, a kid, and pour it on the officers and do everything they want you to do. And then that's sick. The last time that I was here I acted that way, even though I didn't want to, so that I could get out. . . . I'm a five-percenter, and anybody that they know is a five-percenter they put down on their card in big huge letters in red ink that they're five-percenters. And then they put down the name that you have yourself. But when you say that you're a Protestant, then you never see this. But then as soon as something jumps off, they see your card and they see the five-percenter there . . . and you've got the worst of the deal automatically. That's why a lot of dudes tell them that they are not five-percenters when they actually are.

• • •

GH N 7: We both was classified as being aggressive, disgruntled, you know, that type of statement. When I come down to Green Haven, my record went everywhere I went. For instance, on disciplinary action, the first thing they say is, "We notice that you were in the Attica riot, and we noticed here that Comstock says that you was a disquiet inmate and that you was a militant and aggressive," etcetera. This is irrelevant to the charges I might be there for. I might be there for disobeying an officers' request; and this request might be something that I thought was not reasonable. . . . So there's not going to be an institution they really can send me to that will really accept me. From that point of view, right? I also had requested to take up some courses here, and I wasn't allowed, because they considered me to be too aggressive and militant.

• • •

Att R 26: Like, I have been told that I have been ruffling, like, too many feathers. That even if I win this, they will win them all. Even if they don't get me right away, they will get . . . they will get me.

A Man of Militance can extend his concern to encompass violations of other people's autonomy. He can react with resentment if he personally witnesses (or feels he is witnessing) incursions into the rights of others. He becomes emotionally mobilized in environments in which authority-peer confrontations occur, or where rumors of injustice circulate. He enters and escalates conflicts (without much data) where his interests are not imperiled. The real issue for the rebel may not be class membership or group loyalty, but the need to classify any use of power as an abuse of power:

Att R 15: Then I told him, "What happens to one inmate happens to me, because he's part of me." . . . And I was very emotionally involved, you know, and when they dragged a guy by my cell, and I was standing by the cell, and the officer hesitated to go by, because I had a broom handle in my hand, and I said to him, "Why don't you pick him up? You've already got him handcuffed. Why beat him any more than you already have? Everything is under control!" You know, they starve him from the mouth and they act like they're getting pleasure out of it, and sometimes they do, dragging them and beating them.

• • •

GH N 19: You know, like, they give me a work release program, I go out on the street and work and make a paycheck every day, right? Wow, that's good, you know? Even if I did it, I would still be thinking about the guy in the strip cell. And any little thing that an officer says to me, that contains that, "Like we got to do that because of such and such," I would say, "No, man, you don't have to do it, and you're wrong for doing it." Even if that would jeopardize work release. It wouldn't change anything as long as I know that certain thing is still happening in the institution, no matter what they could give me. What kind of job or how much freedom or anything.

In the more extreme versions of such a world view, the presumption of abuse turns into a presumption of danger. Freedom and Safety concerns converge. Authorities may be seen as having malevolent designs and as engaging in outlandish plots to emasculate or destroy people. This view can be stressful in that it creates a sense of vulnerability:

Att R 15: They have psychiatrists or whatever you'd like to call them coming up here and giving the guys drugs and all of this here. That's bad. . . . And the food here, I would say that they must have some kind of drugs in the food. I think so. I think that they are experimenting with a lot of these inmates in here. It's almost tasteless. It's like it has sleeping pills in here.

• • •

GH R E: If you don't go, then they beat you up like hell, you know? They almost killed a man last week. See, when they say you got to do something, that's supposed to be the supreme law from above, you got to do it right then and there, and if you don't do it, then you get beat up. And if you fight back, they try to kill you. . . . Sure it's dangerous. Your life don't mean nothing in here.

• • •

Cox T 1–1: I saw it. They beat the boy, and they stomped him, and they sprayed him, they tore his shirt off, they threw him in the shower and made him choke, and then they came back and put a rag around his neck, choking him in the rec room while they stomped him. And they kept telling him, "You're going to sign a paper, nigger." . . . It got me nervous, because I know what could happen when they start off looking for you. You don't get out.

I: Previously you considered yourself somewhat of a target, that all these guys knew about you, and they were going to try to mess up your bit?

Cox T 1–1: I didn't just think it, man, I knew it. The actually told me in a roundabout way that something was going to happen.

GH N 19: Everybody started yelling. You know, like they're telling the officers, "Give him what he wants; he's supposed to get it" or "Leave him alone." While inmates were yelling, they would get a tape recorder and hold it at the end of the tier, right? This is to get all the noise on the tape recorder, so they can justify their tear-gassing the tier. See what I'm saying? They may even come around and provoke something. I don't know if it's intentional or not, but it happened. You know, like where a dude is in his cell, what can he possibly do or say that would warrant somebody shooting a can of tear gas on a whole tier? And that's how it is.

If one sees oneself as a victim, it is hard to acknowledge one's active role in frequent disputes or confrontations with authority. Conflicts invariably become occasions on which one is arbitrarily assaulted without provocation:

GH N 19: They took me up to Attica, and, when I got to Attica, they tell me not to hit officers, this and that, blah, blah, blah, and they gassed me. I was there three weeks, right? . . . They claimed that I hit a doctor down there. So they were trying to give me another sentence.

• • •

Au N 7: I was locked up, and I was accused of having tried to assault an officer with a broomstick, which was a fallacy. I was sitting in the back of my cell getting ready for the tear gas, but, because I had ordered books from China Publications just for educational purposes and to read for myself and to understand—right?—I was considered a radical, right?

• • •

Cox T 1–1: And then I see dudes talking in their gate, and they tell the dude to get off their gate, and he might get off his gate, but when they go away he might go back there again. And if they come back up and see him there, they might go and call somebody, and they might have somebody come up there then to beat him up. . . . I had my hand up and they told me to swing.

There are benefits in seeing oneself as a David who is singled out by the Goliaths of this world. When one's slingshot fails, there is satisfaction in continued efforts to harass authority through litigation or passive resistance. The point here is not to win (because the cards, by definition, are stacked) but to demonstrate one's ability to retain both integrity and autonomy:

GH R E: The way they railroaded me to jail, I wouldn't work, I'd die before I'd work in any institution. I wouldn't work. I wouldn't even accept parole. If I ain't good enough to get no justice, I ain't good enough to get up in the witness stand and tell the truth. I ain't no good to go on parole or nothing else. They can't make no deals with me. I'll file a fifty million dollar suit against the state. . . . In Attica they locked me up for a year when I told V. I wasn't going to work nowhere. He locked me up for a year. . . . And all they do is run around all day and take the people up there that refuse to work down in the population. They say, "Ready to go to work?" . . . I ain't going to do any kind of work in this institution. But I'm different from a whole lot of guys you got down here telling you that they ain't going to work. Line them outside against a wall out there and put a machine gun in that yard, and "You going to work or else we're going to blow your brains out." I say, "Kill me. I don't give a damn. Get it all over with." Hell, these guys, they'll go to work, man, they ain't going to take no pressure. . . . I don't give a damn if the water gets up to my eyebrows, I still ain't going to give up. I'm from the old school. Never feel like cracking up and doing something. Act normal. . . . You got to have control of yourself before you can have control of other things, and I got all the control in the world.

● ● ●

GH R F: I'm here mainly for not giving up.

I: And how long have you been down here?

GH R F: For a month.

I: For not giving up?

GH R F: And they tried to force this job on me. So they come out and told me I got to take this, but I don't want this. So when you don't want it, they put you down here. . . . But actually you're not compelled to work. I'm not a hard laborer. So, therefore, I don't have to work. The only reason a person will work is to get some money for his commissary and things of this nature. But I will not work. I do not want to work, you know? In other words, "Take this." Why should I? . . . But they going to try and force it upon you. "We want you to." I want to do what's beneficial to me. What I want, not what they want. I'm doing this time. It's not what they want. . . . I was here in '67, '69, and I had a great deal of difficulty here to the point of where they had to break me up, literally. I got in an argument with an officer, and when I was cuffed, they jacked me up, which is the normal procedure.

The equation works if it remains a Formula of Defiance. A person must have control over his resisting, retaliating or aggressing, and he must see himself as goal-directed. Where his feelings get out of hand (where resistance occurs through tantrums), it becomes less clear that the threat is external and that it is possible to resist it. On such occasions (which are rare) autonomy battles can become autonomy crises:

GH N 19: This got me frustrated, the fact that they wouldn't release me from the hospital, but at the same time they wouldn't put me nowhere else. See, because they were saying, like, I was violent. I hit a correction officer in Elmira; I hit a doctor in—which I'm still going to court for right now—I hit a doctor in Matteawan. And you can't go here. I said, "What am I staying here for? If I'm mentally ill, get me out of this institution. What are you saying? Are you saying that I'm mentally ill, or are you saying that I'm sane? You got to make your mind up." They wouldn't give me an answer, you know what I mean? So I started thinking, man, it just got to me. You know, I couldn't control myself. So I attempted suicide, and they caught me. . . . Well, I just got so frustrated, you know? And, like I said, what's the sense of it? It seems like any time I go to the joint, or a different institution, and file proceedings, court proceedings, they just seem to eliminate that by moving me out to another place. And then they go to court and tell the judge, well, it's moot, because he's not in the institution any more. . . . That's what happened; it seemed useless, and I got frustrated, and I just didn't see any sense to it any more.

Responsible and Irresponsible Authority

The relationship between autonomy and dependence is intimate and complex. To pursue autonomy in theory means to sacrifice supports; it means to be left to one's own resources. If one seeks supports, one reduces the range of one's discretion and freedom of choice.

This sort of law, however, is neither logical nor psychological. In an ideal "client-centered" world, unconditional support can be linked to unconditional autonomy. Such a world may exist in expectation and may cause us to bite (or ignore) the hands that feed us. We can vociferously defy those in charge, while we may simultaneously complain about the lateness or inadequacy of our subventions or allowances.

It is equally possible to have neither autonomy nor nurturance. In concentration camps (and to a lesser extent, in homes) freedom and benefits can be consistently withheld. We may have no say about our lives, and our needs may be ignored or frustrated.

In such instances—or in situations that are seen this way—it is hard to disentangle the parameters of resentment. To complain about persons in charge means to bemoan their indifference and the arbitrariness with which they exercise power. These two complaints are linked, in that they point to the sort of all-around inhumanity that casually violates human integrity wherever it can. Authorities are doubly reprehensible, because they cheerfully exercise control or negative functions, while they retreat from their responsibility to provide necessary positive services:

Au R Z: You have some officers that won't even bother to make a call on the phone unless you've got the interview slip. And if you've got the interview slip, it might take two or three days. And this is an emergency problem that has arisen. . . . Intervene right away, rather than let a guy go to his cell, and think that nothing was being did for the next day and the next day. So now you're all frustrated, nothing's being did, and everybody seems to disregard what he's saying. . . . I don't ask for too much here myself, because I know the way the system is. I know they don't care no more about me than they care about the next guy.

• • •

GH R 1: Stress I don't see in terms of actual physical structure. Stress I see in terms of, like I mentioned, the other day I had a visit, and I found out later that afternoon that the visitor sat up there from eleven in the morning until two in the afternoon, and they never called me, and how that is, like, insulting and degrading, and I was furious at the time, and I was, like, I seen red. . . . I just couldn't convey to her that, so I had to try to go over her head, and that was a stress area for me, and it came to a point where I didn't want to fucking talk about it no more. . . . Another stress area is communications. Immediate communication is what is taking place in the street when you are out there in the community, and if you have to do something you pick up a phone and call or get on the bus or get in your car. Here sometimes it takes, like, three weeks for something that takes like ten minutes out there, and that is very frustrating.

• • •

GH N 12: This I believe causes a lot of hostility in a prison, the administration. A person has a specific need, or he needs an answer, he asked a question. I mean, he has something really purposeful, and he has nowhere to go. He has absolutely nowhere to go. . . . The most would be when they didn't let me go to the hospital for fifteen months for my operation, and also answers I needed from the administration, which took months and months, and constantly putting in interview slips and finding out what happened with previous interview slips.

A person can see his autonomy violated if he is subject to one-way (nonreciprocal) communication. The first side of the coin is the circumscribing messages to which the person is subjected; the second side is his inability to bargain, defend himself, or otherwise respond. Not being listened to involves a violation of one's integrity, because it violates equity and lowers the chance to influence one's fate:

Att R 26: Maybe it is they have heard so many kinds that they believe everybody is trying to con them. . . . When I was explaining this to him, he said, like, I was trying to con him—right?—and I just about come off the desk to smash him and tell him, "Lookit, I am serious. I know what the fuck I am talking about, and this ain't no bullshit."

• • •

GH N 12: When I went to the parole board and I seen that the parole board was the same old thing from ten years ago, nothing changed. Maybe they weren't spitting in your face like they used to, but maybe sometimes I feel that this would have been better, because they were more or less telling you more than they were asking you. . . . I can say, "Look, I didn't do it." You know, they're not going to believe that. They're going to go by the record and all that. So an inmate really has no power, no personal authority to really give his side of the story, or even to back it up.

• • •

Cox S 1: And what good is your version of it, because you've got officers who head the release board, they look at it this way—they even tell people this—"you're jail wise." They'll tell you this, you know, "we think you're jail wise. How have you managed to take no tickets and stay 13 months?" That's the average stay here, say about 13 months—and they'll go, "how have you managed to do this?" You know. . . . they believe that you're causing all kinds of trouble, but you're just getting over on them.

Reciprocity of communication builds links between men who are governed and those who are governing them. It makes it possible to negotiate, to question, to build relationships that ameliorate the impact of power. Distinctions can be drawn among the ranks of one's keepers between those one can communicate with ("relate to") and those who are unable or unmotivated to be human or flexible:

GH N 15: The officers up there, if you're from New York City, you cannot relate to them in any way whatsoever. They're all officers that have been upstate all their life, basically farmers. They can't react to any situation. They're not close. Like most of these officers here in Green Haven are from the city. They grew up in the city. I don't mean to say that they're letting us get away with murder or anything, but they can relate to us better. You can sit down and talk to an officer in this place, I don't care if you're white, Spanish, or black or whatever. You can relate fairly well to an officer, because the officers here know basically what it was to grow up in New York City. And I think they have more compassion. . . . I feel that the major problem here is the young new officers that come in, and they want to make an impression, and they want to show that they're the boss, they carry the badge, and they want to get the respect by following everything to the book. You can't follow everything to the book in a state institution, dealing with thousands of inmates, you have to give a little, and the inmates give a little. I think the officer who has been here a year or two has fallen into it where everything is running smoothly, and he knows he doesn't have to stick right to that book. When a new officer comes in, he tries to follow that rule book, and it just can't be done. You can't change the inmate himself after he's fallen into this certain groove. . . . They're just new officers that are just out of the academy. The academy teaches nothing, in my opinion, from the officers that I've spoken to. There's no teaching whatsoever, the proper way to deal with an inmate, or what things to let slide. I think they teach them that they're supposed to be trained killers or something, and they're com-ing into the institution and they're guards. You have a man five foot six who guards an inmate who stands six feet tall and weighs 250 pounds. But you can reason with people, you can reason with anybody. These new officers aren't taught to reason. They're taught, "This is how you do it." After a month or two, then they learn. And even the old-time officers who have been here for years and years, who were considered the rough officers of years ago, have conformed to this so-called new system.

Distinctions can also be drawn between those who hold power lightly and those who exercise it inflexibly. This allows for the chance to challenge authorities selectively. Such a stance is congruent with autonomy concerns, because it can assume that the "good guys" are exceptions to the rules, even where "good guys" are men one deals with and others are an abstraction.

A continuing relationship with men in authority can bring mellowing of adolescent protest and can reduce autonomy concerns. This impact is most dramatic where the autonomy issue has been emotionally highly charged or has been linked to a career of protest. In such cases it is common to witness "conversions" in which behavior is drastically and permanently modified.

Such developments are surprising only if we forget that the rejection of dependence is ambivalent. Adolescence is stormy in part because we re-linquish the benefits of childhood. The rebel may rage loudly because he deplores the failure of those in power to love and nurture the powerless. If this belief is disconfirmed, bitterness can turn into surprise and, even-tually, loyalty:

Cox T 1–1: After a while I remember what could be said as a turning point. I began to fall in with the program. And I admit that, when I first came in here, I had the idea that all police was, you know, like gestapo. And when they kicked me out of school I met an officer that I had to work with constantly all day without—even these officers here, they were pulling for me. Now this don't happen every day, but they were pulling for me. Saying that I was all right and this and that. Other than that there was one officer that I sure liked. Not on a personal basis, but we would associate with each other, he was all right.

• • •

GH R 1: Most of the guys that rebel and reject the environment, the people are just being natural now, and these are people that have some-thing left within them in terms of human values. They come into a situation like this and say wow—this is not where it is at and I cannot fucking adjust to this, and these are the people that are potentially the guys that are going to turn their heads around and be the constructive members of society because they have something within them that tells that this is an environment that is lacking in love and in anything that is worth living about, and the guys in the boxes are the ones that are working to turn their heads around, believe it or not. Those in segregation and the ones with the longest disciplinary records, these are the guys that don't want to come to prison because they don't like the feeling. But the parole board and the administration see it differently. They see a long disciplinary record and say—well this guy will never change and when actually this is the guy that is susceptible to the change.

Other Freedom Concerns

The drive for autonomy is not the only concern that is related to human freedom. Though the adolescent strives for independence, he also strives for identity. To do so, he seeks the chance to rehearse behavior that is uniquely his own and to adopt a life-style, an appearance, and personal possessions that distinguish him from most of the rest of us.

The opportunity for truly distinctive conduct is valued as an aid in dealing with others and in maintaining our concept of self. Institutions that insist on uniformity undermine self-respect and foster apathy and dependence. They encourage pliability (Goffman), but they do so by making the sick sicker and the helpless more helpless (Wing). Most people prize the opportunity for distinctiveness as a way of preserving their sense of identity but also as a means of ensuring their continued capacity for exercising initiative in daily life:

Au R N: No feeling of being able to say anything about your life. It is like everything is shoveled to you. You know, you are in this hole, and everything that you need—your room, your board, your house—is shoveled through a hole at you. That takes all the responsibility away from a person, and then X amount of years later you are out in the streets again, and then you will be responsible, which you never had to be, and it is like being in the other world. . . . And you come in here, and you are given your sheets, and you are given your room to sleep in, and they try to make you as comfortable as they can within security, you know, which is another trick. And then you go out in the street, like I said before, and then you have got a whole different ball game.

• • •

Au N 7: And the lack of movement and freedom and lack of responsibility! I mean, how can you be a responsible member of society if they don't give you any responsibility—how can you make decisions on the street if you can't make decisions in prison? . . . The advantages of being here are that you have some semblance of freedom and some semblance of responsibility and some semblance of making decisions for yourself . . . there is that choice—do this or do this or do this. Even if it is in the choice of, well, will I have to cut my sideburns because the officer said to cut them, I could slide, you know, I could get by, but should

I cut them, you know? Even that choice. . . . Wearing clothes that you want to wear—right?—some men here wear a certain hat. This is their identity. They wear a certain type of hat. Another man might wear a certain type of ring.

Another aspect of freedom is physical freedom, which can mean space, activity, and a chance to move about. Physical freedom may be a critical aspect of the physical environment and may hold a value of its own:

Att R 26: When I came to Attica, you know, this place was a lot better than the county jail. I had freedom of movement. Like, when I walked out of the car to come in the gates, it is the first time—it was snowing out— it was the first time in thirteen months that I have had snow or rain or something fall on my head, and it was just the idea of having just a little bit of freedom around that was good.

• • •

Au R BB: When I got down here, compared to Attica, this place was wide open. No tunnels, no guns pointing in your back every time you moved. It was like, I don't know how to explain it, it was like walking out of a real tight room into a big room.

But, like other physical dimensions, freedom has connotations that transcend physical impact. These connotations may relate to expanding one's sense of self, one's ability to act, and one's control of feelings:

GH R R: And all these gates, it develops a much stronger psychological outlook that you must control yourself. In a sense it brings static, it brings hate. You see all these bars, it's like locking you off from the rest of the world. There's a big 40-foot wall out there, all over the institution. And you have to come through the wall to come in, right? Who's going over the wall?

• • •

GH N 15: Sure, because I get around the whole institution without any problems. I'm not confined to an area, I walk in different blocks. . . . A tremendous sense of freedom. The first time since I've been upstate that I've really felt that I can do this time, and plus involve myself into other things.

• • •

GH R 1: I find that this is an impression that I got when I got here— just the environment had me feeling inhibited. Here is a physical environment that had an impression on me. It is so crowded, and a guy gets in prison any number of years, accumulates stuff, and has to put it in the cell. And one night I couldn't even get out of the bed, there was so much stuff on the floors, and there is only about a foot and a half between the bed and the wall, and you have to find places to stick books and papers, and I do art work, and you have to find someplace for that and the typewriter, and it is just the physical environment—the cell is inhibiting. . . . When I go into a cell at night I am conscious of compromising my own human values, and there is times that I wouldn't go into the cell by my-self. I would have to be forced in. And that is getting into it really heavy. . . . I remember a time when this environment had me feeling like half a man. I would look at a woman, and I would look down at the floor, because it was that type of feeling. I thought it was me, and then I under-stood, in years to come it was just the environment that was causing that feeling, and it was a very unnatural environment.

• • •

Cox S 21: They said, "Do you want to go to segregation?" And I said, "For what?" And they said, "For protection," and so I refused to sign the paper, and they put me down there anyway. And I stayed in F block for five months—that is where you urinate and everything, and you're in the cell. And I stayed there five months, and at the end of the fifth month I seen two doctors, and they said that something was wrong with me, and I was shaking a little. But for five months being down there a person that was half crazy would go all crazy.

It is in this area that prison has its simplest, and its most obvious effect. For an environment designed to confine men physically confines them psy-chologically as well. A prison creates a world that demands constricted acts, thoughts, and feelings. It is a world in which strong and tragic resent-ments are bound to fester and sometimes to explode.

8

Environmental Themes and Variations

WE CONCEIVE OF PEOPLE'S CONCERNS with environment as psychological priorities that vary from person to person and from setting to setting. It is an assumption that we must examine more closely and we must document to the degree that we can.

In Chapters 2 through 7, we outlined what we mean by environmental "concerns." We implied that people, by virtue of being human, require some very basic commodities in the world around them. We suggested that these requirements become individually stronger or weaker because of differences in personal experiences and motives, which determine what a person wants most in order to cope with the world and to survive in it. This means that, while most of us might consider some environmental qualities to be "desirable" or "undesirable," we expect differences in the hierarchies or profiles of these concerns as we explore the subjective worlds of different persons.

We also expect that the attributes an environment has—the "strengths" and "weaknesses" of the environment—will evoke, challenge, or stymie different sets of personal concerns. As a corollary, the same individual will respond differently to two different social worlds. He will find more or less congruence or a better or worse "match" in one social setting than in another, or in a third.

We conducted our interviews in large maximum security prisons and explored the preferences, aversions, and experiences of inmates in those prisons. In these interviews, we included the "self-anchoring" scale we described earlier. All the interviews were coded for the presence or the salience of the concerns we have described in Chapters 2 through 7. Any theme that came up repeatedly or consistently in an interview was recorded as a personal concern of the respondent; the most dominant such concern was coded as primary.

123

The interviews were independently analyzed by two coders, and any residual inconsistencies were resolved in conference. Reliability was calculated for one sample ($N = 77$); and a coefficient of .77 showed that the reliability was good. The finding is particularly impressive, given the complexity of our analysis and given the fact that the number of themes ranged as high as six and averaged 2.9 per interview.

Table 8-1 describes our overall findings; it includes all usable interviews and provides separate totals for (1) the random samples, and (2) the stratified (random) samples comprising identifiable prison subenvironments. The table shows that Freedom is by far the most salient concern of inmates; the theme occurs prominently in two thirds of our interviews and is the primary theme for two out of five respondents.

Feedback, Support, Privacy, and Safety have almost equal prevalence. Structure is less of a dominant concern, and Activity appears to have the lowest priority. Inmates in the stratified samples have roughly the same concerns as those in the random samples. Not surprisingly, however, they show predilection for smaller settings (Privacy); they are also more insulated from outside ties (Feedback) and somewhat more concerned with keeping active.

Table 8-2 shows the distribution of themes for inmates with high, medium, and low satisfaction levels. Satisfied inmates are less concerned about Freedom than other prisoners. The highest ranking theme for the satisfied group is Emotional Feedback, and the group is also relatively interested in Activity. Dissatisfied inmates are less concerned with Support (prison programs) than the more satisfied prisoners. The composite profiles suggest that satisfaction in prison is related to (1) a high value placed on intimate links and on personal rehabilitation, (2) a desire to advance educationally or vocationally; (3) an interest in keeping busy, and (4) a limited disposition to resent authority.

The Relationship of Personal Characteristics to Environmental Concerns

Tables 8-3 through 8-9 provide preference profiles of inmates of different backgrounds and experiences. Table 8-3 shows the environmental concerns of black and white inmates. Black inmates show very high concern with Freedom; this theme is present in three out of four interviews with black prisoners and is a primary theme for half the group. The Freedom theme is also prevalent for whites (56% total; 28% primary), but nowhere to the same extent. The table also shows that black inmates are more interested in material advancement than whites, but less interested in keeping occupied.

TABLE 8-1. Distribution of Environmental Concerns (Combined Samples)

	Total, all Interviews		Random Samples		Subenvironment Samples	
	No. Themes	Primary Only	No. Themes	Primary Only	No. Themes	Primary Only
Privacy	167 (40.99%)	44 (10.8%)	96 (38.2%)	24 (9.6%)	71 (45.3%)	20 (12.7%)
Safety	155 (38.0)	45 (11.0)	98 (39.0)	27 (10.8)	57 (36.3)	18 (11.5)
Structure	111 (27.2)	33 (8.1)	68 (27.1)	20 (8.0)	43 (27.4)	13 (8.3)
Support	183 (44.9)	54 (13.2)	114 (45.4)	33 (13.1)	69 (43.9)	21 (13.4)
Emotional Feedback	170 (41.7)	50 (12.3)	121 (48.2)	37 (14.7)	49 (31.2)	13 (8.3)
Activity	117 (28.7)	20 (4.9)	66 (26.3)	9 (3.6)	51 (32.5)	11 (7.0)
Freedom	281 (68.9)	162 (39.7)	164 (65.3)	101 (40.2)	117 (74.5)	61 (38.9)
Total	408 (100%)	408 (100%)	251 (100%)	251 (100%)	157 (100%)	157 (100%)

TABLE 8-2. Distribution of Environmental Concerns among Inmates of Varying Satisfaction Levels (All Samples)

	Low (0–3) (N=162)		Satisfaction Medium (4–6) (N=145)		High (7–10) (N=84)	
	All Themes	Primary Theme	All Themes	Primary Theme	All Themes	Primary Theme
Privacy	58 (33.1%)	16 (9.9%)	67 (44.4%)	18 (12.4%)	34 (38.2%)	9 (10.7%)
Safety	62 (35.4)	14 (8.7)	49 (32.5)	15 (10.3)	38 (42.7)	14 (16.6)
Structure	41 (23.4)	18 (11.1)	43 (28.5)	10 (6.9)	24 (27.0)	4 (4.7)
Support	59 (33.7)[b]	14 (8.7)	74 (49.0)	25 (17.2)	41 (46.1)	11 (13.1)
Emotional Feedback	59 (33.7)	13 (8.0)	56 (37.1)	18 (12.4)	47 (52.8)[b]	16 (14.0)
Activity	37 (21.1)	4 (2.5)	42 (27.8)	6 (4.1)	32 (36.0)[a]	10 (11.9)
Freedom	130 (74.3)	83 (51.2)	103 (68.2)	53 (36.6)	38 (42.7)[c]	20 (23.8)

[a]Significant at .05 level.
[b]Significant at .01 level.
[c]Significant at .001 level.

TABLE 8-3. **Distribution of Environmental Concerns for Black and White Prisoners (All Samples)**

| | Ethnicity | | | |
| | Black (N=194) | | White (N=132) | |
	All Themes	Primary Theme	All Themes	Primary Theme
Privacy	74 (36.1%)	18 (9.3%)	61 (43.0%)	21 (15.9%)
Safety	63 (30.7)	8 (4.1)	63 (44.4)[b]	27 (20.5)
Structure	53 (25.9)	19 (9.8)	32 (22.5)	10 (7.6)
Support	91 (44.4)[a]	30 (15.5)	46 (32.4)	11 (8.3)
Emotional Feedback	68 (33.2)	23 (11.9)	57 (40.1)	15 (11.4)
Activity	39 (19.0)	3 (1.5)	51 (35.9)[c]	11 (8.3)
Freedom	152 (74.1)[c]	93 (47.9)	79 (55.6)	37 (28.0)

[a]Significant at the .05 level.
[b]Significant at the .01 level.
[c]Significant at the .001 level.

The three dimensions that differentiate between blacks and whites are related to prison satisfaction. Two of the dimensions are negative predictors of satisfaction, and one is a positive one. What impact does this relationship have on the prison experience of white and black inmates? Table 8-4 confirms that blacks are less satisfied than the white inmates. Are the differences in satisfaction related to environmental preferences? For two dimensions, the answer turns out "yes." Table 8-5 shows Support and Freedom themes distributed among black and white inmates of varying satisfaction levels. The table shows a strong relationship between Freedom concerns and dissatisfaction among black inmates, and a link between Support needs and contentment for whites.

Table 8-6 shows the dimensional profiles of inmates of varying ages. The most striking difference occurs for Structure. Structure is the lowest-ranking concern of the younger age groups, and it ranks third highest among the concerns of inmates twenty-nine and over. One out of five of the older inmates have Structure as their dominant concern; for two out of five older inmates, Structure is clearly of consequence.

Safety, on the other hand, is an issue mainly for younger inmates. It is the primary concern of one out of five youthful prisoners and only occasionally is dominant for older offenders. Safety is of *some* concern to 50 percent of the young age group. Younger inmates, on the other hand, show little interest in Feedback. This relates to their marital status, and reflects a here-and-now orientation; it may also make young inmates relatively unwilling candidates for therapy.

Privacy is a dominant issue for 15 percent of older prisoners, and for only 5 percent of the youths. Some 40 percent of young inmates, however, list Privacy as a relevant concern.

Table 8-7 deals with the dimensions that differentiate married and unmarried inmates. Linking to loved ones (Emotional Feedback) is a disproportionate concern for married inmates. It ranks second to Freedom in their hierarchy of concerns; it preoccupies more than half the group and is a primary concern for one of four married prisoners. Single inmates see Freedom more saliently than do married inmates. The Freedom concern

TABLE 8-4. Rating of Prison Environments by Black and White Inmates*

Satisfaction Level	Ethnicity of Inmates			
	Black		White	
Low (0–3)	95	(48.7%)	47	(33.8%)
Medium (4–6)	69	(35.4)	55	(39.6)
High (7–10)	31	(15.9)	37	(26.6)
Total	195	(100.0%)	139	(100.0%)

*Significant at the .01 level.

TABLE 8-5. Distribution of Support and Freedom Concerns among White and Black Inmates of Different Satisfaction Levels

	Black Inmates' Satisfaction			White Inmates' Satisfaction		
	Low (0–3)	Medium (4–6)	High (7–10)	Low (0–3)	Medium (4–6)	High (7–10)
Support	37 (38.9%)	33 (47.8%)	17 (54.8%)	7 (14.9%)	23 (41.8%)	14 (37.8%)[a]
Total	95 (100)	69 (100)	31 (100)	47 (100)	55 (100)	37 (100)
Freedom	78 (82.1%)[b]	54 (78.3)	15 (48.4)	29 (61.7)	30 (54.5)	17 (45.9)
Total	95 (100)	69 (100)	31 (100)	47 (100)	55 (100)	37 (100)

[a]Significant at .01 level.
[b]Significant at .001 level.

TABLE 8-6. Distribution of Environmental Concerns among Different Age Groups (All Samples)

| | Age Groups | | | | | |
| | 16–21 (N=111) | | 22–28 (N=131) | | 29–67 (N=121) | |
	All Themes	Primary Theme	All Themes	Primary Theme	All Themes	Primary Theme
Privacy	44 (39.6%)	5 (4.5%)[a]	63 (48.5%)	19 (14.6%)	44 (36.4%)	17 (14.0%)
Safety	53 (47.7%)[a]	21 (18.9)	44 (33.8)	12 (9.2)	37 (30.6)	5 (4.1)
Structure	15 (13.5)	2 (1.8)	30 (23.1)	4 (3.1)	48 (39.7)[b]	24 (19.8)
Support	47 (42.3)	20 (18.0)	62 (47.7)	15 (11.5)	45 (37.2)	11 (9.1)
Emotional Feedback	32 (28.8%)[a]	7 (6.3)	60 (46.2)	16 (12.3)	51 (42.1)	21 (17.4)
Activity	28 (25.2)	3 (.8)	33 (25.4)	8 (6.2)	41 (33.9)	5 (4.1)
Freedom	86 (77.5)	53 (47.7)	94 (72.3)	56 (43.1)	78 (64.5)	38 (31.4)

[a]Significant at the .05 level.
[b]Significant at the .001 level.

is primary for close to half of the single inmates but for less than a third of those who are married.

Inmates generally rank low in educational achievement. The profiles of inmates who have graduated from high school are similar to those of other inmates, except for the Activity concern (Table 8-8). As a group, the more highly educated inmates place a higher value on their chance for keeping constructively busy.

A background variable we do not have (and possibly will never have) is a reliable index of mental health. Problems of impulse control, emotional lability, or cognitive distortion affect perception in plausible but undocumented ways. There is no way of substantiating such relationships from the background files of inmates.

Table 8-9 lists the only cue that is available to us, the inmate's history of psychiatric institutionalization. We see that former mental patients are

TABLE 8-7. Feedback and Freedom Concerns of Married and Single Inmates (All Samples)

	Single		*Married*	
	Total	Primary	Total	Primary
Feedback	85 (32.9%)	20 (7.8%)	58 (56.3%)[b]	24 (23.3%)[b]
Freedom	190 (73.6)	117 (45.3)[a]	68 (66)	30 (29.1)
Total	258 (100)	258 (100)	103 (100)	103 (100)

[a]Significant at the .05 level.
[b]Significant at the .001 level.

TABLE 8-8. Activity Concerns of Inmates with Different Educational Achievement (All Samples)

	Less than High School Degree		*High School Degree and Higher*	
	Total	Primary	Total	Primary
Activity	73 (25.3%)	31 (10.7%)	25 (43.1%)[a]	3 (5.2%)
Total	289 (100%)	289 (100%)	58 (100%)	58 (100%)

[a]Significant at the .01 level.

TABLE 8-9. Safety and Support Concerns of Inmates with Prior Experience in Psychiatric Settings (Total Sample)

	No Psychiatric History		*Mental Commitments*	
	Number of Themes	Primary Theme	Number of Themes	Primary Theme
Safety	111 (34.2%)	30 (9.2%)	22 (59.5%)[a]	7 (1.9%)
Support	148 (45.5%)[a]	44 (13.5%)	6 (16.2%)	2 (5.4%)
Totals	325 (100%)	325 (100%)	37 (100%)	37 (100%)

[a]Significant at the .01 level.

less likely than other inmates to be concerned about material advancement (Support), while Safety is a disproportionate concern of the ex-patient group.

The Concerns of Long-term and Short-term Inmates

We expect men who have spent varying time in prison to have evolved different environmental concerns. Table 8-10 explores the relationship between time in prison and two of our dimensions. It shows that long-term inmates are more concerned with Structure than those with little prison experience. By contrast, men with less time in prison seem more interested in self-improvement (Support).

Table 8-11 shows that inmates who face very long sentences (irrespective of the time they have spent in prison) are relatively concerned with the stability (Structure) of their environment. Fully one third of the group discuss the issue, and 15 percent see it as the primary environmental concern.

Crime-related History and Criminal Justice Experience

Environmental concerns are affected not only by generic differences in experience but also by those that relate to past contacts with the environment one inhabits. Divorce brings a different perspective to marriage. Dentists look different to patients who are subjected to annual root canals and to those with perfect teeth.

The impact of prior experience is contaminated by personal attributes. Classified truants do not see schools in the same fashion as other pupils, and some of their cynicism is attributable to alienated expectations, values, and motives. Environmental experience, on the other hand, modifies and shapes expectations.

Table 8-12 shows us that inmates with no jail experience are more concerned with Freedom. These inmates are less acclimated to criminal justice settings and may find the custodial regime more unfamiliar and unacceptable.

Table 8-13 links drug offenses to Emotional Feedback concerns. High-Feedback perspectives may relate to the addict's propensity—while in jail—to question his past motives and conduct and to seek restoration of links. The more experienced drug offender is the most likely candidate for this syndrome.

TABLE 8-10. Environmental Concerns of Long-term and Short-term Inmates (Total Sample)

| | Years Served | | | | | |
| | (0–1) | | (Between 1 and 2) | | (More than 2) | |
	Total	Primary	Total	Primary	Total	Primary
Structure	20 (17.2%)	4 (3.4%)	26 (20%)	7 (5.4%)	46 (40%)[b]	18 (15.7%)[a]
Support	63 (54%)[a]	19 (16.4%)	52 (40%)	15 (11.5%)	40 (34%)	12 (10.4%)
Totals	116 (100%)	116 (100%)	130 (100%)	130 (100%)	115 (100%)	115 (100%)

[a]Significant at the .01 level.
[b]Significant at the .0001 level.

TABLE 8-11. Concern with Structure of Inmates with Long Prison Sentences

| | Length of Prison Sentence | | | |
| | Less Than 10 Years | | 10 Years and Over | |
	No. Themes	Primary Theme	No. Themes	Primary Theme
Structure	50 (20.9%)	13 (5.4%)	44 (34.6%)[a]	18 (14.2%)
Total	239 (100)	239 (100)	127 (100)	127 (100)

[a]Significant at the .01 level.

TABLE 8-12. Freedom Concerns of Inmates with Prior Jail Experience

| | No Prior Jail | | Previous Jail Term(s) | |
	Number of Themes	Primary Theme	Number of Themes	Primary Theme
Freedom	186 (75.3%)[a]	108 (43.7%)	74 (63.2%)	41 (35.0%)
Total	247 (100%)	247 (100%)	117 (100%)	117 (100%)

[a]Significant at the .05 level.

TABLE 8-13. Feedback Concerns of Inmates with History of Drug Offenses (All Samples)

| | No Drug Offense | | Previous Drug Offense(s) | |
	Number of Themes	Primary Theme	Number of Themes	Primary Theme
Feedback	84 (35.0%)	29 (12.1%)	60 (48.4%)[a]	15 (12.1%)
Total	240 (100%)	240 (100%)	124 (100%)	124 (100%)

[a]Significant at the .05 level.

TABLE 8-14. Support Concerns of Property Offenders (Total Sample)

| | No Property Offense | | Previous Property Offense(s) | |
	Number of Themes	Primary Theme	Number of Themes	Primary Theme
Support	29 (33.0%)	7 (8.0%)	126 (45.7%)[a]	39 (14.1%)
Total	88 (100%)	88 (100%)	276 (100%)	276 (100%)

[a]Significant at the .05 level.

Table 8-14 contrasts property offenders, who are the modal "mainline" inmates, with inmates who have different criminal histories. The table shows that standard prison programs (Support) are of concern to the "typical" (as opposed to atypical) inmate.

Table 8-15 refers to men who have histories of violent offenses—inmates who are classifiable as a *serious offender* group. These inmates (who

TABLE 8-15. Structure Concerns of Inmates with History of Violent Offenses (Total Sample)

	No Violent Offense		*Previous Violent Offense(s)*	
	Number of Themes	Primary Theme	Number of Themes	Primary Theme
Structure	50 (20.7%)	14 (5.8%)	43 (35.2%)[a]	16 (13.1%)
Total	242 (100)	242 (100)	122 (100)	122 (100)

[a]Significant at the .01 level.

are comparable to serious students, to hospital patients with histories of surgery, etc.) value Structure or stability in their setting.

Environments and Environmental Dimensions

Table 8-16 shows the environmental preferences of inmates in five prisons and reveals differences among them. Attica prison, which houses older, long-term inmates, ranks low on Freedom and high on Activity. Auburn and Green Haven are also adult prisons. Auburn is noted for its programming and progressive staff climate, with considerable leeway in discretion. Auburn inmates seem responsive to programs (Support) but show concern about Structure. Green Haven has been described as very relaxed in its climate. The inmates' Structure concern may be a reaction to this feature.

Coxsackie and Elmira are prisons for youthful offenders. Coxsackie has a homogeneous young population and a strong educational program. High concerns are Safety—a reaction to the social environment—and primary Support (programs). Feedback and Activity rank low. Freedom concerns are high in the two youth institutions, with Auburn—the most youthful of the adult prisons—ranking third.

Table 8-17 suggests that Auburn ranks as the most popular New York State institution, with the "pull" of a relaxed climate and diversified programs. The "profile" of Auburn (Table 8-16) implies a "trade-off": Shops and classrooms compensate for stability that is lost through a "progressive" prison climate.

Our final table (8-18) shows inmates who have varying institutional mobility patterns. We find Safety primarily of concern for inmates who are still in their institution of origin and less salient for those transferred to a second setting. (Additional transfers change the trend, perhaps as a result of safety-motivated moves.) Concern with stability increases with mobility. This may occur because of the disequilibration of moves, or as a corollary of the "old-timer" syndrome.

TABLE 8-16. Environmental Concerns of Inmates in Five New York Institutions (All Inmates Sampled)

		Attica		*Coxsackie*		*Auburn*		*Elmira*		*Green Haven*	
		No. of Themes	Primary Theme	No. of Themes	Primary Theme	No. of Themes	Primary Theme	No. of Themes	Primary Theme	No. of Themes	Primary Theme
Privacy	N	31	14	37	4	31	8	38	11	30	7
	(%)	(33%)	(16.9%)	(39.8%)	(4.8%)	(37.3%)	(9.9%)	(49.4%)	(14.7%)	(34.5%)	(8.2%)
Safety	N	34	9	44	16	24	3	22	7	31	10
	(%)	(36.2%)	(10.8%)	(47.3%)	(19.0%)	(28.9%)	(3.7%)	(28.6%)	(9.3%)	(35.6%)	(11.8%)
Structure	N	17	2	12	1	25	9	12	2	45	19
	(%)	(18.1%)	(2.4%)	(12.9%)	(1.2%)	(30.1%)	(11.1%)	(15.6%)	(2.7%)	(51.7%)	(22.4%)
Support	N	33	11	40	15	43	10	32	9	35	9
	(%)	(35.1%)	(13.3%)	(43.0%)	(17.9%)	(51.8%)	(12.3%)	(41.6%)	(12.0%)	(40.2%)	(10.6%)
Feedback	N	38	14	22	6	33	12	36	8	41	10
	(%)	(40.4%)	(16.9%)	(23.7%)	(7.1%)	(39.8%)	(14.8%)	(46.8%)	(10.7%)	(47.1%)	(11.8%)
Activity	N	32	9	18	2	24	5	22	2	21	2
	(%)	(34.0%)	(10.8%)	(19.4%)	(2.4%)	(28.9%)	(6.2%)	(28.6%)	(2.7%)	(24.1%)	(2.4%)
Freedom	N	51	24	64	40	54	34	56	36	56	28
	(%)	(54.3%)	(28.9%)	(68.8%)	(47.6%)	(65.1%)	(42.0%)	(72.7%)	(48.0%)	(64.4%)	(32.9%)
Total	N	94	83	93	84	83	81	77	75	87	85
		(100%)	(100%)		(100%)		(100%)		(100%)		(100%)

TABLE 8-17. Distribution of Mean Satisfaction Scores
by Five Prisons (Combined Samples)

Institution	Scale Score Mean	(n)
Attica	3.6	(88)
Coxsackie	3.9	(90)
Auburn	5.2	(81)
Elmira	4.0	(73)
Greenhaven	4.0	(83)

Support is less important to inmates with repeated transfers. In the case of such inmates, mobility may disrupt "careers" that extend to the outside world, as opposed to an intraprison (interprison) career.

The Genesis of Dimensional Preferences

We have noted that any dimension of any environment may be attractive to different persons for different reasons, and, while some of these reasons may relate to the persons' past, others may be contextually inspired. An inmate may seek Support to make up for the opportunities he lacked in the community or because it helps him to "do time," or because his prison term is of a duration that is compatible with gainful participation. Support can therefore be correlated with ethnicity, prison satisfaction, prison experience, and shortness of sentence.

Feedback matters most to men who have ties to persons in the community or who feel they have problems. Feedback can therefore be associated with age, marital status, and a drug history. Young, inexperienced white inmates in youth settings are most prone to have Safety concerns, while Structure seems most vital to older, long-term, or career offenders. Structure can also be important in settings where authority is comparatively relaxed.

Activity appears vital to inmates who are relatively highly educated, and it facilitates the prison adjustment of such inmates. Privacy helps older inmates to cope and may lead such inmates to seek small subsettings. Freedom concerns can be salient for single, inexperienced inmates of minority backgrounds. A concern with Freedom invites low morale but may also be a corollary of dissatisfaction.

The same prison offers different opportunities and different threats to different inmates exposed to it; different prisons invite or promote variations in perspective. Combinations of experience and stimuli orchestrate into confluences, some of which are congruent, and some incongruent. The task we face is to enhance—as best we can—the "fit" between the needs of men and the salient attributes of their settings.

TABLE 8-18. Environmental Concerns of Inmates Transferred among Prisons

	Present Institution Only		One Transfer		Two Transfers or More	
	No. of Themes	Primary Theme	No. of Themes	Primary Theme	No. of Themes	Primary Theme
Safety	57 (47.5%)[a]	21 (17.5%)	39 (26.9%)	8 (5.5%)	37 (37.8%)	8 (8.2%)
Total	120 (100)	120 (100)	145 (100)	145 (100)	98 (100)	98 (100)
Structure	18 (15.0)	2 (1.7)	37 (25.5)	7 (4.8)	38 (38.8)[b]	21 (21.4)
Total	120 (100)	120 (100)	145 (100)	145 (100)	98 (100)	98 (100)
Support	53 (44.2)	19 (15.8)	73 (50.3)	19 (13.1)	29 (29.6)[a]	8 (8.2)
Total	120 (100)	120 (100)	145 (100)	145 (100)	98 (100)	98 (100)

The overall column span is headed *Number of Prisons Experienced in Current Sentence*.

[a]Significant at .01 level.
[b]Significant at .001 level.

II

STRESS AND ITS AMELIORATION

9

Inmate Victimization

IN THIS CHAPTER, WE SHALL VIEW A GROUP OF INMATES who face a common modality of pressures and obstacles. We shall trace the inception of stress in these men and describe their subsequent experiences. We shall review the efforts of the men to cope with their fate and we shall catalog their successes and failures. In this connection, we can also record the help and hindrance offered to the men in stress as they try to adjust or survive. Later, in Chapters 10 and 11, we shall deal more closely with stress-reducing supports of the environment and with their effectiveness.

We have selected our subject for this chapter for its conceptual purity and its practical importance. The concerns of the inmates who are our target group lie primarily in one area (Safety), and the sources of their despair are very tangible and easily traceable.

The men with whom we are concerned make up a large portion of the young male prison population. They are a long-standing problem for correctional staff. They should seriously worry us all, because they are more truly victims than are most victims, more vulnerable, impressionable, innocent, and inexperienced.

The condition we shall describe is remediable; it can be addressed, prevented, and ameliorated through interventions. Prisons are dealing with the problem now and sometimes doing so heroically. To improve these interventions, we need to know more about the stress process among the inmate victims, and about the limitations and possibilities of the remedies we are deploying to help them.

The Process of Stress

A stressed person is one who has discovered that familiar environmental transactions—customary ways of coping with the environment—

are hopelessly challenged. The result is typically a period of psychological disequilibrium, which includes disbelief and despair. At some point, the person may regroup and may begin to try to "solve" his or her problem by evolving new adjustment modes. This effort is marked by anxiety, and can include an obsession with the sources of one's stress. In our terms, the person's "environmental profile" becomes *skewed,* with high concern for features of the environment that denote *incongruent* transactions.

Though stress involves prepotent profiles, the reverse is not always true. A person in love can show tremendous concern with Emotional Feedback. Such a person is not stressed, though, unless his or her love is unreciprocated. Where prepotent concerns are stress-linked, the relationship may be complex. The loss of a loved one, for instance, may result in cycles of Privacy and Activity–Social Stimulation, as the grieving person seeks to assimilate the magnitude of his or her loss and seeks for distraction or solitude as the "digestion" or grief process runs its course.

The prepotence of concerns under stress also bears no necessary relationship to the profile of pre-existing concerns. Stress may challenge environmental transactions heretofore taken as givens. An earthquake that destroys my home highlights dimensions of my milieu I had no need to be concerned about before my shelter (with all its casually valued connotations) caved in around me. The effect of stress is that of removing props or tools to everyday life on which we may depend without being aware of the extent of our dependence.

Retirement from work is stressful—to the point of sometimes accelerating death—for men who need Activity. But preretirement activity is something we often take for granted and even complain about. Enforced inactivity brings home a man's incapacity for leisure. By the time the problem is dramatized, the unmet need for Activity may have produced impacts (such as depression and psychosomatic disorders), which make it hard to find new activities.

Stress variously relates to a person's limitations and strengths. All of us can be stressed in every possible respect. We have "thresholds" for stress at every point of our intersection with the environment, and these thresholds will vary. We sometimes fail where we can best handle failure, but we may fail too hard or too often. "The bigger they are," says folklore, "the harder they fall." But it still remains true that lower thresholds are more easily challenged, and that a man under stress may have cumulative problems, in that stress may make him vulnerable to further challenges. This is particularly true in antitherapeutic environments, where the cues to vulnerability are not picked up, or where no allowance for weakness or "personal failings" is made. A stressed soldier may be ordered into combat, or a stressed employee fired, and a person can thus be further driven to despair.

Some environments invoke stress deliberately, so as to reap psychological or social benefits. Police drive by and stare at a youth, to exploit his "guilty knowledge" or fear of authority. Teachers invoke anxiety to inspire work.

Where self-esteem issues are prominent, we find men feeding their egos at the expense of others' misery. This may occur on a large scale, as in the extermination of millions of persons in support of self-images of "aryan purity." An analogous phenomenon occurs on a substantial scale in prisons, where inmates build self-conceptions of manliness at the expense of others deemed "unmanly." This phenomenon, which depicts our society at its worst, concerns us in this chapter.

Inmate Victimization in Prison

The inmates we shall portray in this account are under stress from other inmates. They are "victimized" in the sense of the term as used by Fisher and applied by Bartollas, Miller, and Dinitz. "Victimization" is a process that is defined by Fisher as "a predatory practice whereby inmates of superior strength and knowledge of inmate lore prey on weaker and less knowledgeable inmates" (p. 89). Issues of "weakness" or "strength," "superiority" or "knowledge," must be seen as *relative to victimization, and to no other transactions.* We don't know how "strong" or "weak" the victims or aggressors are in other settings, such as at work, in school, or at home. We know that aggressors select the arena of the victimization contest ("prison lore"), initiate the stressful encounter, and pick the indices of evaluation. The victim walks into situations where his presence lends itself to a game in which the aggressor arranges things deliberately so he can make the victim look as helpless, "weak," and inferior as possible.

The extreme form of inmate victimization is homosexual rape, which is extremely rare in prisons but has been prevalent in some institutions, including the Philadelphia detention facility publicized by Davis. Though rape literally is not at issue in most victimization of inmates, it is figuratively always involved. It lurks (as does execution over the criminal justice system) as the ultimate penalty, the most extreme form of power that may be held over the victim. Moreover, the motives of victimizers and of rapists overlap heavily. Prison rapists and victimizers derive from similar backgrounds, and they select victims who are culturally similar to each other. Moreover, rape is almost always threatened by prison aggressors and is always feared by the victims.

The aim of victimization is complex, and we can describe and illustrate it later. The apparent or superficial object of victimization is sexual exploitation, and it is sex that the aggressor most often demands of the victim. But we noted that rape is an infrequent event. Though it is possible that the aggressor's hope springs eternal, irrespective of his past experience, this interpretation is unlikely. It is more likely that the nature of the aggressor's threat is incidental to his real purpose, which is to be threatening. The latter assumption suggests that the medium in inmate victimization is in fact its message, that the aim of the activity is to provoke stress and to make stress visible. The gain of such interactions would be that implied by Fisher's definition: to "demonstrate" the aggressor's "superior strength and knowledge" and to pinpoint the victim as "weaker and less knowledgeable." The aim succeeds best where victims are unfamiliar with the arena of testing, which includes violence and its threatened deployment.

Patterns of Inmate Victimization

We know that victimization is prevalent in male prisons, but it is hard to assign a number to the proportion of victims that become involved. Davis tells us that "virtually every person having the characteristics of a potential victim is approached by aggressors" (p. 14). The statement may hold true for settings such as East Coast youth prisons and reformatories, and for urban detention centers. But even in those institutions, the victimization rate is hard to establish, though we know the proportion of "inmates with victim characteristics" in the population.[1] This is so because "approaches by aggressors" sometimes have negligible impact, sometimes fizzle out, and occasionally boomerang. If violence results, the aggressor may sometimes catch the brunt of it and thus turn "victim."

Inmates in two New York institutions, when we asked them about their experience with victimization, supplied us with a 28 percent victimization rate. Though our samples were random, this proportion is at worst meaningless, and at best suggestive. One of the two institutions involved was a youth prison, which increases the chances of finding victims and aggressors. Both prisons are New York State settings and contain the sort of contrasting populations (urban sophisticates and rural inmates) that make victimization likely. On the other hand, (1) some respondents were probably reluctant to talk about victimization experiences, and (2) the popu-

---

[1] A "profile" of stigmata delineated by Davis (1968) is applicable not only to inmate rapes but also to lower order victimization. Davis lists victim and aggressor characteristics as follows:
   "Victims tend to be white.
   Victims tend to be younger and smaller than aggressors.
   Most victims are afraid to report their aggressors to the authorities. . . .
   Aggressors tend to be black.
   Aggressors tend to be guilty of more serious and more assaultive felonies than victims.
   Both aggressors and victims tend to be younger than other prison inmates" (pp. 14–15).

lation contained relatively high proportions of serious offenders, which may depress the victimization rate.

Of 152 incidents that were described to us, 64 had been played out in youth prisons and 9 in juvenile institutions. This distribution confirms the prevalence of victim experiences among youths. The finding is reinforced by the fact that the estimated age of victims in these incidents was nineteen [2] and that a cohort of white inmates in the youth prison yielded six victims for every ten respondents.

Tables 9-1 and 9-2 confirm the observation that victimization relates to a contrast or a discontinuity of cultural backgrounds between victims and aggressors (Buffum; Davis; Irwin; Bartollas, Miller, and Dinitz). Table 9-1 shows that four out of five victims are white and that aggressors are to the same degree disproportionately black. Table 9-2 shows a similar disproportion with respect to urban–nonurban origin. While three out of four aggressors come from New York City, four out of five targets are nonmetropolites, with nontargets about evenly divided.[3]

Table 9-3 relates to the familiarity-with-violence question, because it shows that victims are less likely to have been involved in a violent offense

TABLE 9-1. Ethnicity of Aggressor, Target, and Nontarget Groups

	Black	*White*	*Puerto Rican*	*Total*
Aggressor (N=39)	80%	10%	10%	100%
Target (N=107)	19	79	2	100
Nontarget (N=59)	48	35	17	100

NOTES: Differences aggressor–target significant at the .001 level.
Difference target–nontarget significant at the .001 level.

TABLE 9-2. Commitment County of Aggressor, Target, and Nontarget Groups

	New York City	*Other*	*Total*
Aggressor (N=39)	74%	26%	100%
Target (N=107)	15	85	100
Nontarget (N=59)	49	51	100

NOTE: Pairwise differencés significant at the .001 level.

[2] It is possible that our age distribution may somewhat overrepresent the younger age group because our sample overrepresented the youth prison population. The mean of our distribution was 22.8 years, the standard deviation 4.9, and the range 14 to 39.

[3] A number of authors use such dramatic demographic distributions to argue for racial motives in inmate victimization. Scacco, for instance, asserts that "blacks appear to be taking out their frustrations and feelings of exploitation on the other inmates in the form of sexual attack and domination" (p. 5). He suggests that "the black man seeks to even the score against his white oppressors once behind the walls" (p. 72). Our own assumption is that motives may *statistically* relate to ethnicity where the substance or content of motives has little to do with race; our impression is that prison victimization is a phenomenon of this kind.

TABLE 9-3. Threat of Personal Force or Use of Personal Force in the Commitment Offense of Aggressor and Target Groups

	Threat or Use of Force	No Threat or Use of Force	Total
Aggressor (N=39)	87%	23%	100%
Target (N=102)	47	53	100
Nontarget (N=58)	82	18	100

NOTE: Aggressor–target, target–nontarget pairwise differences significant at the .001 level.

TABLE 9-4. History of Residence in Mental Health Facility and of Suicide Attempts among Target and Nontarget Groups

	Residence in Mental Health Facility[a]	No Residence in Mental Health Facility	Total
Target (N=105)	32%	68%	100%
Nontarget (N=59)	10	90	100
	Suicide Attempt[b]	No Suicide Attempt	Total
Target (N=100)	38%	62%	100%
Nontarget (N=59)	2	98	100

[a]Significant at .003 level.
[b]Difference significant at .001 level.

than the other two groups. Table 9-4 suggests that some victims may have been emotionally disturbed in the past. Past stress among victims may, of course, reflect the results of victimization, which can drive men into mental health settings (Huffman) or cause them to injure themselves (Toch, 1975). Aggressors, however, may *prefer* inmate victims who show traces of anxiety or low self-esteem. This follows from the assumption that the "payoff" of victimization can be to "demonstrate" the "weakness" of the victim, thereby "proving" the "strength" of the aggressor.

Culture Shock

In the first act of *The Pajama Game*, the new superintendent of the Sleep-Tite Pajama Factory complains that

> A new town is a blue town
> A "who do you know" and "show me what you can do" town.
> There's no red carpet at your feet
> If you're not tough they'll try to beat you down.*

* From "A New Town Is a Blue Town" by Richard Adler & Jerry Ross. © 1954, 1955 Frank Music Corp., 1350 Avenue of the Americas, N.Y., N.Y., 10019. International Copyright Secured. All Rights Reserved. Used by permission.

When any of us enters a new setting, we usually work on the assumption that our past experience will prove helpful to us. We assume that situations we have resolved in the past will help us to understand new situations, and we assume that the skills we have used to solve past problems will work with new problems. We look for familiar opportunities and familiar challenges that can be dealt with in familiar ways.

Almost everyone scans a new setting when he arrives in it. Such scanning is not idle curiosity but a means of orienting onself to environmental presses to see where they fall in relation to one's needs. The process is similar to that of driving into a new town and locating key features on a map so that one knows how to get places without getting lost.

A stress-free transition presupposes (1) that the information one needs to deal with new settings can be readily obtained, (2) that one encounters no major problems before he has acquired sufficient familiarity to respond to them, (3) that one sees himself as still able to reach his currently important life goals.

Transition stress can be reduced if the new setting provides a moratorium to environmental adjustment, if it supplies data about itself or offers bridging experiences from other environments. The average arrival has the best chance of avoiding stress if he can be helped to see new configurations as comprising familiar features. A cliff one must climb is less forbidding if it contains handholds and crevices such as one has negotiated elsewhere.

At the most stressful end of the spectrum the new arrival is confronted—preferably without warning—with a strange world that firmly challenges his most basic assumptions. Such experiences are sufficiently disequilibrating to be "used" by some settings (such as concentration camps) to make people dazed, helpless, and malleable (Bettelheim, 1960). An unscheduled transition trauma of this kind faces some young male inmates entering jails or prisons in which other young inmates are housed. This trauma can start at the earliest point of entry into the setting with the discovery that one has become target for what appears to be homosexual attention:

Cox R 6: We were standing in the line and they yelled it down, "Three niggers and one homo," like that. . . . And then I heard the guys talking about me, and then the accidental ass-grabbing started.

• • •

Att R2 10: Any new person, they hollered obscenities at them and all sorts of names, and throwing things down from the gallery and everything. They told me to walk down the middle of this line like I was on exhibition, and everybody started to throw things and everything, and I was shaking in my boots. . . . They were screaming things like, "That is for me" and

"This one won't take long—he will be easy." And, "Look at his eyes" and "her eyes" or whatever, and making all kinds of remarks.

The experience of being targeted challenges a number of basic premises of the average young male. One such assumption is that of his own sex role, which he has taken for granted himself, and has assumed that other people will stipulate:

Cox R 27: When you get in your cell sometimes, you get in there and you look at yourself and you say, "Why is this guy saying these things?" I had never thought of that myself. I always thought I was a good looking man and I never thought about myself being a girl. . . . I've sat around a guy a lot of times, I've had my arm around a guy, somebody. We really got wrecked with each other, and then we went out the door and we had a good feeling, a friendship thing, and here I could never put my arm next to somebody. The person would think that I was either trying to make advances or he would turn around and say, "This is a freaky thing, baby." . . . Out there you wouldn't even think about it. You would pick up this *Midnight* magazine or some crazy thing like that, some crazy newspaper or something like that. And you read about a man being sodomized or something. And in here it's something that happens every day, and you have to watch out. . . . When they first start saying things to me like, "Hey baby," I would expect to see a secretary walking by or something. I just could not believe that a male would be saying those kind of things to me. And I thought that the guy must be goofing on me or something, playing jokes. And I knew then after a while that, if the guy had a chance, he would want to kiss me and have sex with me. That is something you say to yourself, "This can't be true." And it's a freaky thing in the head, man. It's really hard to tell you the feeling that you get. It's like threatening your life, only instead he is threatening your manhood.

The experience also raises the question of one's status as an autonomous human being. As a person one usually deals reciprocally with other persons. One's fate always hinges partly, or largely, on one's own actions. One is not prepared to encounter junctures where one is matter-of-factly regarded as an object available for the asking. Yet in prison the way one is defined and verbally addressed may make it clear that one is seen by other men as impotent, that others feel free to question one's capacity to keep oneself from being used or exploited:

PC 3: From one minute to the next you don't know what an inmate is going to say. You don't. You could be discussing a fishing trip for a few minutes and the next thing you know the guy next to him is yelling that he is going to get into your buns or he thinks you're cute or how about a blow job or something like this. But the few minutes that you were talking about this fishing trip your mind was relaxed and you were settled down and then right away somebody has to start. And it's always that way. Somebody has to start. No matter what the conversation is, it always comes into it. . . . He'll say, "How's your buns today?" Just to keep his image up. And then you have to start, because if you don't start on the defensive then they're going to say that so-and-so doesn't defend himself, so we'll ride him a little more.

•   •   •

Cox R 27: Sometimes there is twenty or thirty people in the showers, and they're always making remarks to you, and you don't feel free. I'm used to on the streets, where you don't have any paranoia. Taking a shower is a beautiful thing. Here it's a paranoia thing, where they have you back against the wall. And if you turn around and wash your legs and you're bent over, besides getting remarks you might really get hurt. . . . And you take your shower in thirty seconds, and you feel really stupid, and you just pull your pants down, and there is all these guys waiting for you to pull your pants down. It's a sick thing. Even though the physical pressure is there for a short time, the mental pressure is there permanently. And if you're on the toilet and everybody is just walking by, then it's really an intense thing. I've been to the bathroom in front of people on the streets, and it's just nothing at all like it is in here. You just want to say, "Jesus, leave me alone." But you can't close the door, and it's a cell, and people are looking at you. . . . Sometimes I have some heavy thoughts in my cell, thinking about why all this happened. Is this pressure going to build up to the point where I say I'm actually going to be a fag? I really wonder where and why all this is happening. What I was into. I never dreamed that I was going to be in this condition and in this kind of place and around these kind of people and around this kind of environment, where I would want to leave and couldn't.

The physical environment adds to the impression produced by the interpersonal setting. Confinement adds to the impact of social pressure, because it seems to cut off physical retreat (at least initially) and produces an unfamiliar "back to the wall" feeling—a panic state and sense of resourcelessness.

One discovers not only one's sense of fear but one's lack of preparedness for dealing with fear. Part of the problem rests with the Alice in Wonderland flavor of the new experience, where sharper contrasts seem to be generated for oneself than for others. On the simplest level, one sees the cultural discrepancies that make one a favored target. But one also knows oneself to be mystified, lost, and visibly helpless:

Cox R 29: I can see it from anybody else that comes in from where I live—they just don't fit in with the rest of this population. The population is almost 50 percent, 75 percent, 80 percent from the city—we just don't fit in. . . . They don't act the same and they don't even think the same. It's what I do that is normal. Every one of them that comes through down up north to here has been called a "pussy," and they really have more put on them than guys that come from the city or Rochester or somewhere else. They have had more pressure put on them.

• • •

PC 15: The farmers like me were being approached or lured into something like that. . . . I was scared, and I didn't know how to react to certain predicaments, and I didn't actually know who to turn to, as far as I didn't know anybody. And I didn't know if I should go to the officers, the other inmates, or the homies, people from your home town. I didn't know what the difference was between all these persons. I didn't know one from the other.

Tests of Resourcefulness

If the inmate does not succumb to panic, he learns over time that the threats to which he is subjected are incidental to his dilemma. He is not a serious target of rape but an object of maneuvers designed to test his "manliness" or coping competence. Aggressors and spectators seem concerned with his reactions or nonreactions to aggressive overtures. The man is on trial, and he is fatefully examined. The penalty for failure is accelerated victimization. If a man acquits himself fully, he ensures his immunity to attack.

The issue is Manliness. The criterion is courage. Courage is evidenced by willingness to fight and by the capacity for doing so:

Cox R 27: We just recently got this guy on the division that is from Schenectady, and he's in here. Like, he's sort of a gangster, and they don't say boo to him. They sit back and watch him. They don't say boo to him. They don't pop any shit on him, because he kicks their ass.

• • •

Cox C–2 23: Now, each and every inmate goes through a trial period where someone is going to say, "I want your ass." But if he straightens it out himself, and he gets into a fight or something with the guy, it will show everyone that he is not going to take that kind of shit, you know?— he will be all right.

• • •

P 1: If you don't react to that one word in the right way, you lose something, and then they will test you a little further. . . . Everybody is trying to prove that they're not going to be an underdog. They're not going to be pushed around. And sometimes in so doing they also have to prove that they're going to be more aggressive than you are and they have to show that. And that is the only way that they can prove it.

While the index of manliness is pugnaciousness, the criterion of unmanliness is fear. The person who shows fear when he is under fire from practiced diagnosticians of fear, is classified as unmanly. The assumption among aggressors is that fear is obvious, but the diagnosis may hinge primarily on the absence of aggressivity. This formula is self-serving, because it provides the aggressors—who are manifestly aggressive—with a presumption of their own fearlessness:

P1: And I think the worst thing that can happen to a person is that they come into a prison scared, and the minute a person sees that they're scared the people want to jump on him and get the best shot at him. . . . It's a manhood thing, "Let's jump on this guy and fire him up and show him how big we are." He's scared, and if he is, he's not going to do anything. . . . You can read fear on a man. You can smell it. It depends on what kind of life you're brought up in, and I suppose that a man who came out of Harlem would be pretty tough, and if you put another man right next to him he could smell that fear of the other man. It's just there. It's in the air. You can feel it. It's a tangible thing. . . . If you can't live with yourself and can't possibly handle anybody or anything around you. And if you can't handle yourself, then you're lost, you're gone, there is nothing you can do. If you can't show people that you can be pushed up to a point, and not over that point, then they're going to get you, it's as simple as that.

• • •

PC 2: People in here know just by the way that you act what you're like. I can tell you just by the way people conduct themselves whether you're nervous or cool or what. If you walk around turning your head every five minutes, it's noticeable, and people are going to wonder what it's from.

• • •

VR 3: I was trying to remain composed, and yet still, with all this going around in your mind, you're trying not to let them realize that you're absolutely frightened to death. Because if you let them know you're frightened they're going to make it that much worse for you.

To show fear is to invite further threatening or testing. This sequence implies that we'll find the most substantial exposure to pressure where there is the most substantial incapacity to resist it. The most stressful environmental pressures are invoked against those who are most helplessly susceptible to stress.

Att R2 23: He couldn't take care of himself, you know. He wasn't a con, he wasn't a tough guy. He was like that kind of human being and, like, terrified, and the fucking guys just took advantage of him, you know. . . . I don't know how many fucked him, but, like, there were others that were involved that were just harassing him, you know? They got a kick out of harassing him. . . . it reminded me of a dog in a cage and somebody just sticking sticks in at him and shit like that. . . . The kid went to Matteawan, because I remember the day that he wrapped shit and rags and toilet paper and stuffed it under his bed, and, like, before they sent him to Bellevue they had him clean it up—the hacks had him clean it out, and he wound up in the bughouse. He wound up in the bughouse.

● ● ●

Cox C-2 24: There was this one guy that came up from Elmira. He was real tall, skinny, and blonde hair, and he was really young looking. Okay, he has a baby face, and you can just tell that he is scared shitless, and the blacks, they swarm all over him. They just know, they know that he does not know what is going on, and they just swarm all over him.

For some men, the ability to generate fear in others is evidence (in their own eyes) of an unchallenged or unlimited potency. The extreme of this syndrome is the bully, who feels fearless because his victims, who are carefully selected because they are weak and helpless, are terrified of his senseless violence and brutality. We have described the bully elsewhere (Toch, 1969):

> The clue to his disposition is the habit of invoking violence wherever it can make an impression to be savored. What is wanted is the physical and psychological effect of violence on other persons, which can cement the bully's conviction that there is nothing to fear in fear itself because it is, after all, always present in others. . . . He picks on weak people because the effects of terror are most easily secured with them; he gives no quarter, because lenience takes away the edge or full measure of his enjoyment [p. 161].

The subcultural prison aggressor may be an evanescent stage removed from the bully. He may prefer verbal to physical aggression and may not savor the violence itself. But he does see loss of control in others as evidence of his own "coolness," of the capacity he has to govern his own feelings while other men fall apart. He may seek *power* in the shape of psychological impact, but he may prefer such power to be public—visible to spectators and acknowledged by the victim himself.

Aggressors may strike a number of poses designed to win victims and influence them. Among standard roles aggressors play are the Wily Seducer, the Paternalistic Protector, the Thoughtful Dispenser of Bribes, and the Collector of Outstanding Loans that Looked Like Gifts When They Were Offered. The ultimate gambit, most generally deployed where the victim shows fear, is to dramatically threaten violence or to imply that violence is inevitable:

VR 3: He just kept saying, "You're going to get up there, and there's going to be guys selling your ass for twenty cartons, and you're going to find yourself being raped by five or six guys before it's all over." And this was the story that he kept repeating like a broken record. Either to me directly or to little groups that he could seem to get together.

● ● ●

Cox R 27: So he said, "Okay, angel, that's okay, I'll play it rough with you, and then, after you break, then you'll be mine."

PC 2: Then he started talking about the Rock people there that wouldn't take no for an answer. If they want something they will take it, because they've been doing it all their life.

• • •

VR 6: I just kept on trying to give him these vibrations that I didn't want to have nothing to do with him, but I was getting these vibrations from him that it was more like a threat—either I answer his questions or, like, he is going to strike me or hit me or something like that, or cause trouble.

Environmental discontinuity helps the Dispenser of Threats with his efforts at impressing people. If violence is unfamiliar to the victim, the aggressor can look very dangerous to him. And, though the aggressor may be a chronic loser, with many scars to prove it, he can achieve an immensely satisfying impression of awesomeness at no initial risk:

VR 6: He was a black guy, and he was very tall, really tall, and I remember he had a scar on his neck where somebody—I don't know— maybe just wound something around him in a street fight or something. He looked like a guy with the really, you know, mean look and the real prison look.

• • •

VR 4: And I see all these people walking around here with scars, and I say to myself, "Holy Christ, the life they led compared to mine!" . . . . The thing about it is the people involved in these things—usually I would think about a faggot in this thing, that a homosexual would be a small person or a more feminine type of person or something. But these people that I was involved with were big people. They were tall and bigger than I am. And really it's not just something that you could turn around and say, "Get the hell away from me." It's not something that you could bluff them. It's not that kind of situation.

To the extent to which the aggressor's gambit works, Safety becomes the prepotent concern of his target. The resulting view of prison becomes polarized and dichotomous, with sources of danger being the dominant features of the environment.

Patterns of inmate adjustment eventually become predominantly conditioned by fear. Vigilance is seen as the price of Safety, and perception is tuned to the discovery of danger cues. Other persons are avoided, and behavior is sharply circumscribed. The result is a pattern of conduct that makes it obvious that the target is afraid and thus provokes the aggressors to further aggression:

Cox R 6: I would lock in and wait until all was quiet and everyone was asleep before I would go to sleep. And I was nervous and scared, and I would wake up in the morning before everyone else, and then I would get up and get dressed and be ready when the lights came on. And then I would feel all right. I knew that I was awake and that, if anyone tried to get into my cell, that I could see them when they came to the door.

I: What about the times that you were out of your cell?

Cox R 6: I played the wall. I never let anyone behind me. I'm all right when they're in front of me, but I don't like to have anyone behind me. Even out in the streets, I don't like anyone behind me. I was in the service for six months, and I was taught in there not to trust anyone behind you. So I don't trust anyone at all. I stay up against the wall.

● ● ●

VR 3: I was shaking, nervous. And I stayed in my room. There you either lock in or out at night. And I stayed locked in. I figured, what could happen through a little two-by-two window?

● ● ●

Cox R 27: Yeah, I still keep my back to the shower, and I wash my back and watch everything. It's a weird thing, that if you drop something you don't even bend down to pick it up. You say, "Fuck it, I lost a bar of soap." I'm just not going to be criticized and bend over and get whistles and remarks.

It can become obvious to the disadvantaged but sophisticated inmate that fear reactions in prison have stimulus properties like those of red flags in bullrings. These inmates have no way of curbing their fear, but they can, through determined acts of will, control their fear-inspired conduct. They can prevent new victimization by simulating the stigmata of manliness they observe among inmates around them:

Cox R 29: All my motions, you know, like walking, you know, talking, and any movement at all, I always try to make myself look like if anyone would fuck with me I would kill them. . . . Just keep, like, a mad look, "Don't pull any stunts," you know? . . . You have to be pushy and stuff like that. I know people that have weak legs, and they can't do anything about it, but it is because they have that they are classified as, you know, homosexuals—you know, somebody that they can fuck with, you know? So I always have to keep an alert on my motions and walking, and be very aware of them.

● ● ●

Cox C–2 23: Okay, you have heard of body talk. What is the word for body talk? Kinesthetics. Well, just his bodily movements was attracting attention. I told the guy to deepen his voice and try to act more masculine for these people. He was acting too feminine and carrying himself in a feminine way around here. His body movements seemed to attract people. So, although he was speechless, his body movements—the people were watching and reading his body movements.

● ● ●

Cox R 27: When you're walking by yourself, and I have to walk like a real jerk, because I don't want them to think that I'm feminine. And when

I talk to someone I talk really deep. You almost have to fall into their trip. And I don't like to talk the way they do, with this jive ass and chump ass. It's disgusting to me.

• • •

Cox R 30: I had to prove to these other people that I wasn't a pussy or a punk or anything else. . . . I proved it, you know? A guy even looks at me wrong and I say, "What is the matter with you, have you got a problem?" And he looks at me and says, "No," and I say, "All right," and leave.

Inmates may carry the manliness gambit one step further and may try to "identify with their aggressor." They can affect a violent stance and stage demonstrations of readiness to aggress at a moment's provocation:

PC 12: Well, when I first came to this institution in 1965 I was nineteen years old and fair-skinned and white, and there were a lot of inmates that were nice to me. And they wanted me to do these sickening things. And back then I felt that I had to do something. So they said, "Listen, we'll do this and that," and I said, "Yeah," bang! And now I've gotten to the point where you can say what you want, but just keep your hands off me. Before I did what I thought was a thing from James Cagney movies, and that's what I was going to do.

• • •

P 1: I would walk around a corner, and I would wonder if something was going on. If the corner was over here, then I was over there and making sure that nobody was behind me. And I constantly carried a weapon, and I got into fights, but they didn't try it any more, because they knew that I was carrying a weapon. And I had a sadistic attitude at the time, and I didn't care any more.

• • •

Cox R 27: First I wanted to protect myself, and the only way that you can protect yourself is with violence. And it was getting to the point where after a while I was starting to do pushups every night, and then as I would get tired I said that I would kick that guy's ass as I got stronger. And I almost planned the fight. . . . I noticed that there was a bunch of guys around, and "That is it," I said. "That will show the other guys when I get in a fight with this one that I'm not going to quit." So I fight and get punched a few times, and I punch him a few times, and they see that I'm a man.

The difficulty with role-playing is that the line between the staged self and the real self can dissolve. Men who see themselves as gentle can become prisoners of aggressor roles they play. They can fall victim to a process highlighted by James and Lange several decades ago, whereby feelings are evoked by relevant acts. Inmates may sense changes in their own personalities that are ego-alien to them. They may see themselves reacting aggressively in unscheduled situations and in destructive ways:

P 1: I think that you can talk yourself out of it if you're very slick and if you're mean and have a mean rep. If you have the right eyes and the right look in your eyes and the right way of how anger should appear in your eyes and how hate should appear and malice, and how to project fear into somebody else's eyes. If you can do that, you can do it. If you can do it, you can talk your way out of it. . . . And if I hadn't done something there to boost my own mental morale, it would have been so much easier to do. It's as simple as that. . . . I had to increase my own mental morale, because I couldn't walk around the yard without fearing what would happen to me. And I had to do something. . . . You have to exchange that fear with another emotion. You can't carry it halfway. You can't say that I'm afraid, but I'm going to be brave. It won't work. One or the other takes over at a certain time, maybe the wrong time. And you have to keep your head and just change the emotions completely. It's like running back and running through the field. You can't go back and you can't go ahead. You have to change directions completely. It's what you've got to do. If you can't change your emotions, then you're gone. And you're going to stay weak. I'm still weak today. But it's a different kind of weakness. . . . I finally did defeat the fear, the fear is always there, but the thing that was stronger was the hostility, and that is why there is an exchange of emotions. Instead of engaging in the fear, I forced the hostility until it was a bigger point than the fear. . . . And that is all part of forcing another emotion forward to camouflage the fear. It is a game. It is a game of emotions with yourself. . . . Let me tell you, even though I defeated hate, I destroyed myself. I destroyed everything that ever I felt, and when I came out of the penitentiary it was sickening. If somebody would say hello to me, and they would say it in the wrong frame of voice, it was, it was terrible, and there was no excuse for it. I knew why I was doing it, and I couldn't stop it. It was a thing where you can control hate and you can control fear, but if you come to the point where it controls you, then either way you're losing.

I: And you linked this to your experiences in the penitentiaries?

P 1: Definitely. I never felt like this before. There is no doubt about it. I lost control of myself. You lose control of your emotions.

If a man does not internalize his facade, he may abandon it in disgust or may shed it because it does not work. In reverting to form, of course, a man risks new cycles of victimization and fear:

Cox R 27: In here if you try to rap to somebody or talk to them, then automatically you're talking the wrong way. Like, they've got some kind of code in here that you have to talk to people in a certain way, almost. And I'm trying not to go along with that. Like, when my people come up to see me, I don't like to talk to them with this "Hey, motherfucker, what's going on?" I try to keep myself away from that. Because there is such a pressure on you to either act that way or you're stuff or a squeeze, or there is a thousand names that they will call you.

I: So you're saying that this sex thing causes you to act in certain ways.

Cox R 27: That I'm really not into. . . . Like, I started to grow my sideburns long and my mustache, and I thought that this way I wouldn't look so good, but then after that I said fuck it, and I shaved.

• • •

VR 4: As I said, what had kept me pretty much clear of this individual was my acting like a nut . . . everybody else knew it was an act, but he didn't. He thought this was just the way I was. Always just a mean— he even got to say it, "You're always so mean and always bitching." "That's the way I am." That's how I'd talk, like an underworld character out of an old goddamn movie. . . . He must have had a mentality of a very young fella, a young boy, because I really started acting mean and nasty. And I figured that this would discourage him. . . . I almost acted like a nut to make him think that he better stay away from me in case I went off the deep end one day and started acting like a crazy person and might kill somebody. And I acted like a kook, hollering. At different times I'd see him coming, and somebody'd say, "Here he comes, here he comes." And without looking you knew damn well here he would be coming. And you had to start banging things around and acting like I was something or other and he got me mad. And anybody that would even talk to me would get my wrath. But he was so stupid he couldn't take the hint, he just wouldn't back off, no way in the world. I went down to the counselor again, and I said, "Gee, there's got to be something we can do." I talked to the guards over in the mess hall and explained the situation to them.

The Fight–Flight Premise

The prevailing myth in prison is that there are two ways, and only two ways, of dealing with aggression. One way is to admit defeat and to ask for help or retreat to a protective setting. The other option is to publicly attack the aggressor. Most vulnerable men who interact with other inmates are advised to counter aggression with aggression. The prevailing norm calls for displays of weapons or preemptive strikes:

PC A: I had a friend come in about two months ago, and they put him in D block, and that is the worst block in the institution for homosexuality, for smaller guys and then some other guys that are homos. And I gave him a shank and told him that it would be better if he didn't use it. I said he would do better if he would crack them in the mess hall. Then he wouldn't have any trouble. And then he would be carrying his own weight. I said that, if he mess with the shank, then he would have to use it for all his fights, because everybody that approached him would know that he had one.

VR 6: People was telling me where you had to handle those situations yourself, because if a dude go to a staff member or something they would automatically be labeled as a rat. So I tried to talk with some of the white guys that was here, because they was living on this tier with me, and they tried to give me solutions, you know? The majority of them told me to hit this guy, or anybody that comes up to you, just hit them and make sure that it is in front of a bunch of people, so that they will see where you are at and that you don't mess around.

● ● ●

Cox R 6: Everyone has been talking to me and telling me that I should fight, and I've tried everything else, so now I might as well fight.

The fight-flight norm is prevalent throughout the prison community, including among staff. Custodial officers may advise inmates of the advantages of using violence when one is threatened. This advice reflects the working-class norm (shared by some staff) which—as we have noted—makes pugnaciousness a measure of manly worth:

I: You went to your company officer?

Cox C–2 23: Right. I went and said, "Look, this guy is bothering me, man. He keeps coming out with these sexual remarks, and I want somebody to do something about this guy—tell him something." He said, "Well, there is nothing that we can do about it, and there is nothing that the brass can do about it, so hit him." He came right out and told me, just like that.

● ● ●

Cox R 6: I had told them what it was and described it to them, to the counselors and—

I: How did you describe it to them?

Cox R 6: The same way that I started to describe it to you. And they told me that you can't run away from it. You have to knock them down, face up to them. The first person that you knock out, you get locked up for three or four days, and then you come out and come back down, and you're going to get a lot more respect. . . . I remember one thing that I said to them. I said that these guys were big, and I would have to jump three feet to reach them. And they said that I would have to bring them down to my size. And he told me to kick them in the nuts, and that would bring them down to my size. And he said not to be afraid of lockup. . . . And they all agreed with each other . . . they said that there was a recommendation that I would have to start fighting and that that would be the only way to do things. . . . One guy started out and said, "Why don't you knock him out on his ass?" And the others said, "Yeah, why don't you?" And then that was the solution, and then they sent me out and said, "Next, please!"

Fight–flight thinking excludes other options, such as communication and problem-solving. The exclusion of verbal gambits can even look reasonable where they are clumsily exercised and show little impact. **If a** victim speaks to an aggressor in ways that dramatize his helplessness or that suggest lack of sophistication, the aggressor may feel amused. This reaction leaves the victim increasingly susceptible to fight–flight arguments. And since the inmate may feel cornered (having lodged an appeal and lost it) he may be tense enough to react in fight–flight terms:

Cox C–2 23: You try to talk to them. You try to talk some sense to them and say, "Now look, I am an inmate and you're an inmate." And they will say, ah—"Don't tell me that pussy shit." They will tell you that, you know? And so I figured that talking was no good with this guy, you know, there is only one way to handle him, and that is to fight with him.

• • •

VR 2: Like, he might say something like "Are you ready?" And I don't react to him. And I just say, "I despise you." And he takes it as a joke. Even if I'm serious, he takes it as a joke.

The fight–flight orientation makes sense in the context of cultural norms that are shared by some men, and it may be compatible with their personality and their physical resources. For other persons, the prescription calls for behavior that is strange and unfamiliar, and that demands unrehearsed psychological reactions. Where violence has rarely been exercised by a man, his position may be not unlike that of a cow that is advised to lay eggs:

Cox R 27: The last fight that I was in was in sixth grade. I'm not a violent person and I don't get into that.

• • •

Cox C–2 24: If anybody comes up on me and picks a fight I just turn the other way. It is not that I am afraid, it is just that it is against my morals. Violence, it proves nothing, it proves nothing.

• • •

Cox R 6: My friend who was a homo, he said, "Don't take any shit. Maybe you're not a hard rock on the street, but when you're in here you have to be a hard rock, or you're going to take a lot of shit." And once I got there I couldn't do it. I don't have a fear of fighting, but I just can't do it. I don't believe in it. It takes a lot to get me to fight. . . . So ever since I've been in the institution, the only thing that I can think about is hitting somebody. Cracking the box in my cell and lifting weights, just so that I can build up my confidence. So that I won't back down from a six-foot-two black guy when he comes up to me and act like I'm two feet. That's what I'm trying to do, build up self-confidence. . . . I was cracking up. It was the first time that I cried since I was fourteen, and just the thing of them saying "Knock him down, you don't have to take that stuff." I feel that I should start fighting.

The victim may be caught in a double bind, because he is reluctant to use violence and feels incapable of it, and also because of double messages in the system. He knows that inmates and staff respect a man who fights, but that violence brings punishment and can affect one's chances for parole. Since the positive and negative pressures emanate from the same milieu, they produce confusion, disorientation, and sometimes discomfort:

VR 2: I kind of say, if I do it, then I will have more time. And I've been in here for three years waiting for a call on the charge. And if I don't do it, I keep on going the same way that I'm going here now.

• • •

PC 15: As far as the inmate is concerned, you have to prove yourself to the other inmates, as a man. Whereas to the adjustment committee and to the jury, you're proving yourself to be a fool. That's where it bounces.

• • •

Cox C–2 23: Oh, I felt like I wanted to break out when I just looked at the guy. I just wanted to walk up to this guy and say, "You have been bothering me a whole lot." And just smash him in the face. But, you know, there is a lot of things that makes a guy hesitate about fighting in here, and the record happens to be one of them. . . . I was thinking that I should have hit that bastard when he said it—right?—but then I thought, "No, I just got here, and I can't do something like that. I can't do something like that, because right away I would get the reputation of being a fuck-up and everything with the officers and everybody." So I thought I would wait and lay off and see what happens.

Where the victim does use violence, it is often far from the deliberate deployment of manly force portrayed by myths. Much more frequently, the picture is of a man at the end of a rope pushed an inch too far. The man is fearful, tense, and resourceless; he feels pressed beyond endurance and trapped. His controls snap, he breaks down and explodes:

Cox R 30: We was all lined up—the whole division D–1—and he came up and starts to look at my ass and starts throwing me kisses and saying he loved me and showing me signs and stuff like that. I am standing there and looking at him. . . . I am trying to ignore him, and the whole division starts to look at me and saying, "Yeah—this guy must be a squeeze—he must be a punk." So I turned around, and everybody was looking at me—right?—and I said, "To hell with it," and I went over there and punched the dude in the face. And that broke everything right up. The officer came over and grabbed me.

• • •

P 1: And so when this guy cut in front of me again, I hit him in the head with a tray as hard as I could. And when he went to the ground I hit him several more times before the guard could reach me, and that was the only way. It is regrettable, but it is the only way that you can handle it. And I didn't want to do it, but I did what I had to do to protect myself. It was self-preservation, the first law of nature. I had to do it. . . . You don't even have to do it. Your mind snaps and you do it anyway. And in that second you know that it is either that or you know that it is all over again. And you do it. You don't think about it, and you don't do it with malice in your heart, you do it out of self-preservation and for no other reason.

● ● ●

VR 4: I even had a way of eating. I make it look like I was almost an animal. You know, I'd take the bread and just gouge out a piece of it with my teeth, and just look mean, you know? Or sit there with a fork and look like you're a caveman type. And it really was a game, you know? But nothing stopped this guy, he just couldn't be put off. And he came over, and he came around the table behind me, I knew he was coming, but, like I say, I just kept eating. And when he sat down, he had a cup of coffee in his left hand and he put his right arm around my whole shoulders. . . . I realized that this was it. I had come to the end of my rope and put up with this crap for long enough. And either they were going to lock me up for stabbing him or something. It all happened so fast. I had just come to the end of my rope. And when I jumped off then he stood up immediately. But he still had his coffee in his left hand and I poked at him with that fork, and he backed up, because he really thought that I was going to stab him. I was so angry, but I really wasn't going to stab him. I just wanted to make him realize that I could become violent. And, like, I said, "Back up, and if you ever touch me I'll kill you." And I was just ready to enact it. I was at the end. And there was no guards apparently there at the time, because if there was they would have said something to me. But he backed up and spilled coffee on his hand, and I know he carries a knife. And it wasn't bad enough that he was big, but he carried a knife, and I was glad that he didn't decide to take some violence. And it really upset me so much that I wasn't finished with my meal. And I got up and left.

Where a deliberate aggressive move is made it is frequently tentative and suffused with fear. The non-violence-experienced inmate bluffs without conviction, is unsure of his impact and afraid of possible repercussions. He is apt to feel that he has gone too far and has probably made his situation even worse:

P CC 4: So I went to a different approach where I thought I would tell him where I stood and what I felt and to fuck off and get out of my life. And so I told him that, to put it bluntly, someone would have to knock me out or stick a knife in me before anything would develop. And then I just wouldn't be conscious if it was that development. And then I told him that I was just the wrong dude to fuck with. Cause what happens if you get me to a point I'm like a rat in a corner. . . . After I said it and after I had left him, that's when I was really scared. Because I had played out my cards and I had given him more or less of a choice of what—if he wanted to have any type of a relationship—what he would have to do.

I: Take you off.

P CC 4: Right, and I was scared. . . . It wasn't easy, because I felt that he would see through me. Because I'm not that way naturally. And I thought that he would see through me and laugh at me, more or less.

• • •

Cox R 29: He is saying, "Well, if you are going to bust me in the chops, you know, bust me in the chops." And I says, "I told you, I just want to have you quit fooling around with me. If you want to fool around with me any more, then I am going to bust you in the chops, you know?" And so I sit down and he sits down in back of me. And he sit, and then he get back up and says, "Do you want to fight?" And I was sitting down and he tells me, "What are you going to do?" And I says, "Well, what are you going to do?" And we just looked at each other, and lucky he left the class at that point. . . .

I: And how did you feel after he left? Did you feel a little nervous?

Cox R 29: No. Nervous.

I: A little shaky?

Cox R 29: Yeah. Nervous and shaky, and the adrenalin had built up.

The confrontation of aggressors and victims is a poker game in which the chips are indices of courage. The fight–flight myth holds that violence is instrumental behavior and that it acts as a deterrent to aggression. But if violence works (and it does work), the reasons why it works are usually different from those presumed by the myth. Targets of victimization are chosen because they are deemed unmanly, and they are viewed as unmanly because they show fear or resourcelessness. A man loses his target attributes if he provides demonstrations of fearlessness, or if he sports stigmata of manliness. Violence works because it points to a misdiagnosis of the target. Violence also works because aggressors are not as sure of themselves as they pretend. A victim who reacts nonfearfully becomes an uninviting arena for proving one's manliness. He is uninviting because the confrontation can misfire into a demonstration of unmanliness. It is safer to seek other fish in the sea whose reactions are dependably fearful.

The dynamics of victimization account for the success of verbal communication which suggests that the victim is prepared to stand fast and is unwilling to act intimidated:

PC 3: Every once in a while I would hear a remark, "Hi, cutie," or anything of this nature. And then he would smack with his lips. . . . And so I finally laid my cards down and went over to him and said, "You're disgusting," and, "Do you get any enjoyment out of that?" And his exact words were, "I'm going to get into your ass." And I told him right out, "It's going to be a cold day in hell before you ever think about it." He said, "If I have to I'll hit you over the head and take it that way." And I said right then and there, "That's the only way you're ever going to get anything like that from me." And since that there has been no recurrence, and he has never come back, and we have talks, like discussing a problem of the prison or something like that. . . . I believe that to my understanding that my boldness, which really I consider something to be beyond what I want to do. I'm usually shy and tend to stay away from people. I don't bother with people. And this was one of the few times in my life that I had to stand up and say something about what I disapproved of.

• • •

VR 6: I started to walk away from him and he asked me—he just says— "Well, come here, man, and I want to talk to you." And I just started to ignore him, and I say, "I am not going to even talk to this guy." So I went out in the hallway, and he follows me out and he says, he says, "Look, you tell anybody what I told you and I am going to stick a knife in your heart." And I forgot exactly what my reactions was to that, but I just started to ignore him, and he says, "If you think I am afraid to hit you right out in the hallway," and I stood up and I said, "Okay, hit me." I wanted to get this over with and I don't want it to go any farther. I want him to get his shit off and do whatever he is going to do, and I didn't want to put up with his bullshit—and, well, he goes, "I will deal with you later." And then I had not heard nothing else about that.

Unscheduled explosions can be disconcerting to aggressors, because they disrupt his script and compromise his game. The prospective aggressor may run away, not because he is outgunned, but because his modus operandi is demonstrably inapplicable. He is in the position of a Shakespearian director whose Lady Macbeth embarks on a striptease:

VR 4: And he came down and sat down next to me, and he put his entire arm on my shoulder. And I just blew my top off. And I jumped up and I had my fork in my hand, and I told him that I would kill him. And I didn't intend to kill him. It was just a show to back him off. And I looked so outraged apparently that I must have looked like I was off my rocker, and then he spilled his coffee in his other hand and he backed off. And I told him that if he ever came near me again I would kill him. Either you or me. The hell with the consequences. And that was it. Apparently from then on that was the answer. He realized that I didn't want him touching me. . . . You know, he was a giant of a man. And that's what really had me almost intimidated. Because I didn't know what the hell to do. But as I say, I was lucky enough that when I jammed at him with a fork, he got off my back and then he got on somebody else's. He had backed off that way.

PC 4: And finally one time I was scrubbing the counter with a rag, a dirty, soapy wet rag. And it was dirty. And he happened to come by and patted me on my butt. And I didn't even know it was him. Whoever did it was behind me. . . . And I went around and it was just a reaction. And if I had something else in my hand other than that wet rag I don't know what would have happened. And of course this rag was wet, and all the water came around his face, and he was soaked. And I figured, here we go, if it's going to be any time it's going to be now. And I said, "I'm telling you and I told you before, I don't play. I don't want to play." Another expression is, "Just don't bother me. I don't want to be bothered." And I wasn't trying to be mean or a big shot or anything like that. And I just stood there, and he stood there for a second, and I thought he was going to come on me. But he just took the rag off and dropped it on the floor and then turned and walked away. And about three or four people seen it . . . to have other people witness him, this was a pressure on him, and to have him back off like that was quite a hard thing to do. But that was it. That was the end of the whole thing for him.

There are instances, to be sure, of dramatic—and sometimes lethal—role reversals. A man who looks like a promising target, when subjected to testing, feels that he has a self-esteem agenda of his own. His sensitivity to slights converts the aggressor's overture into the sort of challenge that calls for physical retaliation, much to the aggressor's chagrin:

Att R2 46: And then he started in with various remarks of sexual connotation, and so I stopped and I told him that if he had something on his mind or something that he did not understand or something he wanted to know that we could stop and discuss it, and he come out with some vulgarities, and he told me what, well, he would do to me and whatnot, and I asked him if he was serious, and he said yes. And I walked away from him and went down and got some gasoline and come back and opened up the lid and I threw it in there.

I: So he was inside the cell?

Att R2 46: That is correct.

I: What happened after that?

Att R2 46: I went to segregation and he went to the hospital.

● ● ●

PC 12: In thirteen years I've always acted first, because I saw it coming, and I said, "What are you going to try this time? Don't try it, or you're going to find something that you don't want." And I feel this personally, do unto others as they do unto you.

I: About how many times do you think you've responded to that?

PC 12: About seventeen.

Seeking Sanctuary

The fight–flight prescription provides for retreat, but makes this the less preferred option, in that it entails loss of reputation and calls for diminished self-esteem. A person may gain physical safety, but he cannot at the same time remain manly in the subcultural sense of the word. This tradeoff creates cross-pressures, particularly for those who are partially tied to peer norms.

Most flight in prison requires the invocation of staff assistance, or (to a lesser extent) the help of peers. The first problem arises at this juncture, in that a plea for help is a confession of weakness. There is also the implication—illogical but psychologically plausible—that one's victims' fate is somehow deserved. This assumption is reinforced by the fight–flight syllogism, which makes flight the recourse of the weak:

PC 3: What am I going to tell the guards—that this guy was making advances and that I'm afraid? I don't want them to say that I'm a pussy or something like this. I don't need this harassment. Nobody needs this harassment. It's hard enough for a man to do what he has to do in here.

• • •

Cox R 27: I wasn't going to go in there and say that the guy was trying to stick me, so I said that the guy was giving me hassles. He was trying to mess around with me. But then I think that the sergeant got the idea, because he sent me out and questioned him and then called me in, and I told him that the guy was trying to hassle me in the shower, and I didn't actually come out and say that he was trying to have sex with me. I wouldn't actually admit that somebody wanted to do that with another guy.

• • •

Cox C–2 23: You figure, "Wow, if I talk to this guy about this, he is going to think that I am a real punk," you know? You kind of feel trapped, you know? There is nowhere to go. And you are in there thinking of how trapped you are.

An approach to staff can also be viewed as treasonous. Such a move violates the taboo against "ratting," which is verbally endorsed by most inmates and is regarded as a sacred rule. Approaches to staff are presumed to invite retribution, though they rarely do. The inmate who seeks aid from officials must be desperate enough to risk disapproval, to invite harm, and compromise his self-image. An inmate may willingly endure victimization to avoid more serious subcultural contingencies:

Att R2 41: Like, a lot of people in New York City realize that you don't rat nobody out for nothing, and I am not from New York City, but the same thing goes in Syracuse. Because, if you get caught ratting somebody out, then you are in deep trouble, and that is the only thing that really stuck in my mind. That is the reason why I didn't go to staff about this.

• • •

Att R2 46: One lives by a set of rules that he chooses, and, while I don't follow the rules right down. . . .

I: So then, this gave you some reluctance to go, say, to some employee?

Att R2 46: There was no reluctance. It just wasn't done. How can I portray the role of the criminal and yet try to do certain things in a lawful manner and others in an unlawful manner? And I have enough trouble doing time without trying to be the dual personality.

• • •

I: What about going to a staff member?

Att R2 23: Oh, no. Forget about that.

I: Why is that?

Att R2 23: Because I was a young kid that come up through the streets. I was a gangster, you know, and I wasn't going to no fucking police, you know? This was it. I was a gangster you know—teenage—a twenty-two-year-old gangster, you know?

At some juncture, at least 50 percent of young victimized inmates find themselves going to staff for help *despite* the well-publicized taboo against "ratting." Part of the reason may be the personal background of these inmates, which links them less strongly to the convict code. But the dominant factor is the absence of other solutions, as the inmate sees it, and the extremity of distress:

VR 4: The hell with what these guys think. A lot of them don't go to the guard about anything. And I don't feel that way. I don't have the convict syndrome like in the old movies, the code or whatever it is.

• • •

Cox C–2 23: Look, there comes a time. Really, that was the only time that I have done it since I have been here. I don't feel like I dropped a dime. I feel that I did it because I wanted to stay out of trouble. I think that anyone else that wants to stay out of trouble will do the same thing, and they will not be a dime-dropper. . . . You know, violence isn't the only thing in the world.

• • •

VR 3: I didn't think of their retaliating, because maybe I was squealing or anything. I hadn't really, I suppose, realized. I didn't know that much about prison to know that you have a system all of its own in here. So

I was more or less thinking of trying to resolve the problem. If just speaking to the guy meant he would leave me alone and disappear, fine. It seemed that it got through that.

• • •

VR 6: I remember one conversation, and he says to me, "What would you do if I just took it and if I just pulled your pants down and just took it?" And he goes, "What would you do—would you scream?" And I said I sure would, and he asked me if I would tell an officer, and I said I sure would, and he says, "You are a jive rat. You are a rat, and you would squeal on me—this is what you mean?" and I said, "I sure will, and what other alternative would I have?" So he just sort of laughed and shook his head and just walked out.

Most inmates who approach staff are unsure of the help that they need or can expect. They seek safety, escape, an end to victimization, mediation, advice. They expect protection from current danger and insurance against future harm.

Sometimes what staff does or can do seems too much or not nearly enough. There is spotty surveillance, red tape, overconcern with aggressors' rights. And the most common price of safety (a protective setting) may seem too steep:

Cox C–2 23: Well, the officer should say, "I will talk to this inmate," you know? The officer should have handled it. The officer should have pulled this guy off to the side and said, "You—look, I heard you have been harassing this guy G with sex, and if you don't cut it out you are going to get in trouble."

• • •

VR 8: I went over and told the sergeant, and I said, "That man threatened me." I said, "I want something done about it. That man just threatened me, and I am coming out of the movies and I am trying to avoid him and I have been keep locked because of him before," and I said, "The man threatened me and, you know, something has got to be done." So what does he do but go and lock me up first, and then he locks him up. . . .

I: You say that the staff wanted you to go to protection?

VR 8: Because they said that they couldn't do anything based on my word, or on my word alone, and they had to catch him in the act. . . . He said, "Well we have got to catch him in the act." I said, "Let me ask you this question." I said, "Sergeant, what if a man turns this guy in for homicide?" I said, "What if someone turns him down and he kills them— then what? What do you do, lock him up for the rest of his life? That is not going to solve nothing." . . . Here I am locked up in my cell, and this man is out in the yard looking for tricks or whatever you want to call it— someone to have sex with. And I am locked up, and I am not the one who approached him—he approaches me.

The physical or behavioral cues to victimization are known among staff, who can "spot" prospective victims early if their stigmata are extreme. Preventive intervention is sometimes practiced and may take the form of information-giving, advice, and, where possible, protective surveillance:

VR 3: As I came through the Times Square, this officer must have realized that I was terribly green and terribly frightened, because he pulled me aside and talked to me. He said, "You look frightened, and if there's anything that I can help, or if you want to talk to me, or you have any problem, tell the officer down there to let you come up. If there's something I can help you with." So apparently, from what I understood later, he called the block and talked to the night officer. So therefore the officers were looking out for me. So they kept an eye on me for four or five days. . . . And then later the hall captain talked with me, because he was always a nice guy. And he seen that I was having a problem. He always managed to make sure that I was alone in my cell, because there they could put two guys in one cell. And unless they go into a desperate situation that they were really filled up, he always left me by myself.

• • •

Cox C–2 24: I was warned, more or less, by the police in my county jail, because I had no knowledge, and they said, "Watch out." The police said, "Watch out when people put candy on your bars or offer you this or offer you that, because they are only looking for something in return." . . . The police in there were really good. When they brought me to the reception center, I looked at them when they left, and they looked kind of sad because they were leaving me in this kind of place, and they knew that I was not that kind of person. . . . And I was talking to one of the policemen, and I said, "How is it up there, what is it like?" And he said, "It is a big wall with a bunch of cells in it." And I said, "like in the movies?" And he said, "Right." And then I said, "What are the people like up there? Are they big and burly?" And he said that is hard to say because for the reason some of them are and some of them are not. And then we got into what they act like and why they are there and this and that, you know, and it just came into the subject of sex, and they warned me about it. They said, "Don't accept anything from anybody, and stay as much to yourself as you can." They gave me advice from a person-to-person level—and not from a policeman to a convict.

We have noted that some staff (particularly some prison guards) may counsel victims to fight when threatened. Most staff, however, are in the flight business, which provides protection and furnishes avenues of retreat. Flight advice entails warning inmates to avoid danger situations, and flight interventions involve transfers into protective settings. These settings, which we shall discuss later, keep out potential aggressors and keep the victim in. They are invoked as immediate or as temporary solutions where danger is presumed to exist:

VR 3: I talked with the night officer, he said that he thought that the best thing for me to do was to go to protection. Because he said, "I know the guy that's bothering you, I know what his racket has been and what he's done before. I know what's going to happen; let them get you out in the yard, and it's all over." Because they had been trying to get me to go over to the yard. And the night that I went to protection was the night that they had borrowed my jacket. So the officer says, "Yeah, that's their excuse. You don't get your jacket back until they get you in the yard."

• • •

PC 10: So that was the thing, when the officer came down here one night, I told him what was happening, because I was worried. They wouldn't leave me alone, and they wanted to borrow this and that. And I would give it to them, because I was scared and I didn't want anything to happen. So then this officer came down one night, and he talked to me, and he said, "You know, you should go into protection. I know what's happening and I know that these guys have things that they do to the other inmates, it's happened. And you'll find yourself in real trouble."

I: So you said that you went to protection, but then you came over here again. So you must have not stayed there for very long?

PC 10: Well, I was there for three months.

Protection is not sought or welcomed by most inmates. For some, it is an ego-alien solution, incompatible with their preferred modes of adjustment. Just as fights are noxious to some men, so is flight. While fighting may seem childish and primitive, retreat may be perceived as a confession of impotence or a nonsolution. Past experience may make the inmate reject his "weaker" self. He may see the flight option as a neurotic modality, as the sort of retreat from problems he has once engaged in but has now overcome.

PC 2: I wouldn't want to go to protection. Because if somebody is after you they can get you just as well there as they can any place else. And if it happens on the street, I don't go lock myself in my house. I just walk away and leave it at that. . . . Just that as far as I can remember, when I was younger I used to run away from everything. And after I got married and my marriage fell apart, I made a stand right then that, if anything ever happened in my life again, I would deal with it and solve it right there instead of putting it off and not ever getting to it.

• • •

PC A: I couldn't do time in protection. I wouldn't want to be faced with a problem where I would have to hurt somebody, but I would hurt somebody before I would go into protection. I would take him on. I would stick it out in population and do the best I could in the situation. . . . In protection, then it's like hiding. There is no one to protect me in the streets, and there is nobody to protect me in here. . . . It would hurt my own pride. And then I would feel that I'm much littler in mind. I feel that a guy that has to go to protection because he's scared, he's not fully awake and thinking straight. I know that there is a lot of guys in here that are under a lot of pressure and feel that that is the best place for them. But myself, I've got a lot of self-pride, something like that, and I don't downgrade myself a lot, and I couldn't do it.

• • •

P 1: But what good will it do me to go in there for six months and worry about what is going to happen when I come out? And even if they hadn't, what is going to happen to me when I hit the streets? And how am I going to handle this? I was of course, seventeen, but then in life you're taught that you cannot run all the time. That kind of life.

Where fight is subculturally admired, we can infer that flight is subculturally despised. While manliness is equated with fearlessness, flight—which implies a deficit of bravery—is unmanly. Protection companies are labeled "homo companies," not because they contain homosexuals but because "weak" persons (nonmen) seek refuge there. This negative connotation is advertised and is known to victims. Individuals who have been stigmatized by aggressors can ill afford additional stigmata—connotations that can irrevocably compromise their reputations and may lower their self-esteem:

Cox R 6: When you're in orientation, the lieutenant, he talks about protective custody and stuff, he says that we also have a homo quad—

I: In orientation, that's what the lieutenant calls it—a homo quad?

Cox R 6: Yeah, he says that that is where they have all the fags.

• • •

Cox C-2 23: We would see C-2 in the chow house, and they would say that is where they put all the homos. "Now if you look at C-2, you will see all the homosexuals." I am not a homosexual, far from it, so I don't belong in there. And I don't want to be put in that category in the first place.

• • •

Cox R 27: You feel kind of helpless. . . . But I never let on to the administration here that that is too much of a problem, because I don't want to be sent to the other division and have other people look at me like they think that I have homosexual tendencies. That's what they think. And I don't have homosexual tendencies, but I have other guys that are trying to fuck around.

• • •

VR 2: If I can't handle it myself and handle my bit myself, then I feel funny. If I go to protection, then I say, "Damn, then everybody is going to think I can't handle it."

Finally, the restrictiveness of protection may seem too high a price to pay; the circumscription that is involved may outweigh the gain in security. Protection may demand too much loss of Support and Activity for the quantum of Safety it provides:

PC C4: As soon as I thought about it, I made the decision that I wasn't going to take this stuff. Because I'm in incarceration already, and I would be put farther back into the hole, and this is not what I wanted. And this is what I felt that protective custody was.

• • •

PC 12: Well, what was I supposed to do? Stay there for the rest of my time, become stagnated and not being open to all the programs that they have here to advance myself? The main thing was that if I stayed in protection then I was out of reach of these programs. But what was worse than that was that I couldn't go anywhere.

The Support-Activity–Safety calculus is differently resolved by different inmates. Even though penalties of self-insulation may look uninviting, the magnitude of one's crisis may lower the threshold for tradeoffs:

PC 7: The only thing that I can think of is going into protection and staying there until my time is up or until I get transferred out of here. Or maybe I'll be all right, I don't know.

I: So you've been thinking seriously about this?

PC 7: Yeah, I even wrote a tab to the counselor. I want to talk to him about it and see what he thinks. In protection you don't get to go to the movies or get nothing. You eat in the cell all the time, and you don't get to go out.

• • •

I: How did you feel when you went to protection?

VR 3: I felt safe. And when I first went in there the officer that was in charge of protection introduced me to his clerk and said, "Don't worry about any of the guys in here, they're not going to take advantage of you." And I had no problems while I was in there for three months. And people would borrow things, but they would still pay it back.

I: How did you like living there?

VR 3: Well, the first three or four weeks I thought I would go stark raving mad, because I was locked up twenty-two hours a day. The only time you're out is when you get your meals and come back.

Where Safety needs are extreme, the willingness to make sacrifices may become similarly extreme. Inmates not only may brave the pains of insulation, but may go to a great deal of trouble to be provided with sanctuaries:

I: Well, how did you think you would get into the box?

VR 2: Just request it. Or hit an officer.

I: Did that flash through your mind?

VR 2: Yeah, it did. See, I was going to request it, and then if they wouldn't, then I would hit the officer. Because that's the only way you can do it.

• • •

Cox R 31: Then I went downstairs, and I went to the captain, and I told him that I wanted a transfer and I wanted protective custody right now.

I: Directly after this thing happened?

Cox R 31: Right. And the captain says, "What are you, what's the matter, can't you fight?" I said, "Well, take your badge off and take my place, and see what you can do." And he just walked away. . . . I noticed that he ignored my request, and I made an attempt to commit suicide, because I just lost all hope.

A man *in extremis* not only may brave public connotations of unmanliness, but may be willing to show obvious dependence in demands on staff. Personal vulnerability may bring abdication of autonomy and a childlike or regressive acceptance of staff presence and of womblike retreat:

Cox R 6: I requested a job where I would have an officer present all the time. . . . I said, "You know the problem and you know that these guys are hassling people and you know that these guys want to have me. And I don't want a job where I have to sit in my cell." And I said that I wanted a job where there would be an officer present if somebody was going to try to attack me. So they put me in packaging for a while, and that was just a temporary job, and then I got a permanent job making ID cards, because there was always one officer in there and there weren't too many people in there. So I would work there.

• • •

Cox R 22: And, like, I came back and stuff, and he says, "You have got a problem, don't you?" And I said, "Ever since that thing has happened I have had problems all over." So he put me up in detention, and I told him I am not leaving that tier without an officer. He says, "I can see what you are talking about. . . . All right, I will keep you up there."

• • •

VR 8: One time I just locked my door and I told the officer—I said, "Now, look it, I am not going to work and I am not going to breakfast and I am keep locking my door, because there is a person on this gallery that—that is a homosexual, and he is trying to get me to participate in an act with him, and I am going to tell you something," I said, "I have a lot of psychological problems. My wife is getting a divorce. I am having family problems, and I am liable," I said, "to do something to him that I don't want to do, so I rather you lock me up so that I can talk with the sergeant and we can get this thing resolved, because," I said, "I am going

to tell you—the state and stability of my mind at present, I will do something to harm this man. I will do anything. I will kick him in the balls. I
will take a broom and jam it in his stomach. I will take a razor." And I
said, "I want to be locked up because I will hurt the man if he proposi-
tions me one more time, and I am not kidding." . . . I stayed in my cell
a week. Okay, well, the man was on my company, and we didn't tell him
why I was keep locked because of him. We just told him that I had refused to go to work. And he used to come to my cell and ask me how
come I was keep locked, and I said for refusing to go to work.

The Pursuit of Safety

As we have noted in Chapter 3, a prepotent Safety concern leads to a
scanning of environments for transactions that promote safety or that
compromise it. Settings and routines may be mapped for risk levels of
dangerousness. The environment is catalogued (often similarly by different inmates) for safe houses, mined areas, no man's lands—places to
rush through guardedly in daylight, to avoid at all costs, to circumvent or
flee into:

PC A: Protection-wise, I'll never take a shower in the yard. The only
place that I'll take a shower is on the gallery or in the mess hall. That is
the only two places that I will take a shower. . . . I think a guy is
actually stupid if there is no guards or anyone around to take a shower
by himself, and take a shower without any guards around.

● ● ●

I: What other places at certain times do you see as being particularly
dangerous?

VR 6: Well, let's say over in the school is a big thing because you are
pretty much away from the officers. Like only one officer on each floor
and he will be in the classroom, and it is like the metal shop where you
get behind some of these little work areas and stuff like that. But say
in the shower room or the bathroom, and that is the biggest place—the
biggest place is I would think out in the yard. They have a shower house
where, if you are out there and you want to take a shower, you go in
there, and they have an officer, and he stands outside for all the time, but
still he can go in there and put a knife up to your throat or something
and can say, "If you scream you are dead." And you know, you just say
you are going to have sex with him and you are not going to do nothing
else. You are not going to tell the officer nothing. You just do your debt.

A man may circumscribe his routine to varying extents to meet his
changing perceptions of danger. Like a person who ventures out or stays

home to conform with weather predictions, a psychological "Safety report" governs the conduct of High-safety persons. Like older persons in the transition areas of cities, inmates may lock themselves in when the chances of victimization seem appreciable:

VR 2: Being in jail is bad enough, but being afraid of where you can go is even worse. . . . there is places that there is not any authority around, these kind of places, that people that are being subjected to these kind of things cannot go. Because if an officer is not around this leaves him open for an attack. So I don't go. I avoid it.

• • •

PC 10: My door would be unlocked, and I would still stay in the cell. And then I thought about it, and I knew that I couldn't stay in there all the time. So I said, "You've got to start venturing out." So I started going out in the day and then for a few hours at night. . . . I started watching TV. And then people started getting friendly to me, and I started getting back to the same old thing that I have had before.

• • •

VR 4: He would be any place I would go. And I started not going to those places, the mess hall or the recreation room at night or the yard. And I kept to myself in my room.

Safety transactions involve not only the physical environment but also the social environment. In the physical environment, safety is achieved through selective physical movements. In the social environment the movement is social, and the selectivity involves personal contacts and relationships. The sociogram of the High-safety person aims its arrows at men who are nonthreatening, individuals who form social barriers to danger, or persons who can actively protect one from harm.

A protective setting for victims is not only a place that is inaccessible to aggressors but also one that contains persons who are nonhostile or friendly and whose presence discourages aggression. In its simplest form, Safety takes the form of strength through numbers. This is the case because aggressors are known to prey primarily on isolates:

VR 3: When I came from reception in Sing-Sing, someone there told me . . . "the best thing that you can do is try not to talk to anyone and not associate with anyone. Stay to yourself as much as you can." So that, even when I came in here, that was what I was trying to do. And that's not very wise in a situation like this, because I'm told that if you are by yourself, those are the people that turn out to be real preys of these other people. Because the guy who is a loner, they know that he doesn't have anyone to run to his aid if anything starts.

• • •

Cox C–2 24: So they pushed themselves on me, and they did not approach me sexually, because I did not given them a chance, because I got out of the division that I was in and up to another division, where I have two people from my home town that I know. . . . I talked to my counselor and I told him about it, you know.

I: You told him about the problem?

Cox C–2 24: Right. And I said, "Look, get me up with my friends that I know, and I know I can handle myself, and they can help me and I can help them out, and I could make it a little bit easier—so get me up there." And he said, "All right, we will do it."

• • •

I: Did anyone crack on you directly?

Att R2 41: No, you see, when I was in Jamesville I met about five or six guys that I knew from the street, and I seen that they was in there, and I got right in with that clique, and that kind of protected me.

• • •

Cox R 27: So we all stand together and put the little one in the middle and have the big guys on the outside.

Other Safety transactions involve sponsorship, or protector–protectee relationships. Like staff contacts, such links are dependency links. They require a person who confesses weakness and one who professes strength. The process promotes safety through confrontation, advocacy, or the use of power. It is therefore an approach that combines flight for the victim with fight for the aggressor and sponsor:

VR 8: If a man, a white man, is getting bothered up there, and they go to another white guy, and this guy is a friend to one of the guys in their clique, they will go and tell this black dude to lay off or he might find something in his cell when he comes in at night, or he might accidentally trip going in the shower, and accidents happen, you know? . . . I said, "Well, I don't want to tell you, because . . . I don't know how you guys are going to take this." And this one guy said, "Well, you know, run it down to me, you know, if I don't like it I will let you know. Maybe we can help you with the problem. If something is bothering you." And I said, "Yeah, there's a homo that is bothering me." And he said, "Why didn't you tell me?" He said, "You know, I killed one on the streets," and he said, "I just as soon kill one in here." He said, "Why didn't you tell me that?" I said, "Because I don't want no trouble, you know? You know, if you kill the guy or something, and then I am involved in it, and I didn't want none of this." He said, "Look, I would have gave the guy a warning, and the guy would have left you alone, and the guy knows me, and he knows that I don't play. If I tell you I am going to kill you, I am going to kill you." He said, "You should have come to me the first time," so he says, "Well, I will talk with you later." And he went over and talked with some other guys, and they were, this guy was a weightlifter, and they went down to where he was lifting weights and they said, "We would like to talk to you about something," and he came over and that is when they told him, they said, "You know, a friend of ours got keep locked twice on account of you, and we are upset about it."

• • •

Att R2 22: I had run into this kid from over across here a little way, and the guys were cracking on him. So I told him, "Look, hang onto me and no one will bother you, and if they do let me know and I will straighten them out real quick." And it did turn out that the next day—that night when he went into his cell, a couple of guys were cracking on him— white guys—and I said to them later, "Hey, don't pick on the kid." And they said, "Hey," they said, "what is he, your kid?" And I said, "No, he's a friend of mine. If you mess with him you are going to mess with me. If you mess with me you're going to be in trouble." And that is the way that I put it. And they never bothered him after. He has got quite a few friends now.

The Impact of Victimization

Transactions involve both men and settings. Safety transactions, like other transactions, are joint man–milieu products. Threats can help us feel unsafe, and locks may help to reassure us. But there are men (Custers and Geronimos) who laugh at odds; there are others who panic in seclusion.

Inmates are threatened in prison. More vulnerable inmates are more intensely threatened. Some inmates are harmed, and most are not harmed. Most inmate victims escape, explode, or find friends or sanctuaries. Threats do cease. Fear may wane as pressure eases.

But the pressure may not ease. For some men past danger lives in vivid recollection. For others no bars or walls seem thick enough, no peers are ever friends. Assaulted sensibilities and exploited vulnerabilities may be wounds serious enough to heal slowly, or not to heal at all.

Stress may disequilibrate egos in ways that persist. An individual may feel chronically unsafe or may relive unassimilated traumas time and time again. He may feel unsettled, tense, unsure, and hurt. He may be unable to face tasks in the present. His hurtful past encroaches, charging him with being weak or reminding him of the undependability of the environment:

Cox R 22: When I say it is a problem, I mean when I lay in my room and with the earphones on, and no matter what song comes on this always pops into my mind. It pops into my mind all the time. . . . I see it as a problem, because if someone asks me a question my mind is not in the right place, but I tell him something, and I don't even remember what I told the guy. They have, like, messed up my life. . . . The more

I think of it the worse it comes to my mind. Regardless of what I am doing, once in a while this will pop into my head, and I wish that there was some way that I could get it out of my head. Like, if I am talking to someone maybe it will come off my mind sometime. . . . Because all I have got to do, I will be down and reading a book in my room and stuff, and this will go through my mind, and it will blow my mind apart. I will say, "Damn, I have to start thinking about this fucking shit again." I want to forget it and say past is past.

• • •

Cox R 27: The only time that you feel free from it is when you're locked in your cell, and then you're free from the physical attack but there's still the mental thing, which is really heavy. . . . In Elmira I got ulcers from it. You know, I would be throwing up blood, and then out of frustrations I would eat a lot, and I came in weighing 125 pounds, and I don't know if it was psychologically or not, but I just kept on eating, and I wanted to be big. I got to be 180 pounds. . . . I know that personally I would like to get a few exhales out and sort of calm down a bit. It's gotten so bad that about a month and a half ago I started talking to the shrink, and I said that I'm really feeling a lot of tension, so he's got me on a drug at night and another drug during the day. And I'm in my cell, and I'm fine now. I'm a zombie. I walk around really loaded, and it's all right.

The future, which continues the past, may seem bleak. Being protected in the Now does not change the lesson of life's dirty joke. No plans are possible where hope is dead. It seems pointless to seek short-term safety where long-term security is not obtainable:

VR 3: I felt really such a broken spirit, I guess you might say, that all I could do was crawl under the concrete. So the thing was, as this progressed day by day and the officers were talking with me every day, "Are they still bothering you?" It was building, instead of I was hoping it would level off. . . . I think I was so overwhelmed with so many fears and so many problems that I was confronted with, plus trying to adjust to finding yourself locked in a cell so many hours a day, that it was very difficult for me to even try to figure out things, or to try to get any kind of plan as to how I could cope with the future. It was almost a day-to-day groping, really, of trying to muster through all the fear and anxiety and depression that I had. That there did not seem to be any way of having a little extra corner of your mind that you can say, "Well, this is used for planning and plotting your way through." I was just so overwhelmed by all this.

• • •

Cox R 31: I lost all hope. I felt that it would be quite a while, and life wasn't worth living any more. I lost all faith and all hope.

I: Because you felt that these kinds of things would continue to happen?

Cox R 31: Yes.

A man may retreat to the point of no return. The presumption of dangerousness and the sense of vulnerability linger: All men are aggressors. They are aggressors at all times, in insiduous and unpredictable ways. Communication is impossibly risky, and trust is unthinkable. The only real safety lies in permanent, constant flight:

VR 6: The second or third month is when I really got defensive. The first month, still in reception, I was nice to these people, and I would talk to them unless I had a really good reason to shine them on, and then after a while people would come up to me and I would tell them, "Look, I don't think that I have anything to say to you and I don't really know you."

● ● ●

VR 2: People that knew me when I was on the street, they say, "What is wrong with you?" And I say, "What is wrong?" And they say, "Well, you just seem to be a different person." And this is now. And they say that I don't play as much as I used to. And it's really changed me coming in here. I guess you could say that I'm bitter. I don't like to play no more, and I go to my cell and sit by myself.

● ● ●

Att R2 10: You take a kid and you punish him very hard and frequently, and the kid is going to become either very aggressive or very introverted. I was becoming introverted—I wasn't an aggressive person. I couldn't, I wouldn't do much of anything. I stayed in my cell and just had—I wrote lists of my friends' names and all that.

Like the flight stance, the fight stance lingers. Other men sense fear, and they exploit it. To cover fear, one reacts angrily and explosively. There are inmates who claim that they entered prison as trusting and gentle youths and have left prison as irritable, ungovernable men. The point may hold, and if it does, it is tragic. For it is one thing for prisons to fail to regenerate wolves. It is another thing for prisons to make beasts of lambs.

10

Niches in Prison

MEN IN DESPAIR CHOOSE NOT A WAY OF LIFE but a way to live. Much of the activity and energy of men in stressful situations is directed at making sense of incongruity and at limiting action to those areas that strike them as familiar and compatible with their stress-induced needs. Every community has these marginal copers, who tenaciously cling to survival. We become aware of such persons when their emergency strategies fail, when they become institutionalized or slip into overt despair. Such crises, however, are tips of the stress iceberg or echoes of the underworld of stress. That underworld is narrow, hostile, constricted, and desperately selective. To the men in skid row, for instance, the world becomes a scenario of familiar flophouses, coffee shops with sugar on the table, places and moments of warmth, barber colleges, and police who gently rouse (Love). Their life, while closer to the bone than most, is active and limits transactions with the world to those that can be borne. This point holds for other men in other settings, such as for older persons in the South Bronx, whose personal world involves living in enclaves, going to supermarkets in groups, telephone checks in the evening, and increasing engagement in individual and group protective measures.

Even where environmental conditions appear most malevolent, men create, seemingly from rocklike or diaphanous material, a fabric of life. Such adaptation also occurs in prison. To be sure, in the free world men can often flee stress or defend themselves against long-term debilitating impingements through the careful management of time, props, and people. One can quit a job, divorce a mate, develop relaxing routines. In prison there are few advertised refuges, no neighborhood bar, no supportive family, no late movie or television, few drugs, minimal alcohol, few oppor-

This chapter was prepared by John Seymour.

tunities to push the dull reality of doing time into the background. We have also noted that in prison it is not generally viewed as legitimate, by inmates as well as staff, for a stressed person to seek emotional support or to advertise his vulnerability in the hope of receiving recognition and assistance. And searching for a blatant sanctuary is also frowned upon.

We know that inmates vary in the degree to which they are vulnerable to the stresses of imprisonment. While some inmates show surprising resilience to stress, we have considerable evidence that a more vulnerable group exists (Toch, 1975). These men become salient when they inflict self-injury or are transferred to a clinical setting. We are aware that they exist when we see a novice inmate demanding protection, watch an older inmate exploding with frustration, or see a man continuously limiting himself to mandated group activities. We are aware of such inmates, but they are labeled as weak, intransigent, or loners, and their behavior is diagnosed as an idiosyncratic emotional reaction of no generic importance.

In this chapter we take a broader view of the vulnerable inmate, by exploring the process whereby he ameliorates his stress. We shall see that stressed inmates in prison create their own responsive worlds and that the prison setting accommodates a large number of those worlds.

We shall see that the inmate, like the vulnerable person on the street, can arrange a microcosm that rarely guarantees happiness but usually guarantees survival. He can selectively perceive elements of the prison milieu that either defy his needs or reflect a potential for meeting them. The more salient features of the prison environment—its walls and gates, overlapping security nets, bars and cells, those aspects that have the impact of theater—can fade into psychological insignificance. The inmates attend to a series of invisible subenvironments, with various degrees of movement in or out, population sizes, inmate types, degrees of control and supervision, activities, routines, rules and regulations, behaviors permitted or restrained.

The vulnerable inmate labels certain places and activities as warm or dangerous, as places he feels good in or places he must avoid. One inmate may perceive the prison yard as an arena of Activity, another counts the custodial officers who are available, notes the rules, attends to Structure and Safety in the lounging and playing of other inmates in the yard. The perceptions of the vulnerable inmate are specialized, as are those of the skid row bum who attends to chances of panhandling, the location of police, to fatigue and distance from a place to sleep, and his subway fare or its lack.

The world of the vulnerable inmate is limited to the dimensions of prison that are relevant to his concerns. Where an inmate dismisses from awareness the segregation unit, the restricted movement, and the correctional officers but is vociferous in condemning lax rules, inconsistent orders, and the prison's failure to control the behavior of other inmates, it may be said that the functional world of the inmate is skewed toward Structure concerns and away from stimuli relating to Freedom.

Vulnerability makes one's needs and environmental concerns more salient. These concerns highlight required subenvironments, sanctuaries, or *niches*. A niche is a functional subsetting containing objects, space, resources, people, and relationships between people. A niche is perceived as ameliorative; it is seen as a potential instrument for the relaxation of stress and the realization of required ends. It is this quality of niches that stimulates the creative process of niche search and niche identification. Niche search is usually an explorative process in which a person seeks a specific setting because adjustment appears easier there. Occasionally niches are officially or formally supplied (as in mental health units, hospitals, specialized treatment units). But the most intriguing niches are those which are less obvious, those that are created, sought out, or stumbled into by men under stress. These settings in prison may be work assignments, living units, or programs, and they may feature any combinations among Privacy, Safety, Structure, Freedom, Support, Activity, Emotional Feedback, and Social Stimulation.[1]

Features of Niches

Irrespective of their content or quality, niches have several attributes in common:

1. The process of niche definition is *transactional*. While settings and activities may be formally defined in specific ways, the vulnerable person places idiosyncratic interpretations on these places and activities. He may

---

[1] Some studies of prison life have touched on the existence of subsettings within institutions. Glaser, for example, discusses prison jobs as differentially desirable to inmates and as variously promotive of harmony or conflict. For the average inmate, a "good" assignment (according to Glaser) involves a small, select, isolated, homogeneous group, and the availability of prison resources. Goffman discusses differences between subsettings in total institutions and points to free spaces, group territories, and personal territories as areas that are perceived and used in various ways by inmates.

Stern talks of "niches" in describing school settings whose climates are clearly responsive to specific student needs. In characterizing such settings, Stern writes that "each of these types of schools may be viewed, then, as an ecological niche for a particular kind of student. The independent liberal arts college caters to students concerned with intellectuality and autonomy. Engineering schools also emphasize personal independence, but are otherwise more aggressive, thrill-seeking, and achievement-oriented. The denominational subculture is group-centered, as are university-affiliated liberal arts, business administration, and teacher-training colleges, but each of these differs in its focus. Denominational college life would appear to be more purposive and goal-oriented, less playful and convivial, than that at the large universities, whereas the atmosphere of the business administration programs is decidedly anti-intellectual" (Stern, 92).

respond to the social patterns that dominate in a setting, but he reciprocally influences them.

2. Men may *create* their own environmental niche by shaping, selecting, and construing elements of their surroundings or by presenting themselves in a certain way so as to elicit a desired response.

3. Places selected by vulnerable men are seen by them as perceptually distinct and as regulated or *controlled* by themselves, or by others with their interests in mind.

4. One niche may be almost invisible, a personal and private space carved from an impersonal superstructure; another may be crowded, interpersonal, active, and stimulating. But all niches are *congruent* or compatible with the prioritized needs of their residents.

These attributes of niches can be separately discussed, and can be illustrated by referring to our interviews with vulnerable inmates.

1. NICHES ARE TRANSACTIONAL

Most prisoners enter a prison with a tolerable self-image, even though it may be eroded by the dissolution of a number of formerly held assumptions about one's own competence and effectiveness. We have seen that many who survive relatively intact in the free world find themselves deficient in skills needed to deal with prison stresses, and often this knowledge is not easily assimilated.

A continuing theme surfacing in our niche resident interviews is a sense of being different from the mainline population, of feeling like a stranger in a strange land.

P 10: It was like the whole prison is impossible. The majority of the people have a lot of time here, and I was scared by a lot of people. I am about the youngest in this institution. I don't know how I got here anyway.

● ● ●

P 9: It didn't turn out like I thought it would be. Like, on TV you see it, and you just put on a uniform and lock in your cell and everything is okay. It's quiet. And I was prepared to go to sleep or read. But here there was noise constantly. There was kids screaming across a 40-foot distance. I was bugging out from the noise and these white streamers that they kept throwing across so that they could get cigarettes from the other side. And I kept wondering, "Jesus Christ, what did I get into? I don't belong in this kind of place."

People entering prison generally have some idea of who they are. In prison they are often told explicitly that they are considerably less than they thought. They can be told this by officers, by other inmates, or by their own challenged perceptions and insights. But even when the world is upside down, when events occur in a new wonderland of cause and effect, people orient themselves around the core that remains. Niches are settings that help provide a sense of familiarity in the face of threatening novelty.

EI N G: Print shop. When you go in there they make you feel wanted in the print shop. Like, I'm a white guy, and there is a black guy talking to me, and there is no tension, like I have to start all over and make new friends. You get right into it: "What is happening?" And start rapping and playing cards. And we try to make people feel comfortable in there.
And the officers are okay, and the instructors. Like, there is no way that you can get over in our shop. . . . Everybody is the same there, we don't play roles or put on a front.

One way in which prisoners seek to pursue unique personal goals or protect their sense of being different from the general population is through combinations of Privacy and Activity.

One such inmate describes, from the viewpoint of a long-term inmate, the stresses of doing time with short-term inmates and the routine he has evolved to insulate himself:

GH N 14: These guys that are going home start acting from the day they get into prison like they're eligible for paroles, work release, anything like that. . . . That's what it is. And if they can get a farm job or something like that, they get moved over to J Block, and they're out until eleven o'clock, watching TV. So this is a real party for them. And they make it rough for the guys that are doing a harder time, or a longer time. Because these guys, you see them every day, this guy's going home, this guy's going home. This guy's got drugs on his record, he's got rapes on his record, but due to the fact that he got a good judge, he's getting all these breaks. And you say, "Look at me, I'm doing twelve years for a half-assed robbery that I wasn't even caught in the act of doing." I was arrested two weeks later. So I've got five and a half years in, almost half the bit in. With any luck I might have a furlough, but no, they won't give it to me. I mind my own business, I work hard, I stay out of trouble. . . . Well, this job I have, I work all over the place, inside and outside. Outside the buildings and inside the buildings. I work with no officers or nothing. One civilian. And he knows his business and my business. So it's like we're on the street. We go to work, pick up our tools, this is it, we put up a wall or hang a door, we know what we're doing. And the next thing I know it's three o'clock and my day's work is done. I go take a shower and everything else, and I'm away from the static, I'm away from the congregation, you know what I mean? You know, we're all moving here together, we're all doing this together, something else there. You can say more or less I'm on my own, and I enjoy being alone. I don't like this noise and everything else. If I've got to do the time, I've got to do a job, I'll do it.

In this instance the world of the prisoner incorporates his former, out-side role as carpenter. Normally, in the free world, we carry off a surprising number of roles—husband, handyman, father, worker—and we can shape and discard roles. In prison one's world is more limited. But even though one cannot use the blueprint of one's former life and former roles to con-struct a way of living in confinement, one uses what is familiar. Though the world of job and street is gone, one of assignment and block can be substituted. Often an inmate creatively alters his space for living to follow old modes as closely as possible. But frequently relevant experience is lacking: Youths enter prison with a set of values and perceptions of the environment that are often at variance with its demands. With egos molded into rough approximation of an identity, with flexible, changing, unstable anchorages, and behaviors that even confuse themselves at times, youths can have a great deal of trouble in adjusting to felt restrictions of freedom. Often, as we have seen in Chapter 7, they attempt a masquerade to con-vince the world that they are both controlled and autonomous. The pose under conditions of imprisonment is difficult, particularly in the face of one's own outbursts of indignation and rage. A low-pressure, low-challenge niche can make the struggle easier.

One inmate in an institution reserved for youths, for example, who received numerous disciplinary punishments while at the institution, found a relaxation of pressure and a haven of self-control upon transfer from the school program to the farm, which is known as a high-freedom subenviron-ment:

Cox N 6: On the farm—right?—I realize since I have been out there, out there you can stay out of trouble, and inside you can't. Like, in school he will be teaching you something that is not beneficial to you, and you tell him, and you will get a ticket for it, you know? Like, in the shop I was in and the mess hall, and I wouldn't even know why he wrote it. . . . The work on the outside seems better to me, because you don't have no officer and someone on your back all the time telling you to do this and to do that, you know? As long as you know what you do on the out-side, you do it, and the officer don't have nothing to say. All he wants to know is if you are doing your work or not. He ain't pushy and trying to get you to say something to him so that he can come back and give you a ticket, you know. . . . Like, in here, when you go to work when you finish, you have got to sit around and on the outside once you finish your work, and you have nothing to do, you and the others can go outside and sit down and relax, or even you can go for a walk over to one of the other squares or another quad, and inside you have to wait until everyone is done and sit and wait for them to be done.

It should be noted that this inmate's Freedom niche, the farm, is leg-endary among inmates who have Safety concerns as a dangerous place, full of intransigents who victimize weaker inmates. Groups of inmates with similar concerns may thus recognize a setting as ameliorative, while others see the same setting as stressful or as incompatible with their needs. Niches are recognized for what they are only in relation to one's dominant concerns. People in the niche perceive the niche, and themselves, as different and unique. It is this distinction in part, in combination with the other niche attributes we have mentioned, that results in stress reduction.

2. NICHES ARE CREATED

The active process by which an inmate judges his prison world, locates himself within it, and rearranges it is niche-creating behavior if it reduces stress. The process itself is something more than a means and something less than an end. While searching for a congruent setting an inmate becomes more aware of the degree of personal equilibrium he needs for survival. He experiences his world by spending more time in one place and less in another, searching out friends, seeking safety by finding officers or civilians who are protective, fine-tuning his perception of cues to violence or to behavioral irritants.

A number of factors interact to limit or facilitate niche search. Prior experience with institutional milieus and other learned coping behaviors often enable inmates to recognize resources that may be marshaled or reconstructed. In other instances an inmate is only aware that the prison world contains a number of closely sequenced humiliations and begins selectively to seek sanctuaries to protect himself from collapse.

The first effort of many inmates under stress is to transfer out of the stress setting. The stresses that are encountered are experienced as indigenous to the specific institution one is in rather than as more generic features of the environment, or as reactions precipitated by one's own appearance or actions. The sense of "If I can only get away from officer X," or "If I can only get out of this prison, where these groups are threatening me" prevails early. However, movement out of an institution voluntarily, via transfer, is highly restricted, and in New York it is essentially prohibited during the first six months at an institution. During that period, when an inmate's free-floating anxiety is heavy, the inmate must negotiate the immediate physical and social environment that confronts him. Coping with the disequilibrium involves a long, slow process of controlling, eliminating, and reducing noxious stimuli, and of gathering and harvesting resources that facilitate "doing time."

Ittelson et al. nicely illustrate this transactional process by describing five stages of screening beginning with an *affective* stage. The first response of a person who finds himself in jail is emotional, an anxious feeling, a heightened awareness bordering on suspense, a feeling of fear. The next process, if one resolves the disequilibrium caused by the affect reaction, is one of *orientation*. In a new setting a person tries to determine "what's happening," to know where he is, to find his place within his world. The inmate seeks out cell neighbors, or homies, or responsive staff to fill out the details of his environment. A third process is one of *cataloguing*. Inmates give to people, areas, or roles perceptual identifiers, such as "That guy seems all right," or "That shop seems confused or dangerous." Descriptions of warmth, acceptance, hostility, or coldness are assigned to relevant aspects of the setting. Ittelson et al. state that what happens here is that the individual evaluates a physical setting and social setting by "extending its meaning by functionally relating its various aspects to his own needs, predispositions, values" (p. 97).

Next the inmate creates a *system* for his life in the setting. He establishes a sense of "where I can make it," or "where I can escape this, where I can find people to talk to, whom must I deal with to get by, whom must I avoid." If such questions are resolved adequately, the inmate may achieve a feeling of mastery over his functional world, as well as an assurance of its structure and predictability.

Manipulation follows when the inmate orders, systematizes, and controls component parts of his world to attain his goals. With newly found competence and mastery over heretofore overpowering difficulties, a person can begin to formulate new needs and strategies to satisfy them.

However, the niche search process may not flow smoothly. As with any developmental sequence, obstacles may block progress. Initial assignments may be involuntary or may be geared to test coping skills. In addition, inmates often do not perceive prison settings rationally and logically. They frequently have marginal perceptual clarity and great fear, together producing a tremendous amount of error and distortion at the orientation stage. They may act in ignorance of what is expected of them. They may respond to stress in ritualized or compulsive ways, such as by periodically lashing out.

Some institutions maintain low-pressure settings away from the mainstream for inmates who are clearly helpless. These settings may be small, protected, isolated maintenance gangs with foremen attuned to the special problems of their charges or closely supervised arts and crafts programs; they may be programs that keep one sufficiently busy so that personal problems do not overwhelm, or programs with a great deal of mobility and autonomy. Even for inmates whose niches are thus created for them, the niche process is not passive, however. The inmates, not the staff, ultimately define the niche as a niche.

Any overt expression of Safety concerns, Activity concerns, or Freedom concerns directed at staff responsible for assignment decisions is also a niche-creating type of behavior. While many inmates ask for little, and rarely ask out loud, some inmates know that to escape stress they must signal their vulnerability:

Cox N 10: In reception they [administrative staff] watch you like they would watch someone under a microscope for biology tests . . . that is how hard they watch you. They judge by your actions and by what you say and by how fast you move and this and that where you should go. Now, if you move fast enough and you have muscle they will send you somewhere else. But if you have a problem (like me), nervous or something, they will put you in the division [C-2 division].

When we visited this inmate (Cox N 10) in the Reception Center, he refused to come out of his cell to complete a questionnaire. He was extremely nervous and talked disjointedly about transfers, blacks, violence, and escaping.

Several months later he was selected for interview randomly from a pool of inmates in the C-2 division at Coxsackie, the tier maintained for nervous, weak, intimidated inmates, inmates with emotional problems, and a few overt homosexuals. This time the young man was considerably more oriented to the institutional world, was emotionally controlled, and even expressed confidence in his ability to survive:

Cox N 10: Yes, this is the best institution going. I am not a CO's boy or anything, but I go between the COs and the inmates. It is safe that way. I like to be safe. I communicate with everyone as long as they communicate with me not violently. . . .

If I went to another division though, they would probably tear me apart, because I would have no back. A back is people behind you in a division. . . .

I would never leave C-2.

C-2 is essentially a white company—80 percent to 85 percent white (see Table 10–1). Supervision is heavy within the unit, and during non-program hours inmates are segregated from the rest of the population. Inmates normally do go to program—school, shop, and volunteer programs. A sizable percentage of the population are rural inmates, small groups from Oswego or Poughkeepsie who congregate together, talking about familiar places, with familiar values predominating. The niche is perceived as a nonviolent world in which playing does not have a humiliating or competitive purpose, does not terrify or create scapegoats. Similarly, sexual aggressiveness is minimal.

The division is viewed as a quiet, private, controlled world. Even when labeling by non-C-2 inmates occurs, with descriptions of C-2 inmates as "fags," "punks," or "rats," men like our inmate cling to C-2 as a haven and would rather admit to being "weak" than have to defend a more prestigious but less congruent identity.

One common consequence of niche creation is that the niche inmates may fail to recall the conditions of "outside" life endured before niches

TABLE 10-1. Demographic Characteristics of Coxsackie C-2 Unit Compared to Those of Coxsackie Population

	Coxsackie C-2 Sample		Coxsackie Random Sample	
Ethnicity:				
White	29	(83%)[a]	12	(30%)
Black	5	(14)	20	(50)
Puerto Rican	1	(3)	8	(20)
Total	35	(100)	40	(100)
Residence:				
City over 500,000	4	(11%)	26	(68.4%)
Other city	12	(34)	8	(21.1)
Small town or rural	19	(54)[a]	4	(10.5)
Total	35	(100)	38	(100.0)

[a]Difference significant at .001 level.

were located. Stress features of the prison milieu slip into insignificance when they no longer create pain. Only when the inmate becomes lost again, or strives to fulfill new needs, are stressful environmental characteristics discovered or rediscovered.

3. Niches Are Controlled

Where inmates demand Structure, it is not chaos that they bemoan, it is the prison's failure to control things that need controlling. Older inmates may feel a particular need for environmental stability, in light of changes in the composition of prison populations. Given a shift in the inmate subculture, from a respected coping style of emotional distance and coolness, to one that includes militancy, confrontation, and testing, new needs for stability are generated.

Inmates often search out arenas in which constraints may be self-imposed, or where organization controls dominate and monitor or modulate behavior. Such needs relate saliently to concerns for Privacy, Structure, or Safety. Men whose institutional lives are marginal may also sometimes have to remove themselves from turmoil or scrutiny for a while, to cement holes in their defenses, to regroup and reassess their coping strengths, and to make it through the next day in one piece.

Niches may be perceived by inmates as defenses of the boundaries of self (Goffman). They enhance their ability to escape from violence; reduce the unpredictability of the inmate world; modulate such environmental irritants as noise and incursions upon thoughts and activities; increase the scope for mobility; provide predictable access to areas or possessions; produce more lawful restrictions of autonomy or activity; and facilitate the effective management of time.

Controlling the boundaries of self may be more or less important to individual inmates. Some inmates can tolerate only limited trespass, and they may demand Structure as the means of obtaining Privacy. For such inmates, niches are stimulus oases that limit the kind and degree of information one must share and defend one from chaotic social stimulation:

Att N 4: We got wise guys; any place you go, agitators, wise guys. Now, if you look around the prison, you'll see almost 80 percent in this place. So where's the trouble? It's with them. It's agitating. If you don't go around and visit, maybe you're a loner, you want to be by yourself, or you hang out with one guy. They feel, what's wrong with these guys, punks or faggots or something? I just like to be alone and not hassle with these guys.

• • •

El N 16: Well, there are some dudes in here that have very nasty attitudes. That is why I have the job I have. I'm not more or less in the jail population. I'm out of the population, because I don't like it. And they really get to you. They really bug you.

Niches tend to be small in size, are often personal spaces, and are perceived as relatively closed to movement in and out. Such control over space and movement relates strongly to concerns for personal safety:

Att N I: [In the general population] you don't know when some guy is going to flip out and run screaming down the hall with a knife; and in the OVR program there are only eighty guys in a unit, and I can pretty well judge what their reactions are going to be. . . . There is less available people to see, and so you feel a little bit more secure, because maybe it's a smaller group of friends and it's tighter. . . . One thing I've found since I've been here is a kind of general paranoia of large groups, because you can't control a large group as well as you can control a small group. Out there [in population] you might run into anything. . . . You have all different personalities out there. The general population has to deal with all kinds . . . you might run into someone that doesn't think the way you think, and then that is going to lead to a fight.

• • •

El N B: A lot of fights here. Fights over milk and magazines and immaterial things, TV programs. . . . The inmates like to bend the rules and see how far they can go . . . and the guy that is doing a good bit, he's getting harassed. . . . And the people that are older, they sit aside and do the best they can. Because there's not that many of us. I have to stay out of a lot of people's way, because there is a lot of personalities that are around. . . . My job helps a lot, the officers tighten up there.

Inmates in niches point to the control theme of their niches as one of behavioral thermostats which help predict or take the temperature of a place, as well as increasing the ability to manage "what's happening."

Part of the thermostatic effectiveness of niches is due to the fact that they contain fewer people and permit isolative behavior and defensive coping. However, control has an ego dimension as well, a feeling that one knows where one is in the world and can control one's own emotional responses in light of that knowledge. An inmate must be able to predict not only the actions of others but also his own responses and their consequences on the actions and activities of others. Hadley Cantril notes that

> . . . other people have their own purposes. And we must always remember in our attempts to understand others that their purposes are just as "real" as any of their physical characteristics. . . . We must guess what those purposes are. We must predict what effect our intended behavior will have on others' purposes, how others will see us, and how their reaction to us will in turn affect our subsequent action in the endless chain of events in which we are involved [Cantril, 1958, p. 14].

To increase predictability, we may limit our mobility to areas or settings in which predictability is imposed by fiat or in which we know our capacity to handle familiar stresses:

Cox N 2: You see, this shop is orderly. When I was in the sheet metal shop, it was disorderly. Guys running around and playing like little kids. I couldn't handle it—throwing things at each other and all that stuff. It wasn't like it was supposed to be. Out here in the masonry shop, everybody is quiet and everybody is working on their project, and there ain't no noise and no disorderly conduct from anybody. . . . It's quiet, you see? I don't like to be around confusing things, and that is the way it was over in the sheet metal shop. Over here you got guys that don't use profanity back and forth, and this and all that.

• • •

P 9: I'd be paranoid out in population. The first little hassle I would have, I immediately pick up a pipe and hit him with it. If I were out there in that conflict, that is the first thing I would do.

• • •

EI N 19: It is too young for me and too young in its attitude in the population. . . . I have a lot of problems here. In my work assignment it is different, because you're not confronted with all these people. The paint shop is really small. It used to be hard for me in C Block, you have so much traffic going to court. It's hard for a guy that isn't sure of himself in that block, because he can blow up. I blow up. Everybody blows up. I didn't think I could handle all these problems.

Self-control relates not only to Safety and Privacy concerns but also to Freedom concerns. For High-freedom inmates, staff restrictions replace inmate incursions as irritants, but the emotional responses—anger, frustration, or attacking behavior—may be constants. While some High-freedom inmates may derive stature from calculated confrontations with staff, for most, feelings overwhelm goals, and as a result the men find undesired disciplinary placement, segregation, loss of good time, staff labeling, and possible compromise of parole chances.

Some settings place the locus of control within the individual, relieving him of a sense of overwhelming external control and permitting him to modulate his actions and interaction with authority figures. Just as other settings substitute external controls for weakened internal controls, settings may be ameliorative by relaxing the level of monitoring, instructions, or rules:

Cox N 12: Before, I had problems like this: I would get an order from one officer to do this, and before I even get to the desk, they ask me where am I going, and have you got a pass, and who told you to do this, and who told you to do that, and I just explained it to him again, and go down there and get a more specific pass that explains more, and then they want you to do this and that. They don't, you know, let you choose. You don't choose nothing inside, more or less. You either got to obey or get locked up. They lock you up for the stupidest things. You ask them a question and you can—more or less you consult them about a problem, and the officers, they have got a more or less attitude about you, and he is just like—he will always be ready to lock you up out there, and you can't consult them about nothing. . . . I dropped a bomb, because I just couldn't take all this police and everything. I wanted to get on the farm, because it seemed as though every place that I went there was somebody that was trying to hassle me. . . . You feel more at ease out there. Like, you have got at least a little bit more freedom. The police don't be down on you as much as they do in the building, and you get off and you can do anything. . . . [The harrassment] is still there, but I try to avoid it as much as possible. But it seemed the more that you are away from the crowd or, you know, avoid discussing anything with anybody, I feel better.

• • •

Cox N 20: He's the first guy who don't impress authority on you where you have to do this or that. He's a nice person. [My instructor] trusts the inmate, and that is one of the requirements to get in, he likes you. And so by me clowning around him, there is no harm in it, and it's expected. So to me, it's a nice environment.

Relaxed control serves as a behavioral coolant. Where internal controls are recognized as vulnerable and challenges or tests are kept to a minimum, settings are described as benevolent. For High-freedom inmates, a niche may be a place that never questions their image of themselves as manly, autonomous, and strong:

El N 17: In my opinion, it would be a worse institution [if I no longer had my job], because then I think that I would have more problems than I have now. And the fact that I'm in the foundry now, and I don't have that many dealings with the police, that lightens the burden of my bit. Now, if I don't have my job, then that means that I'm taking the full impact of everything. And there is going to be much more, and I'm going to be in bigger trouble. And I'm trying to get around that situation. I don't want to get in trouble. We're out all day, and we're to ourselves, and we have a civilian here and a police officer here, and they're all right. They don't give us no static, the officer is good people, and we respect him and he respects us. And I think that if I wasn't in here, then there might be a dark hole inside this place.

In some settings, the ability to maximize one's physical control over one's location, movement, and activities results in stress reduction. Physical freedom translates into a sense of personal autonomy, a feeling that one controls one's fate and can increase or decrease one's behavioral options at will or in response to specific situations:

Au N 7: I work in the hospital here in prison, and it is considered a better job, and actually right now in this environment I am doing my own thing. I come to my hospital job in the morning, and I am not in my cell always. I go to pick up the sick call slips, and I move about. I move about more freely than the normal inmate. This is one thing, that I have maintained an identity in being able to move freely. Some semblance of freedom within the walls, right? More freedom within the walls—that would be the first basis of establishing, for instance, identity, because you can move more and also wear clothes that you want to wear—right?—some men here wear a certain hat. This is their identity.

• • •

Au N D: Now, I have to deal with one officer, and I work only a very short period each day. The rest of the day is mine to do as I choose with, which gives me a great deal of time for myself. . . . I don't have to lock in for some counts. . . . I'm pretty much free here.

• • •

GH N BB: Well, when I was in Clinton I was the rabbi squad, which was considered one of the best jobs in the institution. I had the most freedom, and I could walk anywheres I wanted in the institution. It gave me a lot of time to myself. It did give me a lot of time, and I got a lot of reading, and I guess the reading was the biggest part of it, and I enjoyed it and I kept up to date as to what was happening outside.

• • •

Au N L: Up until recently I didn't have to participate in the daily routine —go to the mess hall and wait in lines and things like that—so I stayed by myself, and that is why I took the job. . . . I would say that it was easy doing the time. I would say that there are ways that you can do it. You can avoid complications—that is the way I do it. I avoid them all.

The degree of personal control figures heavily in inmate attempts to maximize coping. A major niche attribute is the ability to control the level of stimulation one is faced with. Privacy in a niche may involve the ability to restrict the entrance of others, the ability to influence the types of behavior taking place in a setting, or the ability to initiate a restricted range of behaviors and to resist the onslaught of alien behavioral patterns.

Niches are usually perceptually isolated, calm, and quiet backwaters. The activity present in the setting, or its dominant routine, may present opportunities to inmates to effectively manage time and energy. The creation of a regimen or the effective use of free and unencumbered moments is related to a sense of personal ownership of time, as well as to the ability to govern the range and variety of one's activities. Some work assignments completely preempt most working hours and constitute very effective consumers of energy:

Att N 21: When I first came in here, I applied for the job as projectionist, and I did it on the streets for eighteen years, and then I kept the job until January, and then I hear about the officers' mess and about how you work there all day, and you're busy and you're away from all the inmates, and all the food is better. So I changed jobs to that, and I can still work the movies too. So I wouldn't give the movie job up. I worked the movies, and weekends and afternoons I'm also a porter just to fill the time in. And then an opening in OM came up, and so I went in there. It's better food and it's away from the rest of the inmates, and there is more benefits as far as you can get your laundry done and you're busy. You go from five minutes of six to one-thirty, and you're busy all day. . . . I like being busy. I can't stand standing around all day. Because in the morning, if I'm not busy, then I'll get up and walk around in circles. I'll get up and walk around or walk into the kitchen or just walk. I hate to be just sitting down doing nothing. That is the way that it was on the streets. I would go to work at five in the morning and get through at three-thirty and then go to the theater at night. I worked on the main job for twelve years and the theater for eighteen. That's the one thing that I wanted to avoid, was the trouble. When there is a lot of people that are around, something might jump off.

● ● ●

GH N 15: Well, as far as myself, I'm an inmate plumber, so I get around very well. I start out at eight o'clock in the morning on pass, and I don't return to my block until four or five o'clock in the afternoon. . . . I'm free to go any place I want as far as my blocks, I handle my blocks. [In my job] I work in the morning, then I go to the mess hall or stop off for coffee if I want. I can go down to my shop, I can take a shower, I can do my laundry. Or on a different day, if there's a show, I can go to the show. In the morning or the afternoon. Same way with the movies on the weekend, I can go either day.

EI N 1: They got a thing where they should have this hobby shop. They have got one down to Green Haven. I asked the officers why they don't have a hobby shop down here. You know, something to occupy their minds. He says that the instruments that they use down there could be used as weapons. . . . Well, you see, I do glass work, painting and stuff. I could do work with them. There is all sorts of things that you can do other than just go to your cell and read a book or read the same book over and over. . . . Like, I work, right? I get up at four in the morning and I have a lot of hours I work, and I see myself when I get back at five. I really don't have that much time to myself, and what there is goes to recreation, right?

Activity relates to self-control (Chapter 2). It is chosen not because of the nature of the work, such as making license plates or mopping a gallery, but because it helps the person to monitor, restrict, and govern his own feelings and actions. An environment that can be easily controlled thus lends itself to a sense of mastery over one's unpredictable self.

4. NICHES ARE CONGRUENT

Some settings most of us intuitively like; we may feel warm as we watch birch logs burning, esconced on a soft couch. In other settings we instantly feel out of place, uncomfortable, ill at ease. Such situations cannot be defined through external descriptions alone. The same warm comfortable couch, with a log fire, magazines to read, and soft music playing may be viewed with apprehension, skepticism, and distrust when we are waiting for a root canal. As Bettelheim has noted, "Physical settings, like people, can also lie" (p. 173). Prisons with pastel walls and custodial officers in blazers may be lying about the purposes of confinement. And prison situations can lie as well. The inmate who enters a facility and notes the overt "friendliness" of other tier residents, the gifts of cigarettes, the gestures of aid and acceptance learns early that these stimuli are not symbols of friendship but may be indices of preempted reciprocity, in the form of sexual favors.

As we have seen, the inmate, like the rest of us, constantly reassesses his world, using his observation of the interactions of other people and the consequences of his own acts, and ascribes increasingly clearcut labels upon subenvironments as fearful, safe, private, active, or supportive. One important component of congruence is the degree to which people in a setting have attributes that bear familiar relationships to one's self. Within niches, inmates often perceive other inmates as having similar characteristics, concerns, fears, and solutions to fears. A group defense, given similar needs and concerns, begins to develop, and interlopers are rejected—particularly those who, in another setting, would be intolerant of the niche resident and might compromise him or interfere with the way he does time:

Att N K: We are a group. We are a group—there is no getting around that. Uh—we are more or less, you could say, a big family. We keep it just about even. There is just about the same number of blacks as whites. And—well, right now there is more blacks, but that don't matter. Uh—once a guy is out there for maybe a couple of days, he sees what the whole outfit is, and he just falls right into it. Since I have been out there, there has been one fight, and that was due to the fact that the kid kept aggravating everybody, and it was going to come sooner or later. But—uh—there is a whole general thing—you can go out there and do your time and be away from everybody.

• • •

Att N B: With this job, working on the coal gang, we had one or two guys out there trying to impress the guys and impress the officers and everything, and I just left them and went over and talked with the guys that were separate from them, the two of them. And I started a conversation with them. And we talked about our families, you know? . . . I think that it is better for someone to have just a few friends than to have a whole bunch that they're going to do the time with. Because, when you're with four or five other guys, they might be running into someone's home and making wine and selling pills and stuff, and it's the man's responsibility. And maybe he thinks that you're the same way when he sees you running around with these guys. . . . And if you find one or two guys, you can just sit around and talk about your families and stuff instead of what these other guys are doing. Because a lot of guys seem to be liking to have the police yelling at them and stuff. So they kind of do things to make them yell.

Cultural congruence is probably the most important aspect of person–environment compatibility in prison. Social grading and scaling, which may involve the measurement of differences in important cultural characteristics of others (race, urban–rural, megalopolis vs. small-town youth, middle–lower class, old con–youth), guides the coping patterns of many inmates. Cultural background and the behavioral patterns of various cultural groups become critical with crowding in a heterogeneous population. There are many more unflattering portraits of inmate types offered by people doing time than there are flattering ones. Descriptions of other inmates as irritants, as children, kids, punks, pimps, rats, garbage, etc., predominate. Inmates, on the other hand, often describe themselves as goal-directed, mature, quiet, and in search of others with similar behavior patterns. Positive peer images are rare and usually involve only neutral regard buttressed by reciprocal neutral regard. The Society prison experts speak of is very different from Middletown. In prison there are no primary ties, few alliances that extend beyond the immediate situation, and few norms that transcend the bounds of one's immediate relationships. Adjusting means the ability to survive and cope with each others' company. Membership in groups is temporal and artificial, and where groups may be friendly, there are few friends. Mutual aid is given, but with an emphasis on reciprocity, not altruism. Cultural dissension is part of a perceived war of prisoners against each other, and sitting out the war is a major goal.

Sometimes inmates find group cohesion and identity in sharing the minor triumph of survival. They understand, through discussion with others similarly situated, that they have comparable concerns and weaknesses. This recognition contributes to the self–other congruence of the niche. While the behavior of others may not be especially supportive, helping, or enhancing, it is not disintegrative either, and may be compatible with one's self-image.

Cox C–2 15: You see, because in C-2, like, you will find a lot of diabetics and a lot of people that have got bad tempers, and, like, there are four or five in there, including myself, who has bad tempers, and those guys are white. I have known them for two and one half weeks, but I feel like I just grew up with them. One guy, his home town is forty miles from where I was, and I used to go there, but I would never see him. It is just that we are talking, and we have things in common, because we all have bad tempers and we all hate niggers. So I don't have to worry about anyone coming and mugging me, because these guys know how to fight and stuff, you know?

Vulnerable inmates see themselves as having characteristics or needs that are at odds with those of other inmates. They not only see themselves as walking, talking, and behaving differently but are apprehensive of the contaminating or contagion effect of exposure, and its impact on their own purposes and identity:

El N 13: Well, the environment controls a person itself. If you are around a lot of people that are illiterate, and quite naturally you are going to act that way—you know?—lose a lot of important ideas that you had in mind. When you are constantly around people that are playing, then you start playing—you know?—so the environment controls the fact that the people you are around is what motivates you to act the way that you do. . . . So I avoid people in here as much as possible, and where I am I can do that.

• • •

Att N L: There are not too many people in here that think like I do. . . . Well, see 95 percent of the dudes in here, they are always talking about the same thing—cars, and this and that—something that maybe you talk about out on the streets. I talk about that, and I do that too if I was out in the streets, but in here you don't want to talk about that. You want to get yourself together. . . . Well, I would say that I have come to enjoy being secluded by myself. It is the mere fact that, once I get involved, it is problems. It is all the same talk and conversation, and I have been down here since 1967—right?—and, you know, it is the same talk.

Att N G: To be truthful, I don't feel like a criminal. I did some things wrong, and I have got some of the attitudes that they have. But I don't carry these attitudes. And I want to change myself, and they don't want to change themselves. . . . I was working in maintenance and then going to school nights for my high school, and I really didn't like the attitudes of my cellmates. I couldn't concentrate, so I went and asked for an assignment in C Block, and I heard there was an opening in the ID, and they said to come in, and I told them that I wanted to get out of D Block and C Block. And so I got the job. . . . There you don't hear the guys. And it's probably because of lack of education and their way of life. It's just confusion. That is what it is. In the C Block you have quiet, and nobody disturbs you, and nobody comes down to your cell, and it's a lot better. It seems like the guys there are trying to improve themselves, and in the other block the guys don't seem to think. Maybe it's because they're from a lower class, and they haven't gotten an education, and that might be part of it.

The Old Con or the white-collar offender, whose coping styles may differ from most mainline inmates in their prison, may select settings as niches because they contain one or more individuals who are similarly oriented and alienated. Groups of such inmates ease each other's status as in-house emigres or exiles:

Att N A: And that is their particular business how they want to do their time. . . . But they interfere with me. . . . I get along with the people that are older than myself and the same age. Now, when I was outside I got along with people of all ages. But I mean, as far as doing time and doing my time better and getting more understanding . . . I get along better with people the same age as myself.

• • •

Au N 6: That is the whole thing. You are away from the rest of the people most of the time. For instance, in my case one of the most difficult parts of being in prison—I am a college graduate, right?—and all my life I had friends on the same level. . . . So you don't have anybody to talk to unless you talk about *Playboy* magazine or something [laughter]. And some of them tell me about what they did, and that can be very shocking, you know? In the hospital [people are different]. One of the clerks, Mr. W., is a cultural person, and I have the same interests as his. I work all day, and we try to get jobs for the people that haven't got one—we write letters for them and prepare resumes and how to go about an interview, you know, that kind of program—and this one man I talk to, he teaches people how to read braille, you know? It's very different there.

In socially homogeneous subsettings, alienated or rejected inmates know whom to speak to, about what, and in what manner. Personal adjustment relates to adequacy of interpersonal functioning. Mental illness rates may thus be higher for persons whose background differs widely from typical characteristics of the community (Wechsler and Pugh), and dropout rates in school relate to incongruence between personal and school characteristics (Pervin). A high-privacy, studious student in a college environment in which sociability and partying is rewarded must create his own subenvironment, or else face stress.

A homogeneous subenvironment allows the person to use familiar adaptive modes and to play roles that are already in his repertoire. Inmates talk about "a place where I can be myself," as a setting in which the prison-induced poses or masquerades can be dropped. This is especially necessary because (as we have noted) stress-induced role-playing is often transparent and can convey to other inmates the sense of desperation it was meant to conceal.

In an ameliorative subenvironment a person may face fewer pressures to conform in ways that are alien to him. Cultural homogeneity breeds familiarity, and a shared pariah status invites mutual tolerance:

Att N 12: Yeah, I feel different now. I feel different than when I was around the blocks. They don't want to do nothing but just mess around, you know, and party and drugs and all this stuff, and I was never into that on the streets, and I'm not into that in here.

• • •

Cox C–2 4: I can't really explain the difference between then and now. Before [in population] I just didn't feel comfortable around them. They didn't talk the same as I do, or walk the same, and they made fun of me. Up here, we're all alike, we're all from the country.

The type of activity that is available in a niche may be meaningful in terms of its possible relevance to job pursuits on the outside, or because it helps the inmate to preserve equanimity or hope. Activities such as reading, correspondence courses, and evening college extension courses often not only serve to pass time but help the person to find or cement his sense of self-worth and identity:

Au N 18: We consider ourselves a culture house. We are like our own nation. We are trying to keep the same train of peace with all the native Americans. . . . I always like to work outside, even though the time that I am doing I cannot get outside of the walls or gates, and it is like being outside with the sun and shit like that. Like, we grow flowers and have flower beds and shit like that. Like, we have a lot of trees that we grow and shit like that. . . . Like, the white pine tree that I planted, the white roots of peace come out of it, and a friend of mine planted a big peace tree, and it is something that you know that you did.

• • •

GH N 4: I was a porter there for about three weeks. Then the first aid unit opened, and I thought I'd like to try that. I tried it, I liked it, it was so fulfilling. Then I started begging, borrowing, I can't say stealing but appropriating books, medical books, and learned, self-taught. Asking questions, because I got interested. As I say, the more I worked around the other people and their weaknesses, the more I learned about myself. Now I get about thirteen hundred people a month through my office that I treat personally. And that's thirteen hundred personalities, besides the officers and the nurses and the doctors. . . . I came over here just to be with the guys I knew. Now I got into the hospital work, and I started working in the hospital, I really got interested in helping people. I found that in helping them I helped myself. And the last four years down here, I have matured so greatly, and I have advanced. I do all the electro-cardiograms. I do all the casting, putting on casts, taking off casts. I used to do all the sutures, stopping bleeding, cuts, abrasions, heart re-suscitations. You name it, I do it. I've saved about nine lives down here. I saved one officer's life. I took him out the front gate and didn't even realize I was out the front gate, because I was interested in the patient. I didn't know he was an officer, or a baby raper, or black or white. When you come in, you're a patient. You know, like, my outlook on life has changed with this job. My craziness has diminished with this job.

Staff–inmate relationships surface as a niche attribute. Inmates may see themselves as more similar in values, interests, and behavior to staff than to other inmates. In response to known staffing patterns, inmates choose areas or assignments in which staff roles are flexible and friendly, and inmate overtures meet with responses. Officers and civilians may respond to inmates coldly, within formal definitions of their role, or may personalize or transcend their functions. While chaplains must hear confessions, they may also informally counsel, call an inmate's mother, or act as a protector. And while a psychiatrist must counsel, he may also greet one in the hall or share a cup of coffee brewed with a dropper in a cell. For inmates, a niche may expand or contract with the attractiveness of inmate–staff personal affiliations.

Many niche inmates are seeking not empathy, but the type of concern that they most need when they face situational pressures, such as a note threatening violence or a family problem. The staff person provides a resource to go to when an extra phone call is needed, or a furlough—or he simply is available as a partner for light conversation when the pressure mounts. The criteria usually rest in the "human" quality of staff response to inmate stress:

Att N B: We have one guy out there now that is all right. He's out there on the streets, and he's all right. When he comes on the other side he has to put an act on for the guys that are in here, the sergeants and the officers. He don't want to, but he has to. . . . But not where we work. . . . He's a pretty good dude. He's one of the best ones in here, because when he is around here he's okay, you can speak with him. But when you come back inside the gate, then you can't speak with him, it's because of the other guys. He's changed then.

• • •

Au N 7: In a job like this, in opposition to a job in a shop or a job somewhere else like this, you are in closer contact—in everyday closer contact with the civilians and with the officers, and you develop a rapport, and I found that the biggest thing of this is if I know a civilian, and I know his wife through him, and I know his kids, and I know what his house looks like, and he brings in pictures and does this—now I can't very well hate this man, because I know too much about him. I have developed a rapport.

• • •

Cox S 8: That mason shop, if I had to do a whole four years, I would do it working there in the mason shop. I would do it working there, because in there, in the mason shop, I just feel a whole lot relaxed. As soon as I walk in the door, I feel a whole lot relaxed. . . . The supervisor is an all right guy. He cracks jokes with us, makes you laugh every once in a while. If he sees you standing over there, and he sees that you're feeling bad, he comes and tries to cheer you up. And rap to you about certain things, what's bothering you. . . . That's why I like it so much. That's why I picked that when I came.

Inmates with strong Freedom concerns feel most comfortable with staff persons who actively enhance their perceptions of themselves as mature and respected by tailoring the levels of control to the self-perceived maturity level of the prisoner.

El N 3: It is better here to me, it is better, and they don't be pressing you too much, and you know what to do, and they figure that you are grownups, and the officers are grownups, and they are not going to be on your back all day telling you like they be telling you, and chewing at you.

• • •

GH N BB: I was in the buiding all the time, and everyone got to know me, and they respected me and the way that I carried myself, which is one of the most important things when you are in the jail. If you can get the respect that the authority has—it was a big ego trip to me, kind of like I was always called by my first name or "mister" instead of just a number or last name.

Niches as Growth Environments

The best niches are those that not only provide refuge with a minimum of labeling, but also enhance self-understanding and improve one's ability for coping with stress. Learning experiences in such niches are modulated, graded, and geared to the person's resources and vulnerabilities.

The social learning potential of this type of niche may be illustrated with reference to a special treatment program established by the New York State Department of Correctional Services to house "problem inmates." The population, many of who have shown vulnerabilities to various sorts of prison stresses, is more formally defined and more explicitly selected than that of less formal niches. As can be seen from Table 10-2, differences exist between the demographic characteristics of inmates who are in the

TABLE 10-2. Comparison of ACTEC IV Population with Random Sample of Adult Male Inmates

	ACTEC Sample		Random Comparison Sample	
Ethnicity				
White	25	(86%)[b]	81	(38.2%)
Black	4	(14)	131	(61.8)
Total	29	(100)	212	(100.0)
Conviction offense				
Violent	14	(38)	84	(39.6)
Nonviolent	7	(24)	122	(57.5)
Sex-linked[a]	8	(38)[c]	6	(4.9)
Total	29	(100)	212	(100.0)
Mental health commitment on record				
Yes	19	(63)[b]	25	(10.5)
No	10	(37)	213	(89.5)
Total	29	(100)	238	(100.0)
Suicide gesture recorded				
Yes	12	(41)		
No	17	(59)		
Total	29	(99)		
Institutional protection placement				
Yes	15	(52)		
No	14	(48)		
Total	29	(100)		
Residence				
City over 500,000	14	(48)	175	(79.5)
Other city	8	(28)	31	(14.1)
Small town or rural	7	(24)[c]	14	(6.4)
Total	29	(100)	220	(100.0)

[a]Statutory rape, incest, sodomy, sexual abuse, and pedophilia.
[b]Significant at .001 level.
[c]Significant at .01 level.

ACTEC program, as it is called, and a sample selected randomly from large prisons. The population of the unit is disproportionately white, a higher proportion of the ACTEC inmates have been convicted of violent and sex-linked crimes, a majority of the unit population has a record of mental health commitments, a large proportion (41 percent) has suicide gestures recorded in the files, a majority have been in voluntary protection during imprisonment, and a substantial proportion of ACTEC prisoners (24 percent of the total) are from small towns or rural backgrounds.

Being developmentally and culturally unprepared for the prison milieu he sees around him, the ACTEC candidate requests help, transfer, or voluntary segregation. If he cannot find a place among the niches available in his facility, he may effect a transfer to ACTEC. It is, in many ways, the end of his line.

As one inmate describes ACTEC and the sequence of events that led to his placement there:

ACTEC 3: It started, I guess, about two years ago. I was getting fed up with institutions and always having to try to stay out of trouble and stay away from this and stay away from that, and it becomes a big hassle after a while, because you have got to run from this and run from that, you know? Because, if you have got a big bit like I have, you have got to try to stay out of trouble to get back out there. No way, you know? . . . You have got all kind of hassles in prison. Number one, if you are young you are marked—right?—for anybody. They will try to make a kid out of you if they can, a homosexual, right? That is mark number one. Then mark number two, you have got your different groups. They look for weak spots, and they will try to set you up, you know? These are all the kind of things you have to watch for, and if you are young you are ignorant— you have never been in jail before, so you don't know the ropes. Right? See, I am from Kingston, so I am not from the city, so you meet very few guys upstate from the same area. . . . Everything is a problem. It was like a whole new world. You have to cope with the officers, and there is a lot of harassments going on, but they wasn't the biggest problem. The biggest problem really in a sense was the inmates. Well, it was a matter of twenty-three or twenty-four hours you are going to hear shit. There is always someone looking for a reputation. That is another thing to watch out for. . . . There is always hassles—every day. Some hassle always comes up somewheres, you know? The only place I didn't find it was ACTEC, you know?

I: And what was your initial impression of the place when you first arrived there and you were new?

ACTEC 3: I nearly had a heart attack. I was sitting in the lobby, and the officer from the unit that I was going to come down to the lobby, and he stuck out his hand, and he said, "I am so-and-so, and nice to meet you, and wait until you see this"—I nearly had heart failure. I just knew that there was a trick involved someplace. For the first three days, really, I was watching everything and everybody, and I said, "Wow!" I couldn't believe the place, you know? So it was just like a college campus, but you can't go off of it. . . . . The inmates were learning to deal with themselves—their problems and whatever happened to be their hangup. If it was violence, they would learn to deal with it. If they had a bad temper, they would learn to deal with it. We didn't have to, you know, out and out twenty something hours a day, deal with other people—deal with the shit that they are going to be slinging at you, because everybody was too wrapped up in trying to find themselves and dealing with themselves and stop all the bullshit and the liberality instead of keeping up that big front—that tough guy, gangster. The majority of the roles was dropped, you know? . . . Back in that old environment you learn to deal with the fists, and you have got to deal with the fists. Usually there is no two ways around it. You can only run for so long. And when you keep backing away, then there is other people saying, "Wow! What is the matter with this guy?" you know, and now you are getting it from both angles. There is only so much—now you are getting pressure from all angles, and that is kind of hard to take. . . . You see, in our unit you have a lot of guys, and they learn to help themselves and also help each other instead of hurting each other. Now, if you are pent up and something like that, and you have a problem or someone is bugging you, I don't go around needling you and giving it to you, and giving that to you to have to put up with on top of what you have. If I see you are bugged out, then I will say, "Hey, what is wrong, and maybe I can help you." "What is the matter?" you know? If the man says, "Nothing, leave me alone," you just say, "I am trying to help you, and I am here if you want to talk to someone. I will listen and do what I can to help." And he still might not want to talk, so you walk away. But yet it is there, and after a while he might say, "Well, let me get some of this shit off of my shoulders."

The program manual for ACTEC describes Unit IV as designed for "male adult inmates referred from other facilities who are disturbed, emotionally upset, demonstrating strange and unusual behavior," and unable to cope. The population consists of formally referred inmates meeting these rather vague criteria.

The program elements of the unit, particularly when contrasted with traditional psychiatric and counseling practices of the Department of Corrections, are unusually group-based. Community meetings address an array of institutional stresses and problems (noise, immaturity, assaultive behavior, threats, gambling, homosexuality, furloughs, counseling, visits), and they are frequently held and mandatory. Evaluation of stress management, manipulation, and fragility of ego supports occur during these sessions, where personal relationships are explored and crises defused. Staff and inmates try to discuss their unit's problems before they erupt into crises, dissipating anxieties before they produce conflict.

Inmate counselors, complementing the professional staff, are active within the unit and have developed rapport and acceptance. Program parameters maximize support from trained officer volunteers and peer counselors. With the help of these resources, inmates can explore their vulnerabilities while they slowly go about the business of personal growth and development:

ACTEC 4: In a way, you see, one of the reasons that I don't particularly care about the population that I was in, is that I couldn't straighten up. I couldn't do the kind of things that I want to do in the population. I could never build up myself by being in the population, because it's not geared for this thing. I could never grow personally in the population, because there is nobody thinking anything positive. You have to grow mentally and physically, and you have to be in an environment where you can do that. And the population is not the place that you can. You can grow, but there is negative side effects from your growth. And me personally, I want to do something better for my life, and so I don't want to be in an institution. I want to change.

Assignment to Niches

Few staff in institutions think in niche-finding terms. Staff persons use niches, but in an informal, casual way, taking inmates from areas where they have been threatened or where they have obvious difficulties and referring them for reclassification and reassignment. And while niches may exist, they are not always made available to those who need them. A Catch-22 situation evolves wherein the most prominent, protective, and supportive niches may be given as assignments to cool, solid, adjusted inmates, while inmates with difficulties are sent to sterile special housing compounds or to assignments with few ameliorative supports.

Staff may see "niche seeking" as directed at procuring "good" assignments or attempts "to get over," to manipulate status or prestige, rather than as a way to escape stress.

The niche process needs to be explicitly recognized, with mental health as its designated goal. Niches must be mapped; inmates with special problems must be identified. The limited yet prevalent view that corrective treatment and intervention are a function of mental health professionals is inapplicable to environmentally induced stress (Toch, 1975).

In some institutions referrals are made, interventions occur, and problems are defused by officers, the most abundant staff resource and the resource that intersects most with the inmates. A community model, using increased assignment options and discarding stereotyped roles, is clearly compatible with a niche network. At ACTEC, for example, inmate counselors were trained to meet and defuse inmate problems as they arose and to serve as data gatherers and referral sources for the professional staff.

A more difficult problem is that of stigmata and labeling. Some niches are relatively informal and hence invisible. When the niche is made more visible and more definite, some elements of Privacy, Safety, or Support can be destroyed. Labels now placed on inmates in some special settings (bug, rat, queen, punk) add further liabilities to the inmate's capacity to handle his time.

Increasingly, however, there are inmates who respond to the labeling question with the rejoinder, "You've got to be kidding." They would rather carry a card declaring "I am a lamb," and be treated like a lamb, than find themselves facing the ever present wolf with anonymity.

The solution may lie in the graduated differentiation of macro-settings. Congruence with a subenvironment does not necessarily imply congruence with the larger environment, or vice versa. What is important to remember is that milieus are adaptable and subdividable. It is essential to begin to think about internally reconstructing milieus. It is easier to change a man's perception of his world and his position in it, to give a man strength and to teach him to cope, when he is not engaged full-time in a fight for his survival.

11

Living in Protection

Incarcerated persons have a legal right to safety. In recent years court cases have established that any convicts who claim they may be harmed are entitled to "protection." "Protection" becomes a legal status under which inmates may elect to serve their entire sentences. These prisoners then live under conditions similar to those found in disciplinary segregation: They are isolated from the rest of the prison population; they are confined to their cells for all but a small part of the day; they are not able to participate in institutional activities. Indeed, some officials fail to distinguish between disciplinary and protective segregation. As the judge in one case involving sexual assault recently noted, "A threatened inmate can go to the hole."

Many prisons have forms of organized "protection:" Men who cannot survive in the population live together on a floor or in a cell block separated from the rest of the prison. They are segregated from other convicts, and spend their time in a closely guarded unit within the larger world of the prison community. The number of inmates in a protection unit may not exceed, say, thirty out of a total institutional population of 1,200. The importance of this group, however, in many ways goes beyond their limited numbers.

Protection is an area of concentrated problems. Suicide attempts are common. Men lose control ("bug out"), tear up their cells, and scream in rage. Many protection men have a history of mental illness. Prison, a difficult environment for resourceful and healthy men, is doubly hard on those who are brittle. For some disturbed men protection in prison is functionally equivalent to the mental hospital in society. Protection becomes a refuge, a place with few demands, a shelter from stress, a last-

Chapter prepared by Daniel Lockwood.

ditch niche. Some prison staff, in fact, use protection as a mental health unit, seeing it as one place where men can be observed while undergoing crises that do not warrant formal commitment.

We interviewed all but three of thirty-four inhabitants of a prison protection unit. The inmates seemed glad to talk to us. One man, for example, a forty-year-old black inmate who was diagnosed by the prison psychiatrist as suffering from "full blown schizophrenia, paranoid type," told us:

The doctor here, she called me to come up here, but I didn't go, because I didn't think I needed medication or anything. So I told her I didn't want to go. And you're the first people that I've been able to talk to about this to get it off my mind.

In other cases, men related experiences that they did not share with others in prison because they involved violations of inmate norms. In one case, a man had been an informer seven years before in a gambling incident. The incident had caused him to be fearful and anxious ever since. From shame and embarrassment he had never discussed his concerns with anyone.

Our interview generally explored breakdown catalysts from the perspective of the men involved. We specifically aimed at feelings and reactions to stress, and these were openly shared with us. The following, for example, is a target of sexual aggressors who talks about his feelings of vigilance, sensitivity to stimuli, fear, tension, and anger:

Well, you're constantly on guard instead of being able to sit down and relax and maybe read a book or something of this nature. You have to be constantly on your guard and keep your ears open at all times, and you have to be constantly on the defensive. And somebody might walk up and make a snide remark, like, "How's your buns today?" or something like this. And right away you jump right down their throats, because you're constantly on the defensive, because you're so keyed up. And it puts a terrible strain on a person.

We came across men who were in protection for purely situational reasons. Often it was difficult to distinguish such men from men who were taking refuge from subjective problems. Some men who were suffering from delusional fear were intensely sincere and convincing. In those cases, the social history in the files complements the interview and "validates" or "invalidates" the occasions for stress.

With staff, we sought perceptions of the function of protection. We aimed to learn how staff saw their clients and what they felt the purpose of protection must be. In addition, we wanted to understand the process whereby men are sent to protection. We also explored with staff their conceptions of alternatives to protection, and the obstacles they saw to employing those alternatives.

Prison files provided us with background data about the men we interviewed. The files also gave us information about any attempts that the protection inmates or the staff were making to move inmates out of protection to other prisons or to other settings within the same prison.

We were also able to observe daily life on the protection gallery. Interviews were conducted in a secluded place around the corner from where the men's cells were located. We were able to stroll around the hall, talk to the men in their cells, and observe their physical living conditions.

At the time of our study, the protection men were housed in single cells along one long corridor. A corridor alongside on the other side had a similar line of cells. This other corridor (in which we conducted our interviews) was a "protection within protection" area for men who could not get along on the main corridor, and also a staging area for drafts of prisoners being transported to other prisons.

The protection unit was isolated from the rest of the prison. Entry could be gained only through a locked door, and surveillance was exercised to ensure that the door allowed only authorized staff to enter the unit. Inmates were not allowed to communicate with the protection men in any way.

The protection unit had its own yard. Men were allowed one hour of outdoor recreation in the morning and one hour in the afternoon. Otherwise, most of the men remained in their cells except for the brief periods they needed to take a shower every other night, to get trays of food and carry them to the cells, or to do work assigned by the protection officer. Prison staff (doctors and counselors) generally came to the protection gallery if they wished to see an inmate. Almost the sole time the inmates left the area was for visits. Then, inmates were individually escorted by an officer to the visiting room. Men could send slips to the library requesting books and could relay orders to the commissary. When such articles arrived, the protection officers checked them to remove any messages they might contain.

Protection men lived in seclusion, where they were truly protected from other inmates. In exchange for Safety, they sacrificed the freedom of movement that is available to other prisoners, the opportunity to participate in school, and the access to other prison programs. They relinquished their weekly movies and the sports in the yard. In exchange for their safety they lived in quarantine, spending twenty-two hours a day in their cell.

Two officers worked the protection gallery. One served from 7:00 A.M. to 3:00 P.M., and the other from 3:00 P.M. to 11:00 P.M. Both men were older, experienced prison employees who had requested their assignment to protection. These officers had a difficult, frequently anxiety-ridden job. They had to be alert to suicide attempts. They had to handle men in crisis.

They had to keep order among a group of tense, volatile persons who often feuded among themselves. They faced inmate conflicts that were bitter and often had delusional overtones. One man, a former mental patient, arsonist, and check forger, who had been a resident on the gallery for two years, told us:

Since I've been here I've got my head split open. I had fifteen stitches. The guy that locked next to me was a Spanish guy, and he couldn't talk English. And we, me and another guy, were talking, and he couldn't understand us. I was trying to explain to him that we weren't talking about him, and he just couldn't understand, and bam . . . with a metal tray.

Such incidents were common, and the officers working the gallery had to see these events as a fact of daily life.

Both staff and inmates in protection view confinement in cells for twenty-two hours a day as necessary. They see it is necessary to protect men who are in danger; to observe mentally unstable individuals; to preserve order among explosive inmates; to protect "normal" men from a few psychotically dangerous and unpredictable ones.

Men go to protection on their own and through staff referral, and requests for protection usually are routinely granted. Sometimes men are sent to protection by mental health staff, counselors, or custody supervisors, though this is an uncommon practice. For the most part, men are in protection because they have invoked their legal right to sanctuary.

While inmates may exercise free choice to get into protective segregation, prison staff try to discourage this option. Staff's goal is to get men out of protection into a normal situation. A counselor is assigned to the Special Housing Unit and has weekly interviews with each man. In addition, the men are seen by mental health workers and by administrators up through the level of superintendent. If a man stays in protection, the counselor and his department (the "Service Unit") see this as a sign of failure, because the inmate is not improving himself in a program. The mental health workers also fear that the protection experience may aggravate psychotic conditions or cause a suicidal man to become obsessed with morbid ideation. The thrust, therefore, is to reintegrate the protection man into a general prison population.

Protection men are told by staff and peers that the parole board looks unfavorably upon those who spend time in protection. "How can you make it in the street," they say, "when you can't even make it in prison?" And staff see protection as a management problem as well as a failure of the rehabilitative goal. A basic aim of prisons is to see that things run day to day with a minimum of trouble. Protection men are "trouble:" Because these men don't work, prison administrators fear that other men may come to envy their lot. They fear that other men will feign fear to "lay up." This fear creates pressure to make protection as spartan an environment as possible so that it does not become a haven for men who do not wish to participate in the plans staff make for them.

Prisoners work and are encouraged to go to school part time, to join voluntary associations, and to participate in recreational activities. There is danger in a prison where no one does anything; there are also no rewards or punishments. For fighting, men are locked up. For minor infractions, a movie may be taken away. This process works only if men care about movies or about being locked up. If inmates are concerned only about their private lives and their immediate space—expressed in feet—the prison cannot intervene effectively to carry out management (custodial) or rehabilitative (program) goals.

Different groups in prison have different perspectives on protection. Officers and their supervisors are concerned with removing men from sources of danger. Their concern is to put the inmate in a safe place, interview him, check his record, and find the names of his enemies. If such names are available, assignments can be arranged to separate men who are in conflict. But most protection cases refuse to give up names and often have no names to give up. Custody staff must be content with noting "unknown enemies" on requests for protection. Inmates are then removed from the population and are no longer of concern to line staff in population.

Once a man is in protection, however, administrators have a management concern to do something about him. We have mentioned that their aim is to get the man out, into a setting where he can be treated like a regular inmate. Referrals are made to psychiatrists: Can the mental health worker or the Service Unit counselor work with the man to evolve a suitable plan for leaving protection? If successful, this intervention is only the beginning; even if the psychiatrist or counselor can emerge with a plan for transfer or change of assignment, there is no assurance that the plan can be carried out.

The plan to get the protection case out of total lockup and into population may encounter a series of obstacles. Institutions that can accommodate the Safety needs of the inmate may have criteria he does not meet. An occupational rehabilitation program may offer a haven but may see itself as designed for severely impaired persons. Other institutions may have no cell space or may prefer persons within a certain age range. There may be difficulty in communicating to the "central office" the perceived timeliness or urgency of a transfer. The protection man himself may resist attempts to move him. He has, after all, once decided that protection "solves" his problems. He may see attempts to deprive him of his sanctuary as ill-informed, as dangerous actions by malignant and alien forces. He may prefer protection in one prison to population in another prison because he is closer to where his family lives: A visit every few months may seem insignificant but may supersede other concerns. Staff trying to "help" the protection man may thus have to struggle with their beneficiary.

While staff seek alternatives for the protection man, his daily existence becomes a concern of the protective custody officer. Will the inmate commit suicide? Will he "bug out"? Will his behavior endanger others? Can he endure his cell time? From experience, the protective custody guard knows that men often "escape" from their own violence rather than fleeing from external enemies. The protection officer possesses and deploys skill and experience to diagnose and defuse accumulating explosiveness. The world of protection is a small one, thirty or so men locked in an isolated area with one officer. The officer, who has known some of his men for years, must rule this world carefully, sensitively, and impartially. He may write out disciplinary reports for infractions. He may dispense a job on the gallery that lets a man out of his cell. He must help sick men with their problems and administer to their needs. Above all, he must handle crises. Managing violent disputes, suicidal gestures, and psychotic episodes become a routine custodial task on the protection gallery.

Another perspective that impinges on the protection gallery is that of men in population. To them, a protection man might be a "homo," a "pussy," a "punk," or a "snitch." Even if they know nothing of the man's situation, they might see the man as a "creep" who is weak and must do time in "pediatrics." Inmates in prison are careful whom they associate with. Living physically close, prisoners are separated by substantial social distances. We noted in Chapter 10 that many men socialize only with those in their own group. Outward appearances identify and catolog "ins" and "outs" to other prisoners. One's associates help to proclaim one's public identity. To be seen with a "pussy," unless one is an obvious "player," is to be a "pussy" oneself. To be seen with a "snitch" is to be a person who disregards the inmate code that ostracizes harmful informers. A protection man, on leaving the unit, must thus be treated warily. This can snowball, because a man others stay away from becomes a man to be shunned.

Protective custody is an escape hatch with a boomerang. It can be a sanctuary from which there is no return, a short-term solution at the cost of long-range social consequences.

Typology of Protection Men

For purposes of analysis, we have divided protection men into four groups:

1. targets of sexual aggression
2. perceived informers
3. avoiders of retaliation
4. men with generic fears or phobias

In general, protection men tend to be white, and more than half have been residents in a mental health facility. A history of suicide attempts characterizes half the group. In other respects the inmates are heterogeneous.

TARGETS OF SEXUAL AGGRESSION

Targets of sexual aggression (cf. Chapter 9) differ from other protection inmates in that they are a younger and less jail-wise group. They are mostly white and tend to come primarily from rural areas or small towns. We infer that these men are vulnerable partially because of their age, ethnicity, and experience of prison life.

What is the typical process whereby a target of sexual aggression comes to enter the protection unit?

Sexual aggressors have been making remarks to S ever since he arrived in prison two months before. Some of these remarks, to S, sound like threats. As the weeks go by, S feels progressively more fearful. He only leaves his cell when absolutely necessary. He comes back from work one day, and finds a note has been thrown through the opening of his door. The note reads as follows:

"Yo S
Check this out if you don't give me a peace of your ass I am going to take you off the count and that is my word.
I be down a very long time So I need It very Bad I will give you 5 Pack's of Smokes If you do it OK That is my word So if you Want to live you Better do it and get it over with there are Three of us who need it. OK.
5 Pack of Smoke Each OK S
from
?"

After reading the note, S's fear turns to panic. He calls the officer supervising his area and tells him he wants to go to protection. The officer puts S's cell on "keep lock." A sergeant comes to interview S. S tells the sergeant "unknown enemies are trying to kill him." The sergeant writes this down on a form and gives a copy to S. In a day or two (during which S stays in his cell), he appears before a committee made up of various staff members. They review his case and ask him for more information. S refuses to expand on his request. After a review by the prison warden, S is escorted to a separate area of the prison. He is now in "protection." He is locked in a cell. His belongings, which he has already packed, are brought to him.

S stays in his cell for two days. The officer in charge shows him the other men on the gallery. If S says none of these men are enemies, he becomes a member of the protection unit. His life becomes simple to describe: he spends twenty-two hours a day in his cell, two hours in the yard, and he showers every third day. In his cell, he reads, sleeps, washes, relieves himself, and eats. He may listen to his radio or to a cassette player using earphones. As time goes by, if the officer in charge likes S, he may let him out of his cell more often. He may assign him a simple task that allows S to wander about on the gallery.

Once Inmate S becomes established in the protection unit, he learns that he may be there for quite a while. He has acquired a stigma. The stigma that attaches to S's stay in protection not only makes it hard for him to return to population; it may also preclude transfer as a suitable alternative. The following section of an interview with a man who had lived in protection for almost thirteen years describes how S's decision to come to protection may be irreversible:

When I came in here I was twenty-two and the guys tried to make me a homosexual. They made advances to me. And rather than to stay there— you either have to stay there, stand your ground and fight them or they take you off. So I went to protection. But if you stay your ground and you decide to fight them and you hurt somebody, then the institution doesn't back you up anyway. They say you're supposed to see an officer. Then if you go see an officer you're a rat. So any way I looked at it, I was going to get myself in a bind anyway, so I went to protection. After once the guy's in protection, in prison, a number of guys in population know you, guys that didn't know you before. They see you going back and forth, or they see you out in the yard. So they say this guy is definitely a faggot or a rat. And that's not really the case with a lot of guys that are in protection. Somebody can't stand the noise at night or something like that, so then they come to protection. But then after I'd been in protection I went to the box, and the only guys that I knew in the box were the guys that I knew in protection. And then I went out to the gallery, and then all these other guys that I had never seen before, right away they put a label on you. You don't even have to do nothing. You just walk by, and they know you're protection. So that makes it impossible, the way that I look at it, for me to go back in population.

This inmate once attempted to resolve his problem by a transfer:

Inmates go to different prisons, you see, and you're bound to run into somebody that you know. And the first thing that comes out of their mouth is that the guy was in protection before. And if you look anything like a category where you might be appealing to them, forget it, because they're not going to let up on you. They'll just keep hounding you.

I: How did you wind up getting protection at [another prison]?

I seen some individuals there. I figured that I could foresee what I was going to have to go through again.

I: And it was the easier way out?

Yeah, but then here's what happened. I went in protection at . . . and I decided that I would stay there for a couple of years. And then I went to the population and I stayed there for about a month, and then it started all over again, but a certain individual there decided to become over friendly. And a lot of them times they use upstairs [protection]. Like, "What were you upstairs for?" Christ, there was forty guys up there in the gallery. And you feel embarrassed to say to them that somebody made homosexual advances to you.

I: How do you see yourself doing the rest of your time?

I'm not going out in the population. No way, because I can't handle it. And now that I've been in all these different prisons, so many inmates know me and they know my face and they know that I've been in protection. So I know that I'm going to have troubles.

Some men in protective segregation have gone directly from reception to protection without trying out any program in population. In their cases fear may have been inspired by rumors picked up in jail while awaiting trial. In addition, men may have had advances made to them while in jail or in reception. When fear sparked by rumors or attacks becomes too great to endure, the men sign themselves into protection.

While most moves from reception to protection are made at the initiation of the inmates, there are also cases where staff recommend transfer to protection from reception. One particularly frail looking young man told us,

Well, the sergeant [in reception] said that it would be best for me to be over here, because he said people like me sort of look good and stuff like this, and people out in population get advantage of you. So I just come over here.

Vulnerable inmates who go into population from reception may be singled out and intimidated, but they may put up with such harassment rather than ask for protection. However, when an especially dramatic advance is made, the cumulating pressure may combine with the stress from the precipitating incident to create a crisis for an inmate. This crisis may be a strong, obsessive panic reaction.

Panic-stricken inmates may request protection. Because they see no alternatives available, they give up their life-style and activities in search of sanctuary. Their other concerns become subordinated to the concern for Safety. Such feelings do not generally spring from one incident. As noted in Chapter 9, the precipitating event may occur after a buildup of tension. The decision to go to protection is made after a vulnerable individual passes a period of time feeling pressure on a daily basis.

I came here August 17th, 1973, and I stayed out in population for four months. And I was working in A Block, I was working in utilities, and I was going out in the yard, you know? But then I had several people approach me, trying to rip me off and stuff like that. I had been sitting out in the yard watching television. And then I had five big colored guys come up to me and tell me, "We're looking for a piece of ass." . . . And I had a couple of people threaten me and stuff out there. And one day I didn't feel very good, right, and this colored guy on the company, he goes down and tells an officer to open the end gates. So the officer cracked the gates, and I'm just lying in there, and he comes in there. . . . I told him, "Man, you just better get out of my house, because I don't feel good." So he did leave, but—

I: Was there anything in particular that happened that day so that you decided, "I've got to do something"?

Yeah, well, somebody came in my cell and told me, "You better give me some pussy." And I told him, "Look, I'm no broad and I can't help you out." And it just aggravates me that I've got to put up with all this.

Sometimes panic may lead to socially damaging acts that aggravate the situation. For example, an inmate may become so excited that he tells an officer the names of the persons who have threatened him. Then he may be compelled to go to protection because he has broken the inmate code to the point that his life is in danger. At minimum, a man who reports another convict to officials will be ostracized. If a person in this situation does go to protection, he has a more difficult time returning to the population than one who simply fears sexual aggression. An offender in prison can attribute his imprisonment to the testimony of a witness. His hatred for witnesses tends to be projected onto men in prison who cooperate with the staff. The convict who "rats" on those who make aggressive advances to him is a "sissy," because he is an object of sexual attention, a "punk" because he will not fight, and a "snitch" because he has told a staff member about his problem.

In looking closely at the events leading to a request for protective segregation, we often must determine if the fear felt by the convict is a reasonable reaction to an objectively dangerous situation or an overreaction to a setting that may appear terrifying but is objectively safe. It is not easy to separate the real from the mythical. In prisons, information about sexual matters tends not to be shared. In addition, codes of masculinity prevent open discussion of fears and apprehensions (Toch, 1975). As a result, there is fertile ground for delusions to grow to self-destructive proportions.

There is obviously a realistic basis for panic reactions that follow a string of homosexual advances. Single cells do not offer men complete security. Some cells can be opened from the outside by broom handles. Aggressors may tell a busy officer to "crack" a cell where a victim lives, and the guard may think the man in the cell has asked to be let out. Doors are frequently left open during the daytime. In addition to gaining entrance to a victim's cell, an aggressor may know areas of the prison where an inmate can be attacked ("taken off") with impunity. Paradoxically, prison reforms add to the fears of vulnerable inmates. Such is the case in one prison where men are now allowed to stay in the yard until ten o'clock and can circulate from one yard to another.

It is not a casual worry for a man to find that other convicts can gain access to his cell or that there are places in his daily travel pattern where he can be "taken off." Above all, vulnerable inmates learn that no amount of supervision, no physical barriers, can prevent their being the object of threats and advances ranging from simple pleas to physical violence.

The impact of danger is increased by the knowledge that men have of rapes that may have occurred in their prison or other prisons. Many of the most up-to-date institutions, especially maximum security prisons, have one or two known cases of sexual assault in the course of a year. If such an institution has 2,000 inmates living in it during the course of a year, the rate per 100,000 is about 50 to 100, a higher rate than for most serious crimes on the street. The rate is more significant when we consider that potential victims come from a minority of the prison population.

A person may have physical stigmata that increase his chances of victimization. One "stigmatized" inmate notes that

. . . they judge a guy on his facial appearance, if he has—it doesn't necessarily have to be girlish, but if he has smooth skin, and it really doesn't make a difference, black, white, yellow, Indian. I know a lot of Indians have that problem. And the guys that have the worse troubles are the ones with slender builds. Holy Christ, they never leave them alone. You know, guys with thin builds. And they are placed in this category. Especially if the guy has a feminine voice. And it doesn't have to be that feminine, but if it's just a little mild or something, you're in trouble, you've had it.

Sex victims in protection are frequently different from other convicts in some striking respect. Two men, for example, had hearing problems. Others suffered from stuttering or mental retardation. Most were social isolates. In some cases, physical or mental impairments led to social isolation, for convicts are quick to stay away from those they perceive to be "loose" or "goofy."

PERCEIVED INFORMERS

"Informers" in protective segregation are either in extreme danger or combine an evanescent reputation for informing with pre-existing psychological fragilities. We can divide protection informers into those who are realistically fearful and those who are delusionally fearful, though the line is not always easy to draw.

We interviewed a New York City Puerto Rican with a long history of violent arrests and prior convictions who had testified recently in a murder case against a man who had friends in the prison. This inmate was attacked by cronies of the person he had testified against on the day he arrived in prison. In objective danger, he was bent on completing his entire sentence of three years in protection. He exemplifies the formal function of protective custody, i.e., to shelter persons in imminent danger of deadly attack.

A second man in the group came to protection because he was severely beaten after advising the victim of a homosexual rape to tell an officer what had happened to him. The inmate had missing teeth, testifying to the objective quality of the danger he perceived. A third man was labeled a "rat" because he had continued to associate with an inmate he had befriended in the county jail who was subsequently recognized in the population as a government witness. The man was told by his prison associates that he had better go to protection or they would kill him, and his protestations of innocence were to no avail. This man was paradoxically already severely depressed over the nature of his crime (killing his wife in a jealous rage), and his depression caused him to make several attempts on his life while in protection.

In contrast to these cases, some men combined an occasion of fear with a predisposition to be excessively fearful. The men whom they testified against were sometimes long gone from the prison population. Unlike the witness who was attacked the day he arrived in prison, these men had no overt threats or physical attacks made on them. The fact of having transgressed and the thought that others might know were sufficient to tip the balance in favor of guilty panic.

We saw two protection inmates who had testified before a commission investigating the Attica riot. One of these men, released in 1972, went into protection when he returned on a new charge in 1974. The other had been in protection almost since the riot. These commission witnesses lacked concrete substance for their fear, since they had only testified about riot events in general, as did hundreds of other men at the time. The inmates had had no threats made against them, and the riot had occurred four years before.

Several self-perceived informants had spent time in mental health facilities. They had made attempts on their own lives. At times, during the course of their confinement, they were placed in hospitals for insane criminals. Pronounced well, they returned to prison—and protection. Here, protection served the informal function of a sheltered environment for paranoid schizophrenics in remission.

Predispositional factors are the major reason for these men's presence in protection, but their acts (such as testifying) placed them in a position that gave them an internal and public rationale. Prison officials can do little in such cases but grant protection. Given the difficulty of separating psychological from situational reasons for perceived danger, lives would be risked if authorities superseded inmates' judgment of their need for protection. Moreover, for those who perceive danger with limited cues, protection may be the most hygienic subenvironment available in a prison.

It becomes obvious that even men with delusional fears attest to the strength of inmate norms against cooperating with officials. Whether norms become the ingredient of chronic fear or form the basis of actual threats, the antagonism between inmates and state employees is a stimulus to conflict, violence, and danger.

AVOIDERS OF RETALIATION

Another group in protection comprises those who fear retaliation for harm they have done to others. In these cases it is not only the action of the protection man against others that causes the flight to protection. It is also the protection man's inability to resolve his conflict in population and to cope with the pressure of social disapproval.

Prison is an environment where violence lurks behind every abrasive event. The perceived severity of conflicts can escalate in the minds of participants, who cannot avoid each other in the closeness of confinement. Even more disconcerting for men involved in unresolved conflicts is the fear that their antagonists may incite others—unknown to them—against them. Such fear becomes fear of every unknown face and every new arrival in the tier, shop, or school.

In our sample, we have a black holdup man from Harlem who is serving a sentence for killing a man who happened to belong to the Nation of Islam. The inmate is convinced that Muslims must avenge the death of one of their members. Ever since a cousin of the victim arrived in prison three years ago, the man has been sequestered in protection, and is convinced he would be unsafe in any prison in the system. He was transferred from another prison in the hopes he would feel safer, but he began to feel animosity directed toward him. He also "discovered" another cousin of the murder victim in the new prison.

Another man had once sold someone bad dope, consisting of "dummies" made up of baking powder placed in glacine envelopes to resemble heroin. He also had an enemy in the brother of someone he had injured in a gang fight in Buffalo years before. He is a twenty-nine-year-old white from Buffalo with more than twenty-two arrests or convictions. Six arrests are for violent offenses. A long-term addict on the street, this man was firmly committed to a deviant life-style and had made enemies by his violence and by his unscrupulous ways of earning money. After fighting one of his enemies in the prison yard, he was placed in disciplinary segregation. From there he went to protection to avoid retaliation, or (as he likes to think of it) to avoid possible loss of good time by having to "stick someone" to defend himself.

In sharp contrast, we see a twenty-six-year-old white, middle-class businessman in prison for a real estate swindle. Leaving court after sentencing, he was chained to another offender, a riot indictee, who tried to shoot his way out of the courtroom. The man with the gun was subdued, but his actions affected subsequent courtroom security. Henceforth, riot indictees had to be escorted from court pens with their feet shackled and their hands handcuffed behind their backs.

When this man went to prison, the rumor began to circulate that he was responsible for the riot indictees' having to be chained. He was threatened, ostracized, and beaten up.

Another man perpetuated the fear of a conflict that began in the county jail while he was awaiting trial. The dispute began when the man changed television channels. An inmate television fan placed a sharpened toothbrush to his throat and told him that if he ever watched television again he would be killed. The inmate thereafter avoided his adversary. When he arrived in prison, afraid that his awesome enemy might have told others to harm him, he went directly to protection. Even though the man's adversary was not in the population, he was so filled with apprehension from the incident in the jail that he could not face the risk he saw in the prison yard.

This unsophisticated offender underwent a culture shock upon finding himself the object of aggression. Like many protection cases, he illustrates the fact that men who cannot meet threats with bluff and bluster or equanimity (being "smalltime" or white-collar offenders or men from rural, small town backgrounds), may have few resources in conflicts. Unaccustomed to violence, they may resolve personal disputes on a lower level of aggression than seems called for in prison. When they come into contact with men from areas and ethnic groups that handle disputes with confidence, they feel unsure of themselves to the point of bankruptcy. They cannot evaluate or decode verbal antagonism (which does not imply physical violence), nor can they respond to it.

The "tough" black holdup man from Harlem folds up when confronted with a religious group from his own subculture. The heroin addict-dealer, a lower-status white from Buffalo, brings with him the enemies he has made on the street by cheating his customers to feed his habit. The middle-class white-collar criminal and the rural white sex offender have disputes with types of men they have not encountered before. Such persons are brought in touch with their deficits and liabilities, particularly in handling aggression.

MEN WITH GENERIC FEARS OR PHOBIAS

Our protection sample contains several men who had not been involved in incidents causing them to be fearful. One of these men made a suicide attempt and was placed in the protection gallery by a psychiatrist. Another went to protection six weeks after returning from a hospital for insane criminals, finding life in the population too stressful. A third fled from noise and crowds and conflict, which to him resembled ghetto street corners he had viewed apprehensively from car windows before coming to prison. A participant in three jail and prison riots lived in fear of another riot.

These men have had years of experience in prison, and they are older than the average inmate. Some are white, one is black, and one Puerto Rican.

The perspectives of these inmates fall into three rough categories. One group features men who are characterized by unremitting irritability. For such men, humanity is an unrelieved press, and the presence of others is painful. Such a man may try, as best he can, to avoid people by insulating himself, ignoring their presence, or "shutting them off." Noxious impingements accumulate despite such efforts, and as tension increases and despondency deepens, the person may (1) try to achieve withdrawal through sleep, (2) attempt self-injury, or (3) try to obtain mood-controlling medication. The chaotic subjective world of such inmates requires an outside world that is sterile and has the womblike quality of psychotic quiescence.

A second pattern is one in which vague but imminent danger lurks everywhere. The person "feels" himself discussed, "sees" himself stared at, "hears" veiled threats. He becomes obsessed with the notion of his vulnerability to danger, of the chance that others have to stab him while asleep or to poison his food. Segregation may be protective for other persons, but is far from reassuring to these patients. It harbors unpredictably "crazy" men. Its guards are corruptible. Its locks are no barriers to infiltrators. The safety of its walls is tenuous and permeable.

While some men "externalize" impulses by locating them "outside," there are other men who try to do this also, but fail. There are inmates who have in the past expressed their violence through crimes whose explosiveness haunts their nightmares. They harbor guilt and unresolved doubts related to their past acts ("Could I really have done what I'm accused of?" "Was I provoked?" Was I framed?"), and more crucially, they face a reality of current and future (potential) violence. This sense of one's imminent violence translates into (1) fear of retaliatory threats by others, (2) perception of violence in others, and (3) fear of one's propensity and capacity to respond violently to provocation.

A person of this kind may oscillate like a yoyo between the fear of others and the fear of self. To help such a man cope, an environment must protect him from threat and must isolate him from stimuli that tempt him to explode. No milieu can do this job perfectly, but segregation (when it is improved upon through rigorous self-restrictions) can come very close.

The Environment Profile of Protection

Protection is generally liked by its residents, though it gets mixed reviews. Positive and negative valuations of protection are summarized in Tables 11-1 and 11-2. Not surprisingly, Safety is the most frequently mentioned positive attribute, followed by Privacy and Social Stimulation. Activity is the most frequently mentioned negative attribute, followed by Support. Clearly, we see a tradeoff inmates are forced to make when they decide to maximize Safety (and Privacy) at the expense of other values. Ironically, a frequent complaint is that protection is not safe enough. Since tighter security means more confinement, the more extreme the need for Safety, the greater the price it exacts.

"Segregation" is the favored form of punishment in prisons throughout the country. The use of enforced cell time as a punishment implies that confinement is painful, uncomfortable, and to be avoided. Court cases have officially defined excessive cell time as "cruel and unusual punishment." There is an assumption that long periods of time spent in a cell

TABLE 11-1. Positive Evaluative Statements Related to Protection

Frequency:	
8	It's safe here.
6	Inmates are better behaved here.
3	People get along better here.
2	You have more privacy here.
2	There are fewer people here.
2	You don't have to fight here.
2	Officers treat men well here.
Other (1 each):	It's a smaller area here.
	You have peace of mind here.
	It's calm and tranquil here.
	You can read and study, get more accomplished here.
	There is no trouble here.

TABLE 11-2. Negative Evaluative Statements Related to Protection

Frequency:	
12	The cell time bothers me.
6	There are no rehabilitation programs.
5	It's not safe enough here.
2	Staff discriminate against protection men.
2	There is no work here.
2	There is not enough sports equipment.
2	There is nothing to do.
Others (1 each):	Can't play cards.
	You have to eat in your cell.
	There's not enough recreation.
	There are no church services.
	There are no movies.
	It's depressing.
	It's rough being alone.
	You can't get help when you're sick.
	People "bug out" here.

are debilitating. How does this picture square with the way protection inmates react to and evaluate their environment?

Twelve of the thirty-one men we interviewed complained about isolation and cell time, but the others told us it did not bother them, that all areas in the prison are the same, or that they preferred staying in their cells to being out of them. Several of the men refused to avail themselves of their recreation periods. Men with mental histories claimed that isolation was therapeutic and soothing to their nerves. A former mental patient wrote the following note in protest against being transferred out of protection:

> I do not want to go to the Diagnostic and Evaluation Unit because, sir, I am getting along very well in protection company. Sir: my nervous have calm down about 80% and I am on Librium 3 times a day and most of the time on this company it's quiet, and the officer lets me work here, that too calms my nervous down, and I get enough rest every night. And we go out in the yard, 2 hours a day. All this is just enough for me! Thanks. So Sir, I do not want to be evaluated by any psychiatrist.

Several men in protection found it a place for constructive study. One nonreader learned to read and was able to work on a correspondence course in the ministry. Another completed numerous "cell-study" courses. Still others painted, read, and wrote letters. These men were pleased to have time to themselves so they could improve their skills.

Other inmates passed their time passively. They listened to the radio on their earphones. They slept long periods of time. Others read novels and magazines, claiming to consume one book a day. These men were content to mark time in their cells aimlessly, without definite goals.

Other inmates seemed to suffer. Two, in particular, who had been accustomed to considerable physical exercise, found that immobilization made them restless and nervous. One of these two men offered a rare minority report on the adverse effects of confinement. He told us:

It was just like you wake up one morning and everything that is said and done irritates you to such a point where you want to lash out at something. It may be the result of the confinement, or what have you. It's just like you wake up one morning and your cell is like an accordion door. Now you don't know which way to turn. So being a hostile man you turn hostilities out and you break up the cell, maybe. . . . See, a man can stand only so much confinement. If a man doesn't have some kind of release, to keep off his frustrations, right? Let's say that you put him out in the yard and he exhausts himself. Then when he comes in he can cope. But he has no way of throwing off his frustrations. And he can't drive himself to exercise in the cell. So he's in there. And there's nothing to do. And he has everything in the world, and there's no way for him to release. He's just sitting there. Now the four walls are going like this. And he can't stand it no more, so he breaks something. So he starts breaking up his cell. . . . I've experienced all this.

Protection men are not representative of men who are segregated in prison. They have, for the most part, a preponderant need for Safety, and/or a consuming desire for Privacy. Their environmental profile is specialized, skewed, and strongly overdetermined.

Preferring sanctuary in protection to life in a prison population, such men perceive themselves as having made a free and knowledgeable choice. One shudders at the fate of these men should the alternative of protection not be available to them.

III

ENHANCING ENVIRONMENTAL CONGRUENCE

12

The Prison Preference Profile

THOSE WHO ARE INVOLVED with the human mind—irrespective of academic discipline—share a common dilemma. They promise themselves and their informants to convey undistorted information, but they are obliged time and again to destroy the integrity and richness of their data.

Only a biographer can afford the luxury of capturing the essence and uniqueness of a research subject. He can afford this luxury because conveying biographical information is an end in itself, because a reader comes to a biographer to learn all he can learn about an individual human being. The biographer's reader doesn't care whether what he learns applies to other human beings; at most, he assumes that the protagonist of the biography is "an embodiment of the spirit of his age" or conveys the "best" the "worst" or the "average" in human nature.

Unfortunately, the social scientist's mission is to study people for what they teach us about other people. The premise is always that the information we obtain must "transfer" or "generalize"; this means that we must delete nontransferable facts, though they may convey the essence of a man's perceptions, thoughts, and values.

In our discussion so far we have strained to reflect what people have told us in interviews. By retaining the flavor of protocols, we may have exceeded the conventional norms of the scientific game. We may stand accused (as in the past) of a "have-tape-recorder-will-do-research" approach, featuring "excessive use of transcripts" (Simirenko).

"Excessive," of course, is in the eyes of the beholder. We have felt a need for illustrations to convey transactions with milieus that we heard people tell us about, and on which we felt people depended for survival. It would be hard to talk about the importance of environmental features to

This chapter has been prepared in collaboration with John Gibbs.

flesh-and-blood people without stepping into their shoes; it would be similarly misleading to limit the range of illustrations, because this range conveys the variation we encountered for each theme, even in the homogeneous environment we studied, and among relatively homogeneous groups.

But once we have traced our portrait we can turn to our "scientific" mission of helping others to apply knowledge elsewhere. This entails different sorts of facts—facts that are easily replicated, amended, and corrected.

The Instrumentation of Environmental Preferences

Our interviews were designed to explore individual perceptions of environment, and to map personal preferences and aversions for environmental qualities and dimensions. The information reflects the unique perspective of the person who provides it. We lose this uniqueness in coding, but we may recapture it, or some of it, by resuscitating our protocols.

This process is neither easy nor cheaply replicable. We can justify expense in exploratory research, but no agency, however well-staffed or humane, could defend routine use of clinical interviews in the processing of clients. If "matching" men and environments is to be undertaken, it must be done with tools that are readily administered and easily interpreted. We need quick, reliable instruments that yield profiles of environmental preferences.

The social sciences turn to biological or physical sciences for "objective" tools and techniques. Since our concern is with "psychoecology," we look to psychophysics for models of possible instrumentation. But psychophysics deals with *unidimensional* judgments, which show that one sound sounds louder, or is lower in pitch, than another sound, or that one line looks longer or shorter than another. Psychophysics does not seek a profile of the perceiver's perceptual proclivities along several physical dimensions, nor of the relative weight he places on different parameters of judgment.

There is an offshoot of psychophysics, however, that accomplishes this very end and measures multidimensional preferences of physical attributes. That offshoot is experimental esthetics, which combines the exploration of psychophysical responses with that of emotional responses to stimuli.

The first treatise in experimental esthetics was published by G. T. Fechner, who is the father of psychophysics, and who applied psychophysics to the realm of esthetics. Fechner recognized, of course, that esthetics taps variables beyond those of perceptual processes. Woodworth (1938), in discussing Fechner's work, notes, for example, that "it should not be assumed in advance that the forms and colors current among a group are necessarily preferred by the majority of individuals. The group standards might be affected by economic and social factors cutting across the psychological factor of individual likes and dislikes" (p. 370).

Among methods of experimental esthetics, one that nicely explores relative judgments or preferences is that of forced choice "paired comparisons," which was introduced by J. Cohn in 1894.[1] In this technique, items or objects are presented to a person two at a time, and he must select one member of each pair as subjectively preferable to the other.

The procedure of forced-choice paired comparisons has a number of advantages for our problem of measuring environmental preferences.

Different aspects of environment are commodities that are conjointly desirable or undesirable to a person, and the paired comparison procedure (unlike absolute ratings) is sensitive to minute differences in desirability or undesirability. A man may individually rate the Devil and the Deep Blue Sea as unambiguously noxious. But some environments feature Devils and Deep Blue Seas, and it is important to know which of the two sub-environments produces less anguish.

It is also much easier for respondents to make relative judgments, because absolute judgments (discrete items) provide less of a frame of reference against which to judge. A man may dislike spinach on the menu of a state dinner but may devour it when starved. A scale that features spinach in the abstract creates a quandary about which context to assume.

Finally, paired comparisons permit reactions to a rather large universe of items in modest space and time. A pair of items provides two judgments, and an item that is paired twice maps its status relative to two different sampling domains. Though the method is uneconomical if each item is to be paired with every other item (the number of pairs required becomes quickly astronomical) the method works nicely with categories—such as environmental dimensions—for which representative items are available.

A problem with the procedure is that comparisons can be arbitrary or nonsensical. A man who is forced to choose between decapitation and a firing squad may find both experiences equally unpalatable; when comparing aardvarks to lemurs he may see the choice as one of supreme indifference. But neither problem is beyond correction or control. Nonsense can be prevented through item construction from pools originating with respondents; arbitrary choices show up as unreliability in statistical analysis.

Other difficulties with the paired comparison method are common to "objective" measures generally and relate to the ideational poverty of items and to their potential unrepresentativeness. The first of these issues is "built in," because a psychometrically defensible item must be simple and uncluttered. It must be devoid of complexity and multiple connotations and of overtones and/or undercurrents. The second problem is related: It has to do with the fact that an item is a pinprick of reality, a very

[1] Woodworth notes that "paired comparisons" is a mistranslation from Cohn's German writings, which refer to "comparison by pairs" (*paarweise Vergleichung*).

small sample of its universe. To enhance representativeness of items we limit the universe they represent by making the range of items more homogeneous. Unfortunately, this invites redundancy and restricts the range of the content we can cover.

The Prison Preference Inventory

As environmental dimensions emerged from our inmate interviews, they had variegated multiple connotations and ranged from the mildest to the most extreme (or overdetermined) concerns. The dimensions also included feelings, values, and ideas that are not appropriate stimuli for judgment. We compromised by making up paired comparison items for each of our dimensions that

1. referred to relatively tangible feelings or conditions in the environment
2. tapped areas within each dimension that seemed to recur with frequency
3. included both positive (preferred) and negative (objectionable) connotations.

We experimented with plausible items that were not included in our dimensions, and these recovered the additional dimension (Social Stimulation) that was not featured in interviews. This made sense, because we know that different methods of inquiry tap different levels of concern and relate differently to a person's self-perception and to his willingness or ability to disclose information.

The Prison Preference Inventory is designed for prison use and contains some items (having to do with custody, housing programs, rules) that would not be found in a School Preference Inventory, a Factory Preference Inventory, or in other environmental profiles. There is also one dimension (Safety) that is probably not a prominent feature of many other environments. The instrument contains items, however, that are very likely to have universality; it also covers dimensions that should be as valid for a monastery or a kindergarten as they are for prisons. Questionnaires could in part easily be constructed to yield comparable information for a variety of settings. Hospital patients could be asked whether they prefer a nurse who cares (Feedback) to a nurse who knows her business (Support), or a dependable nurse (Structure). A wife could express preference for a "liberated" husband (Freedom), a loving husband (Feedback), or a good provider (Support). Students could choose between quiet periods (Privacy), fun-loving fellow students (Social Stimulation) and protection from bullies (Safety).

Such inventories are, of course, not born full bloom. Their construction entails large item pools, requires repeated pretestings, and entails analyses of data from several instruments.

Statistical Properties and Construction of the PPI

The PPI is designed for raw (unweighted) scoring, is symmetrical in structure, and gives each item the same hypothetical total score. The number of pairs in the instrument is the minimum number (56) that permits the eight dimensions to be paired twice with each other. There are roughly equal numbers of positive and negative items (to control for response set) and a range of items of varying (but matched) estimated social desirability.

The Freedom and Activity dimensions, for instance, contain the following items:

ACTIVITY	FREEDOM
I'd prefer:	I'd prefer:
getting a good job in prison	staying away from guards
keeping active	inmates who know their rights
being busy all day	a guard who overlooks
housing in which I keep busy	infractions
a very busy day	staff who let me run my life
an active program	having no guards around
no time to be bored	not having a boss
	as few rules as possible
	no supervision
	no one checking up on me
I'd be more bothered by:	I'd be more bothered by:
too much time to think	staff who are on my back
sitting around	inmates who are rats
having nothing to do	guards giving petty orders
thinking too much	being told what to do
lots of idle time	a lot of rules
being bored	
a lot of freedom	

The questionnaire experienced five revisions in the process of construction. At each stage we pruned, modified, and exchanged pairs in an effort to produce a more well-rounded and reliable instrument. Our first step in item analysis was to compute item–dimension correlations. Those items showing a respectable correlation with the dimension they represented were assigned to our employable item pool and were retested in subsequent versions.

The items that did not correlate highly with their dimension were relegated to a "risk pool." The second step was to look closely at our "risk" items to determine whether they were salvageable in terms of high association with a dimension other than their parent dimension or their ability to discriminate between demographically defined groups. With these types of information we were able to arrive at increasingly homogeneous item clusters.

Table 12-1 compares the reliability coefficients of the original and final version of the instrument for samples of New York State prisoners. Here we see that the reliabilities of six out of eight dimensions substantially increased between the first and final version of the questionnaire. The average adjusted parallel test coefficient (Spearman–Brown) increased by 40.5 percent, and the internal consistency measure (KR 20) was improved by 48.7 percent on the average.

The results of the first administration of the PPI showed that our "interpersonal" dimensions (Support, Feedback, and Social Stimulation) were not very reliable and needed considerable refinement.

Despite such limitations, the early effort yielded promising findings. Not only did the first version of the instrument contain solid dimensions, but many items proved able to discriminate between inmate groups in ways that made theoretical sense.

Table 12-2, for example, compares the item preferences of younger and older inmates in intake and prison populations. We note that the younger inmates are more concerned than the older inmates about their personal relationship with staff; they seem more dependent on staff. They prize guards who are friendly (5), gregarious (16), or protective (1); they are more appreciative of privileges (18) or guidance (13); they are upset about guards who "won't help people" (37) and about situations where "no one cares" (39).

Younger inmates place more weight than older inmates on filling time. They prize housing that "lets people rap" (19) and are irritated about slack time (41), lack of recreation (45), or being locked up (47). The last item relates to a third concern of younger inmates, which is the issue of feeling safe. This is highlighted by the emphasis on protective guards (1) and on "a place where you can be safe" (64); there is also the disproportionate worry about having to be "scared of people" (46), about "inmates who are dangerous" (51), and about inmate bullies (55).

Older inmates, as compared to younger inmates, show a more substantial need for structure and stability. They prize guards who are consistent (5) or who are understanding (16); they are irritated with guards who are inconsistent (37); they prize "fair and firm discipline" (25). They reject

TABLE 12-1. Reliability of the Original and Final Questionnaire Dimensions for Two Independent Samples of New York State Prisoners

Dimension	Original Version			Final Version		
	Parallel Test Coefficient	Spearman–Brown	KR 20	Parallel Test Coefficient	Spearman–Brown	KR 20
Privacy	.38	.55	.49	.54	.70	.66
Safety	.52	.69	.61	.49	.66	.54
Structure	.32	.48	.37	.38	.55	.61
Support	.003	.007	.15	.34	.51	.62
Emotional Feedback	.16	.28	.31	.52	.69	.63
Social Stimulation	.23	.38	.28	.42	.53	.44
Activity	.30	.46	.41	.27	.42	.45
Freedom	.35	.51	.47	.53	.69	.66
$\bar{X}$	.28	.42	.39	.47	.59	.58

TABLE 12-2. Items in the Early Version of the PPI That Discriminated Between Adult Inmate and Youth Inmate Random Samples (in Rank Order)

Item Sets	Proportions of Sample Selecting Each Alternative	
	Youthful Inmates (N=234)	Older Inmates (N=229)
5. Guards who are consistent	17%	48%[a]
Guards who are friendly	83[a]	52
19. Housing that keeps out noise	39	59[a]
Housing which lets people rap	61[a]	41
37. Guards who are inconsistent (−)	16	36[a]
Guards who won't help people (−)	84[a]	64
41. Talk of a riot (−)	58	76[a]
Time on my hands (−)	42[a]	24
39. Tension in the air (−)	48	65[a]
No one who cares (−)	52[a]	35
18. Knowing I can get privileges	25[a]	10
Knowing my people still love me	75	90[a]
34. No rules at all (−)	52	67[b]
A lot of noise (−)	48[b]	33
1. Guards who leave me alone	46	60[b]
Guards who protect me	54[b]	40
25. Packages and money from home	68[b]	54
Fair and firm discipline	32	46[b]
xx. A place you can be alone	36	49[b]
A place you can be safe	64[b]	51
45. A prison with no recreation (−)	42[b]	29
A prison with no rules (−)	58	71[b]
46. Not knowing things (−)	67	80[b]
Being scared of people (−)	33[b]	20
47. Being locked up (−)	45[b]	33
Having nothing to do (−)	55	67
51. Inmates who are dangerous (−)	67[b]	55
Inmates who are rats	33	45[b]
55. An inmate bully (−)	63[b]	51
A disloyal woman (−)	37	49[b]
16. Guards who understand people	87	98[b]
Guards who enjoy a good laugh	13[b]	2
13. Teachers who get me to study	71[b]	60
Staff who are warm	29	40[b]
17. Inmates who let me work	79	89[b]
Inmates who do me favors	21[b]	11

[a]Difference significant beyond the .001 level of confidence.
[b]Difference significant beyond the .01 level of confidence.

"no rules at all" (34), "a prison with no rules" (71), and "not knowing things" (46).

Older inmates seem more concerned about their privacy and peace of mind, and about irritants and disturbances. We see this in the composite emphasis on "housing that keeps out noise" (19), "a place you can be alone" (XX), "inmates who let me work" (17), "guards who leave me alone" (1), and "tension in the air" (39). Not surprisingly, older inmates show more concern than younger inmates about the stability of their family bonds (items 18, "knowing my people still love me," and 55, "a disloyal woman").

The initial questionnaire was administered to a large random sample and to the sample we described in Chapter 11 of inmates in the formal protective setting. We would expect self-segregated men to have stronger Safety concerns than men who choose to live in the general prison population. Table 12-3 confirms this expectation.

Table 12-3 also shows that the prisoners in the protective setting seemed relatively unconcerned with Activity and Freedom. This makes sense if we consider that restrictions and inactivity are the price the inmates must pay to secure the safety of physical insulation (Chapter 11).

For a first effort, the original version of the instrument showed enough promise to merit the investment of our time—and the time of inmates—to further improve the questionnaire. The final version of the PPI is the product of testing a total of 1,604 New York inmates. Our fourth attempt was an instrument in which each dimension was compared with each other dimension on three occasions, thus producing an 84-pair questionnaire. Although the questionnaire was too lengthy for practical purposes, it allowed us to test a larger number of items in a single administration. The best-performing items from this long questionnaire were incorporated into the final version of the PPI.

In the sections that follow, we will describe several different institu-

TABLE 12-3. Environmental Preference Profiles of Adult Inmates in Population and in Protection

Dimension	General Population	Self-Segregation
Privacy	6.30	6.82
Safety	6.52	9.27[a]
Structure	8.88	8.75
Support	6.54	5.81
Emotional Feedback	6.81	7.20
Social Stimulation	6.45	7.09
Activity	7.95	6.50[b]
Freedom	6.75	5.36[b]

[a]Significant at .001 level.
[b]Significant at .05 level.

tional samples and populations and their PPI profiles. We'll also discuss the reliability of the PPI and the relationship among its dimensions.

Institutional Samples

Our first sample consisted of 291 New York inmates housed in the Clinton Reception Center, which is located near the Canadian border. This intake facility receives all adult males sentenced to prison in the state. An inmate usually spends three to four weeks in reception before he is assigned or transferred to a prison for male adult felons.

The majority of men in the Clinton sample are young: 73.2 percent are thirty years of age or younger, and the mean age is twenty-eight. The modal inmate is black (59.6 percent), single (53.7 percent), and at one time was addicted to drugs (56.1 percent). Most of the sample have had previous experience with criminal justice institutions. Almost all (96.4 percent) have histories of criminal arrests. Half (53.6 percent) have served a prison term, and half (50.7 percent) have served time in jail. Property offenses are the most common crime appearing on arrest records (87.9 percent) and are also the most common commitment offense (67 percent). The mean, mode, and median for minimum sentence are 2.4, 0, and 1.3, respectively. The averages for maximum sentence are (mode) 3, and (median) 4.9.[2]

A sample of inmates newly arrived at six Pennsylvania institutions yielded 314 questionnaires. The institutions included in this sample are two maximum security facilities located near urban centers, one medium security facility that confines youthful offenders, two walled prisons in rural areas, and one maximum security prison that is surrounded by a fence.

In age, the Pennsylvania inmates are comparable to those in New York. The mean, median, and modal ages of the sample are 27.2, 24.7 and 20; 75 percent of the group is thirty years of age or younger. The Pennsylvania sample contains more (55.4 percent) whites than the New York sample. More Pennsylvania inmates (74 percent) are single; fewer (60 percent) have been sentenced for property offenses, but most of the sample (75 percent) have been previously convicted of property crimes. Half the inmates have served prior jail terms, and 36.3 percent have served previous prison sentences. About a quarter of the prisoners have a history of drug addiction, and 17.9 percent have a history of alcoholism. The mean, median, and modal minimum sentences are 5.3, 1.9, and 1, respectively. The averages for maximum sentence are 5.5 (median) and 5 (mode).

A random sample of inmates from the Connecticut Correctional Institution, Somers, provided 201 completed PPIs. Somers is a maximum secur-

---

[2] The mean was distorted by 25 men in our sample who were serving life sentences. In our coding scheme a life sentence received a value of 88.

ity prison and is located close to one of Connecticut's metropolitan areas. In contrast to Clinton—which is a prison fortress—Somers is surrounded by a fence.

Like the New York and Pennsylvania samples, most of the Connecticut sample is young (its mean age is twenty-eight, and 72.8 percent of the sample is thirty years old or younger) and single (74.7 percent). Like the Pennsylvania sample, the Connecticut sample is predominately white (52.7 percent), but a higher percentage of Connecticut prisoners (40.6 percent) are confined for violent crimes. Connecticut inmates have also received longer sentences. The mean, mode, and median for minimum sentence are 5.1, 2, and 3.9, respectively. Maximum sentence averages are (mode) 10, and (median) 9.1. These averages for maximum sentence are much higher than for the New York and Pennsylvania samples.

The typical Connecticut prisoner is a property offender (58.1 percent), was below the age of twenty-one when first convicted of a crime (67.6 percent), has attended high school (73.1 percent), and was employed at least half-time prior to incarceration (53.6 percent).

A sample of California inmates was drawn at the Northern Reception Center located at the California Medical Facility (a psychiatric prison) in Vacaville and from the Southern Reception Center at Chino. These two reception centers process all of California's male adult intake population, except for death row inmates. The sample consists of 327 inmates who had completed their intake routine, had volunteered for the study, and were paid to participate. These inmates not only responded to the PPI but also completed a set of instruments for the California Corrections Department's Research Division.

This sample is nonrandom, because inmates who had not been tested and certified as sixth graders (25 percent of the intake population) were excluded and because the volunteers overrepresented whites, high school graduates, and men from Northern California. The mean, mode, and median age for the sample is 28, 22, and 26, respectively. The majority of the inmates had not yet reached thirty years of age (67 percent). Whites represent about half of the sample (54.6 percent), while blacks and Mexican Americans comprise about one fifth and one fourth of the group (17.5 percent and 23.3 percent) respectively. The pool of respondents is equally divided between married (47.1 percent) and unmarried (52.9 percent) prisoners, and most of the men (63 percent) have at least one child.

The average California respondent has attended high school (76.4 percent) and has been permanently employed (58.1 percent), earning $3,000 per year or more prior to his incarceration. One third (34 percent) of the sample reports a history of regular heroin or other opiate use. Three fifths of the group (59.1 percent) have a record of prior felony conviction, 36 percent have served previous prison terms and two thirds (66.5 percent) were previously confined in jail.

The administration of the Prison Preference questionnaire to the population of the Federal Correctional Institution at Lexington yielded 512 completed questionnaires. The Lexington population is 54 percent male and 46 percent female. Again, the majority of the inmates are White (54.2 percent). Mean and modal ages of the population are 31.7 and 26.0, respectively. Most of the inmates have attended high school (56.1 percent) and 29.5 percent have had some college education.

The Lexington sample differs from our three other samples: it contains women and a sizable proportion of highly educated inmates. But Lexington is also different in other respects. The institution is a therapeutic prison and is composed of "units" that offer different programs to different subpopulations. The presumption at Lexington is that each unit can provide tailor-made programs that match the needs of its subpopulation. To the extent to which this presumption holds, we can test the PPI's usefulness as a measure of environmental congruence.

The Reliability of the PPI

One method of judging the utility of an instrument for research, classification, or prediction is to evaluate its reliability. In theory, "reliability" is the proportion of the score obtained by the instrument that is a hypothetical "true" score. The greater this fit, the more faith we have in the instrument. In practice, reliability is pretty much a measure of consistency.[3]

We have an obvious measure of consistency in the PPI, because one of the statements from each dimension is paired twice with one of the statements from each of the other dimensions. This means that each of our dimensions can be divided into two separate scores that can be compared to each other. For example, two Privacy scores would each be composed of a Privacy item paired with a Safety, Structure, Support, Emotional Feedback, Social Stimulation, Activity, and Freedom item. Since there are seven items, each of the two Privacy scores can vary between zero and seven. If the sets of items that make up the two scores for Privacy are measuring the same dimension, we would expect the two scores to be fairly close. If we computed a high Privacy score for a respondent using one set of items, we expect the person to obtain a high Privacy score using the second set of items.

The correlation coefficients that appear in the Parallel Test column of Table 12-4 summarize the relationship between the two item set scores for

---

[3] The coefficient of reliability is statistically defined as the variance of the true or universe score divided by the variance of the observed score. The observed variance consists of true variance and error variance. As error variance increases reliability must decrease, since true variance is fixed (see Cronbach).

TABLE 12-4. Reliability of the PPI Dimensions

Dimension	New York (N=299)		Connecticut (N=201)		Pennsylvania (N=314)		Federal (N=512)		California (N=328)		Average (N=654)	
	Parallel Test	KR 20	Parallel Test	KR 20	Parallel Test	KR 20	Parallel Test	KR 20	Parallel Test	KR 20	Parallel Test	KR 20
Privacy	.70	.66	.73	.64	.67	.63	.67	.66	.70	.65	.69	.65
Safety	.66	.54	.76	.72	.70	.60	.66	.62	.72	.73	.70	.64
Structure	.55	.61	.58	.53	.56	.45	.49	.43	.53	.50	.54	.50
Support	.51	.62	.66	.51	.52	.52	.37	.34	.38	.32	.48	.46
Emotional Feedback	.69	.63	.68	.62	.68	.61	.67	.57	.66	.66	.68	.62
Social Stimulation	.53	.44	.54	.46	.50	.47	.56	.52	.53	.40	.53	.46
Activity	.42	.45	.58	.56	.53	.51	.52	.48	.57	.58	.52	.51
Freedom	.69	.66	.78	.71	.73	.65	.68	.64	.74	.67	.72	.67
X̄	.59	.58	.66	.59	.61	.56	.58	.53	.60	.56	.61	.56

each PPI dimension for the samples and populations of prisoners we have described. These coefficients tell us that the dimension reliabilities and the total (average) reliability of the instrument are respectable [4] and also show that the reliability coefficients are fairly consistent across the institutional samples and populations. We can also see that Privacy, Safety, Emotional Feedback, and Freedom are the most reliable dimensions in each sample or population.

A second technique for statistically assessing the reliability of an instrument is a measure of internal consistency known as coefficient alpha.[5] We used a formula known as the Kuder–Richardson 20 formula to compute this coefficient, and the results appear under the KR 20 column of Table 12-4. These measures reflect the *strength of the relationship among the items* that constitute each dimension. An instrument cannot "consistently" measure when there is a lot of variation among its items. We may recall the fact that coal miners once used canaries to determine the amount of coal gas in mines. If the canaries died, the level of coal gas was considered hazardous. Chirping birds signified that the mine was safe. But if a miner brought one very healthy, large bird and one very emaciated, underdeveloped canary into the mine, how would he judge the level of coal gas? If he vacated the mine when the sickly bird died twenty seconds after entry, he might lose a day's work, but a miner could reach a toxic state before the hardy canary gave up the ghost. The miner's instrument for measuring gas lacks consistency, because the components of his instrument, bird large and bird small, do not vary together.

We see in Table 12-4 that the pattern of the KR 20 coefficients is very similar to that found for the test coefficients.[6] Again, Privacy, Safety, Emotional Feedback, and Freedom are typically the most consistent dimensions.

---

[4] Reliability is related to the length (the number of items) of an instrument. The PPI comprises eight instruments composed of fourteen items each. When we take into consideration that thirty items are typically required to reach a reliability of .80, it is apparent that the dimension reliabilities could have been increased substantially by adding items.

Some authors suggest that a reliability of .90 should be achieved before an instrument is used in an applied setting. We feel that in order to meet this standard we would be required to lengthen the test to the point where it would be impractical to administer to large samples of inmates. Reliability could also be increased by reducing the range of content covered by the items in each dimension. Redundancy would increase reliability at the expense of meaning.

Another factor to keep in mind is that instruments measure most accurately the abilities or sentiments of individuals at the high end of distributions. Although to date we have no empirical evidence, it follows that the PPI would be most reliable for those inmates who are of special classification interest because of preponderant concerns (see Cronbach, p. 174, and Nunnally, pp. 226–259).

[5] Coefficient alpha is based on the average correlation among the items and the number of items in the instrument; see Nunnally, p. 210.

[6] KR 20 is typically lower than the parallel test coefficient.

The Typical PPI Profile

Table 12-5 and Figure 12-1 show that the pattern of PPI dimension scores is fairly similar for each institutional group. Figure 12-2 displays the composite picture. Here we see that the profile of the average inmate peaks with a Support score of 9.9 followed by a Feedback score of 8.3 and an Activity score of 7.8.[7] Safety, Social Stimulation, and Structure cluster in the 6.3 to 7.3 range, and Privacy and Freedom are the lowest-ranking concerns, with means of 5.4 and 4.5, respectively. The discrepancies we find in dimensional scores relate to Activity, Freedom, Safety, and Structure. The Connecticut inmates seem less concerned about Safety and seem to express more interest in Freedom than the other samples; the Lexington population registers a lower score on Activity, and California inmates score lower on Structure.

The correlation coefficients that appear in Table 12-6 represent the average relationship among the PPI dimensions. These statistics have been

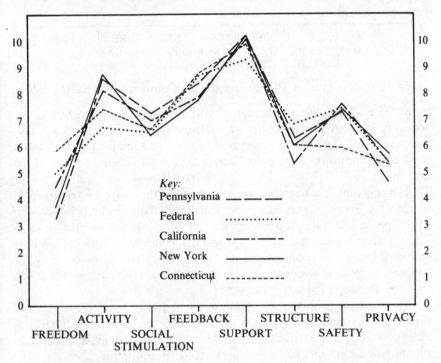

Figure 12-1. Average PPI Dimension Scores for Each Sample

[7] The high support score in these profiles is consistent with the findings of Glaser, who reports that "learning a trade or in other ways preparing for a better job opportunity outside of prison was the first interest of most inmates in every prison we studied" (p. 113).

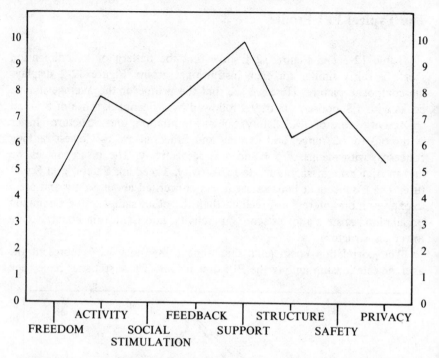

Figure 12-2. Average PPI Scores for the Combined Sample (N=1653)

corrected for attenuation—meaning that they represent the strength of association between dimensions if we assume that the dimensions are perfectly reliable. The relative absence of positive relationships in the matrix is a standard artifact of the paired comparison forced-choice format of the instrument.

Privacy shows a negative association with the more "interpersonal" dimensions, Support, Feedback, and Social Stimulation. The prisoner who values peace and quiet and who prefers to be alone tells us that he considers interactions required for programs, companionship, or intimate relationships relatively unimportant. The inmate who shows concern for Support, Emotional Feedback, or Social Stimulation appears willing to do with less Privacy to satisfy these needs.

The strongest positive relationship in the matrix is between Privacy and Freedom. The man who builds a buffer against his environment sees all intrusions, including staff, as undesirable; an inmate involved in conflicts with guards seems well advised to seek retreat as an option.

Freedom is negatively associated with Safety. An inmate who is sensitive to danger in prison sees close supervision as a safeguard. The inmate who wants to be independent of staff considers himself capable of handling dangerous situations.

Freedom–Support and Activity–Feedback are inversely related. The

TABLE 12-5. The Average PPI Dimension Scores

Dimension	New York (N=299)	Connecticut (N=201)	Pennsylvania (N=314)	California (N=327)	Federal (N=512)	Combined Samples (N=1,653)
Privacy	5.8	5.4	4.7	5.5	5.5	5.4
Safety	7.4	6.0	7.3	7.6	7.5	7.3
Structure	6.1	6.1	6.4	5.4	6.9	6.3
Support	10.2	9.9	10.2	10.1	9.3	9.9
Emotional Feedback	7.8	8.8	8.4	7.9	8.7	8.3
Social Stimulation	6.5	6.7	7.3	7.0	6.6	6.8
Activity	8.7	7.4	8.6	8.1	6.7	7.8
Freedom	3.7	5.9	3.3	4.5	5.0	4.5

TABLE 12-6. Average Dimension to Dimension Correlation Coefficients

	Safety	Structure	Support	Emotional Feedback	Social Stimulation	Activity	Freedom
Privacy	-.25	.01	-.45	-.51	-.64	-.26	.25
Safety		-.34	-.10	-.07	-.27	-.24	-.49
Structure			-.30	-.23	-.40	-.19	-.15
Support				-.15	-.23	-.06	-.43
Emotional Feedback					.09	-.42	-.40
Social Stimulation						-.15	-.14
Activity							-.30

inmate who is concerned with autonomy is not interested in programs that mean additional restrictions or contact with authority. A prisoner who finds it necessary to be busy may be blocking out thoughts of significant others.

Assessing the Validity of the PPI

Unlike reliability, there is no direct way of determining the validity of an instrument. A valid instrument is one that measures what it is supposed to measure. When we deal with the content of a person's mind, the criterion for validity is usually *plausibility*. If we look at our data in the light of everything else we know, the relationships that emerge should make sense. In the next chapter we shall describe findings that suggested to us that the PPI may be tapping meaningful relationships. After we summarize and discuss these findings we will turn to more practical matters. In Chapter 14 we shall consider the uses of the PPI and the deployment of other classification measures.

13

Patterns of Preference Profiles

SIMPLE ORGANISMS HAVE SIMPLE environmental concerns. A plant wants its world to provide nutrients, sunshine, and water. Environments that do not furnish these commodities—such as absentminded professors—produce droopy, unhealthy-looking plants.

But even the simplest organisms vary in the priorities they assign to commodities they may require. Some plants are sunbathers; others thrive happily in shade. Some insist on being drenched, while others husband small droplets of water. The amateur gardener who fails to inform himself about the differing environmental requirements of his leafy friends is apt to discover that he has arranged incongruent environments for them.

Though preference profiles are difficult to trace back, experience with past environmental challenges and with past adaptations plays a clear role in shaping one's concerns. A cactus with its ancestry in sand expects little water, but flowers that grow in swamps need moisture.

Concerns are shaped by career junctures. Young plants may have to be fertilized to promote growth; older plants seem to regard fertilizers as irrelevant. There are linkages between supplies and demands. A dog who is fed table scraps may sneer at dog food, even if dog food contains truffles.

In human concerns, personality (an intervening variable) muddies the sequential picture. An ambitious man may be Support-oriented, but his ambitiousness (High $_n$Achievement) may be hard to trace (McClelland). We may translate Privacy concerns to introversion, but we may be unsure why some persons become more introverted than the rest of us.

In assessing our profiles, we must determine whether they make sense in terms of whatever else we know about a person. Ideally, this means that

This chapter has been prepared in collaboration with John Gibbs.

high points and low points of a profile should correspond to known personality characteristics, to a person's career juncture, to his patterns of past experience, to highlights of his socialization, and to the life problems he faces.

In comparison to what we want to know, what we actually know is meager. Our ancillary data mostly relate to demographic indices in inmate files, which are not dependably recorded. We can firmly rely mainly on two or three basic items, which we obtained very reliably with several samples.

Our first findings (Tables 13-1 to 13-4) relate to age. Table 13-1 shows that in two samples relatively old inmates were less concerned with Freedom issues than younger inmates. This difference makes sense from several vantage points. Developmentally, an older person is more apt to have resolved dependency issues and identity concerns. He is more apt to have defined the borders of his autonomy and to feel less sensitivity about having these borders violated. Situationally, an older person may be less prone to evoke authoritarian moves, which means that Freedom issues have less chance of arising. A custodial officer may be more directive

TABLE 13-1. Distribution of Freedom Scores by Age

	Connecticut Sample					
	25 and Younger		26–30		Over 30	
	No.	(%)	No.	(%)	No.	(%)
Freedom scores:						
Low	13	(14.8)	6	(14.0)	17	(38.6)
Medium	44	(50.0)	17	(39.5)	15	(34.1)
High	31	(35.2)	20	(46.5)	12	(27.3)
Total	88	(100.0)	43	(100.0)	44	(100.0)

Chi square = 13.5078.
Significant at the .01 level.
Contingency coefficent = .26769.

	Federal Population					
	17–25		26–35		Over 35	
	No.	(%)	No.	(%)	No.	(%)
Freedom scores:						
Low	37	(27.0)	48	(33.8)	41	(40.6)
Medium	51	(37.2)	47	(33.1)	42	(41.6)
High	49	(35.8)	47	(33.1)	18	(17.8)
Total	137	(100.0)	142	(100.0)	101	(100.0)

Chi square = 11.39.
Significant at .05 level.
Contingency coefficient = .171.

toward a youth, who evokes his paternal role, than toward an age-mate or a man who is his senior.

Table 13-2 shows that Support decreases with age. This trend may be related to career stages. Young men are vocationally and educationally in transit, while an older man is more likely to have arrived. Even at equivalent achievement levels, the younger person may have more hope of changing his fate. There is a greater presumption among the young of being entitled to environmental supports. This situation is probably parallel to that of the plant that must be supplied with nutrient supplements before it reaches maturity.

A converse of Table 13-2 is Table 13-3, which shows that younger inmates may have less concern for Feedback. The support system here is interpersonal and refers to bonds that are established in life. The Feedback curve is most probably U-shaped, peaking early in life (with attachment to parents), decreasing with the search for personal autonomy, and increasing with linkage to a new family constellation.

The most striking profile difference we found for age was that relating to Structure, which is displayed in Table 13-4. In four samples the concern with Structure increased with age, and in three samples the difference

TABLE 13-2. Distribution of Support Scores by Age

| | Federal Population | | | | | |
| | 17–25 | | 26–35 | | Over 35 | |
	No.	(%)	No.	(%)	No.	(%)
Support scores:						
Low	33	(24.3)	44	(33.3)	52	(47.7)
Medium	64	(47.1)	42	(31.8)	29	(26.6)
High	39	(28.7)	46	(34.9)	28	(24.8)
Total	136	(100.1)	132	(100.0)	109	(100.0)

Chi square = 19.53.
Significant at .001 level.
Contingency coefficient = .223.

| | New York Sample | | | | | |
| | Under 26 | | 26–30 | | Over 30 | |
	No.	(%)	No.	(%)	No.	(%)
Support scores:						
Low	24	(30.4)	24	(32.0)	13	(22.8)
Medium	26	(32.9)	27	(36.0)	33	(57.9)
High	29	(36.7)	24	(32.0)	11	(19.3)
Total	79	(100.0)	75	(100.0)	57	(100.0)

Chi square = 10.17.
Significant at .05 level.
Contingency coefficient = .21.

TABLE 13-3. Distribution of Emotional Feedback Scores by Age

Pennsylvania Sample

	22 and Younger		23-27		28 and Older	
	No.	(%)	No.	(%)	No.	(%)
Feedback scores:						
Low	28	(45.2)	15	(27.3)	17	(27.9)
Medium	27	(43.5)	24	(43.6)	26	(42.6)
High	7	(11.3)	16	(29.1)	18	(29.5)
Total	62	(100.0)	55	(100.0)	61	(100.0)

Chi square = 9.41.
Significant at the .05 level.
Contingency coefficent = .22.

Connecticut Sample

	25 and Younger		26-30		Over 30	
	No.	(%)	No.	(%)	No.	(%)
Feedback scores:						
Low	30	(34.9)	15	(36.6)	5	(11.6)
Medium	28	(32.6)	17	(41.5)	23	(53.5)
High	28	(32.6)	9	(22.0)	15	(34.9)
Total	86	(100.1)	41	(100.1)	43	(100.1)

Chi square = 10.7535.
Significant at the .05 level.
Contingency coefficient = .24391.

is dramatic. In ecological terms, it makes sense to think of the young as needing less stability than persons who are older. Youth entails an exploration of opportunities, and any experimentation with options requires tolerance for flux. Once habits are established, we need predictability. When we are settled down, we require an environment that is correspondingly stable.

It is not difficult to see relationships among some of the parameters we have traced. Stability, for instance, goes hand in hand with a tolerant view of authority, while emphasis on autonomy is compatible with low emphasis on Feedback. It also makes sense to conceive of "prototypical middle-age" profiles featuring Low Freedom, Low Support, High Structure and High Feedback, and of a "modal youth" profile comprising High Freedom, High Support, Low Structure and Low Feedback.[1]

---

[1] The data also contain trends that suggest age differences in the other profile dimensions. As with the interview data, younger inmates show a tendency to have lower Privacy scores and higher Safety scores. They are also more likely to score high on Social Stimulation. The relationship of Privacy and Social Stimulation to age is also noted by Glaser (p. 93). Glaser simultaneously observes a Safety concern among young inmates in youth settings (p. 195).

TABLE 13-4. Distribution of Structure Scores by Age

	Federal Population					
	17–25		26–35		Over 35	
	No.	(%)	No.	(%)	No.	(%)
Structure scores:						
Low	54	(40.0)	35	(24.1)	19	(17.6)
Medium	61	(45.2)	73	(50.3)	46	(42.6)
High	20	(14.8)	37	(25.6)	43	(38.8)
Total	135	(100.0)	145	(100.0)	108	(100.0)

Chi square = 27.38; Significant at .001 level; Contingency coefficient = .257.

	New York Sample					
	Under 26		26–30		Over 30	
	No.	(%)	No.	(%)	No.	(%)
Structure scores:						
Low	28	(34.6)	18	(23.4)	10	(18.9)
Medium	43	(53.1)	39	(50.6)	21	(39.6)
High	10	(12.3)	20	(26.0)	22	(41.5)
Total	81	(100.0)	77	(100.0)	53	(100.0)

Chi square = 15.85; Significant at the .01 level; Contingency coefficient = .26.

	Pennsylvania Sample					
	22 and Younger		23–27		28 and Older	
	No.	(%)	No.	(%)	No.	(%)
Structure scores:						
Low	22	(34.4)	24	(42.9)	14	(23.3)
Medium	27	(42.2)	18	(32.1)	18	(30.0)
High	15	(23.4)	14	(25.0)	28	(46.7)
Total	64	(100.0)	56	(100.0)	60	(100.0)

Chi square 11.26; Significant at the .05 level; Contingency coefficient = .24.

	California Sample					
	18–23		24–29		30 and Over	
	No.	(%)	No.	(%)	No.	(%)
Structure scores:						
Low	40	(38.8)	29	(43.8)	28	(25.9)
Medium	40	(38.9)	35	(31.2)	37	(34.3)
High	23	(22.3)	28	(25.0)	43	(39.8)
Total	103	(100.0)	112	(100.0)	108	(100.0)

Chi square = 12.54; Significant at the .01 level; Contingency coefficient = .19.

Ethnicity

Ethnicity is a composite variable, and it is hard to tell what aspect of it is at work in determining particular differences. Among inmates, blacks are mostly urban, while whites may be rural or may be of small town origin; blacks are typically more disadvantaged than whites; there are also subcultural differences relating to socialization, gang membership, and neighborhood mores. In the case of blacks, there may be some ideological contributions related to black consciousness or Black Power.

With such complexities in mind, we view Table 13-5, which shows lower Freedom concerns for whites than for blacks. An explanation might include the assumptions that (1) black inmates have somewhat better chance of early contacts with peer subcultures and of a restricted range of experience with adults, (2) most authority figures are white, which increases the distance between black inmates and staff, and (3) anti-authoritarian beliefs may be more prevalent among black inmates, while conformist middle-class views may be more common among whites.

Table 13-6 shows a disproportionate concern for Support among black inmates. This concern is easily interpreted, because it links plausibly to a

TABLE 13-5. Distribution of Freedom Scores by Ethnicity

| | Pennsylvania Sample | | | |
| | Black ($\overline{X}$=3.7) | | White ($\overline{X}$=2.9) | |
	No.	(%)	No.	(%)
Freedom scores:				
Low	6	(8.5)	30	(31.3)
Medium	35	(49.3)	33	(34.4)
High	30	(42.3)	33	(34.4)
Total	71	(100.1)	96	(100.1)

Chi square = 12.74.
Significant at the .01 level.
Contingency coefficient = .27.

| | New York Sample | | | |
| | Black ($\overline{X}$=4.0) | | White ($\overline{X}$=3.2) | |
	No.	(%)	No.	(%)
Freedom scores:				
Low	43	(35.2)	33	(51.6)
Medium	45	(36.9)	19	(29.7)
High	34	(27.9)	12	(18.8)
Total	122	(100.0)	64	(100.0)

Chi square = 4.778.
Significant at .09 level.
Contingency coefficient = .16.

TABLE 13-6. Distribution of Support Scores by Ethnicity

	Federal Population			
	Black ($\overline{X}$=10)		White ($\overline{X}$=8.9)	
	No.	(%)	No.	(%)
Support scores:				
Low	41	(28.1)	76	(39.4)
Medium	50	(34.2)	73	(37.8)
High	55	(37.7)	44	(22.8)
Total	146	(100.0)	193	(100.0)

Chi square = 9.66.
Significant at .01 level.
Contingency coefficient = .166.

	Connecticut Sample			
	Black ($\overline{X}$=10.7)		White ($\overline{X}$=9.3)	
	No.	(%)	No.	(%)
Support scores:				
Low	16	(25.0)	45	(45.0)
Medium	28	(43.8)	39	(39.0)
High	20	(31.3)	16	(16.0)
Total	64	(100.1)	100	(100.0)

Chi square = 8.5.
Significant at the .05 level.
Contingency coefficient = .22.

TABLE 13-7. Distribution of Feedback Scores by Ethnicity

	New York Sample			
	Black ($\overline{X}$=7.3)		White ($\overline{X}$=8.8)	
	No.	(%)	No.	(%)
Feedback scores:				
Low	47	(37.6)	15	(22.1)
Medium	54	(43.2)	22	(32.4)
High	24	(19.2)	31	(45.5)
Total	125	(100.0)	68	(100.0)

Chi square = 15.39.
Significant at the .000 level.
Contingency coefficient = .27.

	Connecticut Sample			
	Black ($\overline{X}$=8.6)		White ($\overline{X}$=9.0)	
	No.	(%)	No.	(%)
Feedback scores:				
Low	20	(31.3)	27	(28.4)
Medium	31	(48.4)	32	(33.7)
High	13	(20.3)	36	(37.9)
Total	64	(100.0)	95	(100.0)

Chi square = 6.0.
Significant at the .05 level.
Contingency coefficient = .19.

person's prior opportunities. A man who has had few chances to advance educationally or to acquire skills is more apt to prize the remedial opportunities available in institutions.

Table 13-7 shows higher Feedback concerns among whites than among blacks. This difference may also be a composite product, reflecting (1) the availability of significant others in the community, and (2) subcultural positions that emphasize personal links or that recommend being "cool" and tough. Coolness relates to autonomy, because it frowns on personal dependence.

Marital Status

Table 13-8 shows that single inmates have lower Feedback concerns than married inmates. This difference makes a validating case for the Feedback dimension. It tells us that men who have ties show corresponding concerns that link them psychologically to their loved ones.

TABLE 13-8. Distribution of Emotional Feedback Scores by Marital Status

| | Pennsylvania Sample | | | |
	Single ($\bar{X}=8.0$)		Married ($\bar{X}=9.9$)	
	No.	(%)	No.	(%)
Feedback scores:				
Low	54	(40.6)	6	(13.3)
Medium	55	(41.4)	22	(48.9)
High	24	(18.0)	17	(37.8)
Total	133	(100.0)	45	(100.0)

Chi square = 13.54.
Significant at the .001 level.
Contingency coefficient = .27.

| | New York Sample | | | |
	Single ($\bar{X}=7.4$)		Married ($\bar{X}=8.1$)	
	No.	(%)	No.	(%)
Feedback scores:				
Low	45	(40.2)	25	(25.0)
Medium	43	(38.4)	41	(41.0)
High	24	(21.4)	34	(34.0)
Total	112	(100.0)	100	(100.0)

Chi square = 6.8.
Significant at the .05 level.
Contingency coefficient = .18.

Veterans and Novices

We noted in Chapter 8 that prior exposure to an environment can have a measurable impact on one's orientation and mode of adjustment. Table 13-9 depicts Privacy scores of reception populations that contain some inmates who were previously in prison and some who were not. Despite overall differences in imprisonment rates, the findings run parallel. Almost half of each novice group scores low on Privacy, while one third of the veteran group has very high Privacy scores. Prior experience with prison increases the need of the inmates for Privacy.

Several factors may be at work: (1) The inexperienced inmate may need information from his peers to orient himself to prison; (2) the experienced inmate may be more aware of privacy violations that await him in prison; and (3) the inexperienced inmate may tend to be younger and more gregarious.

TABLE 13-9. Distribution of Privacy Scores by Prior Prison Term for the New York and California Samples

New York Reception Sample

| | Prior Prison Term | | | |
| | None | | One or More | |
	No.	(%)	No.	(%)
Privacy scores:				
Low (0–4)	47	(48.5)	20	(19.0)
Medium (5–7)	32	(33.0)	48	(45.7)
High (8–13)	18	(18.6)	37	(35.2)
Total	97	(100.1)	105	(99.9)

Chi square = 20.36.
Significant at .000 level.
Contingency coefficient = .30.

California Reception Sample

| | Prior Prison Term | | | |
| | None | | One or More | |
	No.	(%)	No.	(%)
Privacy scores:				
Low (0–4)	86	(42.4)	36	(31.0)
Medium (5–7)	89	(43.8)	39	(33.6)
High (8–14)	28	(13.8)	41	(35.3)
Total	203	(100.0)	116	(99.9)

Chi square = 20.25.
Significant at .000 level.
Contingency Coefficient = .24.

Returning inmates do *not* seek Privacy simply because they are sensitive to danger cues. Table 13-10 shows that prison veterans (and criminal justice habitués generally) score lower than novices on the Safety dimension. Table 13-11 makes the same point for parole violators in the Connecticut sample. Seasoned inmates are less concerned about the dangers of prison than their less-seasoned counterparts. If nothing else, familiarity breeds confidence in one's ability to negotiate interpersonal threats.

TABLE 13-10. Distribution of Safety Scores by Prior Criminal Convictions and by Prior Prison Experience for the California Sample

| | Prior Convictions | | | | Prior Prison Experience | | | |
| | None | | One or More | | None | | Some | |
	N	(%)	N	(%)	N	(%)	N	(%)
Safety scores:								
Low (1–6)	36	(27.1)	84	(44.0)	66	(31.7)	54	(46.6)
Medium (7–9)	46	(34.6)	73	(38.2)	80	(38.5)	39	(33.6)
High (10–14)	51	(38.3)	34	(17.8)	62	(29.8)	23	(19.8)
Total	133	(100.0)	191	(100.0)	208	(100.0)	116	(100.0)

Chi square = 19.
Significant at .0001 level.
Contingency coefficient = .24.

Chi square = 7.7.
Significant at .02 level.
Contingency coefficient = .15.

TABLE 13-11. Distribution of Safety Scores By Parole Violation for the Connecticut Sample

| | Nonviolator (X=6.3) | | Violator (X=5.0) | |
	No.	(%)	No.	(%)
Safety scores:				
Low	40	(32.5)	23	(52.3)
Medium	49	(39.8)	15	(34.1)
High	34	(27.6)	6	(13.6)
Total	123	(99.9)	44	(100.0)

Chi square = 6.3. Significant at .05 level. Contingency coefficient = .19.

Employment Status Prior to Confinement

In the Connecticut and California data we have an index of preconviction life-style, because inmates were asked about their job histories in the free world. Past employment status is correlated with age, but it may be a variable in its own right. Employment and unemployment involve different routines, calling for different orientations toward one's environment.

We find significant relationships between (1) Social Stimulation, (2) Privacy, (3) Structure and past employment (Table 13-12), and between Support and type of prior employment (Table 13-13). Those who were unemployed before they were arrested are more likely to value Social Stimulation than those who held a job; they are also less prone to value Structure. Work experience is relevant on both counts, because hanging out in poolrooms is more conducive to gregariousness than life on an

TABLE 13-12. Distribution of Three Dimension Scores by Employment Status Prior to Confinement (Connecticut Sample)

	Unemployed ($\bar{X}=7.2$)		Employed ($\bar{X}=6.3$)	
	No.	(%)	No.	(%)
Social Stimulation score:				
Low	18	(24.0)	32	(34.8)
Medium	33	(44.0)	46	(50.0)
High	24	(32.0)	14	(15.2)
Total	75	(100.0)	92	(100.0)

Chi square = 7.0.
Significant at .05 level.
Contingency coefficient = .20.

	Unemployed ($\bar{X}=4.9$)		Employed ($\bar{X}=5.8$)	
	No.	(%)	No.	(%)
Privacy score:				
Low	21	(27.3)	21	(23.3)
Medium	39	(50.6)	33	(36.7)
High	17	(22.1)	36	(40.0)
Total	77	(100.0)	90	(100.0)

Chi square = 6.3.
Significant at .05 level.
Contingency coefficient = .19.

	Unemployed ($\bar{X}=5.8$)		Employed ($\bar{X}=6.4$)	
	No.	(%)	No.	(%)
Structure score:				
Low	24	(34.3)	17	(19.1)
Medium	30	(42.9)	38	(42.7)
High	16	(22.9)	34	(38.2)
Total	70	(100.1)	89	(100.0)

Chi square = 6.4.
Significant at .05 level.
Contingency coefficient = .20.

assembly line and is less likely to inculcate stability and the value of a steady routine.

Past employment is correlated with Privacy concerns. This fact may partly reflect (1) the impact of the young, gregarious, previously unemployed group on mature inmates, and (2) the results of a more serious and businesslike orientation toward life. Table 13-13 draws a different picture:

TABLE 13-13. Distribution of Support Scores by Employment History for the California Sample

| | Stability of Prior Employment | | | | Length of Prior Employment | | | |
| | Permanent Jobs | | Temporary Jobs | | Less than 6 Months | | One Year or Over | |
	N	(%)	N	(%)	N	(%)	N	(%)
Support scores:								
Low (1–9)	70	(37.6)	34	(25.8)	48	(27.9)	59	(39.9)
Medium (10–11)	81	(43.5)	57	(43.2)	73	(42.4)	64	(43.2)
High (12–14)	35	(18.8)	41	(31.1)	51	(29.7)	25	(16.9)
Total	186	(99.9)	132	(100.1)	172	(100.0)	148	(100.0)

Chi square = 8.2.
Significant at .02 level.
Contingency coefficient = .16.

Chi square = 8.9.
Significant at .02 level.
Contingency coefficient = .17.

It confirms that there is a pragmatic or reality base to many inmates' Support concerns. Men who need Support most—whose past ill prepares them for the future—are often aware of their deficit and concerned with remedying it. However (as suggested by Table 13-12 and by our correlation matrix in Chapter 12), such men often lack concerns, such as Structure, Activity, Privacy, Low Social Stimulation, or Low Freedom, that might increase their congruence with programs.

Patterns of Adjustment

A questionnaire version of the Process Reactive Index (Zigler and Phillips) was administered to the 201 prisoners at the Somers Institution. The instrument consists of twenty-four statements concerning past social behavior, educational experience, and economic, employment, and marital status. In responding to the questionnaire, a person indicates whether a given factual statement holds true in relation to his own history. If a person's response agrees with a pre-keyed answer (True or False) for a statement, it contributes to his total score. If an answer does not match the keyed choice, the respondent receives a score of zero. The total "process-reactive" score is the sum of scores for all the statements and can vary between 0 and 24. Higher scores describe a more effective support system in the community, which is presumed to facilitate emotional and personal adjustment.

The average process-reactive scores for the Somers sample are 13.7 (mean), 14 (mode), and 13.8 (median). With a standard deviation of 3.8, 68 percent of the 201 respondents score within a range of 9.9 to 17.5. The modified process-reactive scale proved reliable in terms of internal consistency. It yielded a coefficient alpha of .69.

We divided the sample into three process-reactive scale score categories, attempting to obtain an equal proportion of the sample in each class. High total scores related positively to (1) being married; (2) being employed prior to confinement; (3) being older; and, somewhat less dramatically, to (4) age at first conviction.

When we view these findings in light of the items that the scale comprises, we are not surprised, because some items are measures of background characteristics and others are closely linked. Almost half the items are concerned with marriage or employment. The higher scale scores for older men may be partly explained by the fact that both marriage and employment are related to age.

It makes sense that those who were first convicted at a relatively tender age would have a more checkered employment career and would find it more difficult to obtain employment than those with a clean conviction record for a longer time. Our data confirm that those with early convictions are less often employed prior to incarceration than those convicted for the first time when they were over eighteen. Our results also confirm that those convicted at an early age are typically younger men than those convicted later in life—at least, in the Somers sample.

Relationship between Prior Adjustment Patterns and PPI Dimensions

Table 13-14 displays the relationship between family membership and Emotional Feedback concerns. It tells us that men who are parents or who plan to return to their families after release tend to be oriented toward outside ties while in prison. Such men have a tangible stake in preserving the salience of their external world by de-emphasizing the importance of more immediate presses.

Parenthood is negatively related to Freedom concerns (Table 13-15). This is hard to understand, but it may link to a higher maturity level of men who undertake parental responsibilities. It is also possible that persons with children are less likely to be obsessed with their own child status vis-à-vis authority.

Another question associated with Freedom is Question 23, which deals with youthful affiliations involving "a grown-up who came to meetings." Positive experiences with early authority figures may make it easier later to accept the role of authorities as legitimate. Dependence may also be a relatively stable personality trait.

Another item associated with Freedom is past institutionalization. Chronic residents in total institutions seem more concerned with restrictions than those with less confinement experience. Resentment may well be cumulative. Institutional experience, on the other hand, seems to breed familiarity as well as contempt. Table 13-16 shows that experienced in-

TABLE 13-14. Family Membership Items Relating to Emotional Feedback

| | Feedback Score | | | |
	Low	Medium	High	Total
	No. (%)	No. (%)	No. (%)	No. (%)
Item 1:				
When I leave the prison, I will live with my wife.				
True	12 (23.5)	16 (31.4)	23 (45.1)	51 (100)
False	37 (31.6)	52 (44.4)	28 (23.9)	117 (99.9)
Total	49 (29.2)	68 (40.5)	51 (30.4)	168 (100.1)

Chi square = 7.540.
Significant = .05 level.
Contingency coefficient = .20724.

| | Feedback Score | | | |
	Low	Medium	High	Total
	No. (%)	No. (%)	No. (%)	No. (%)
Item 4:				
I have fathered children.				
True	22 (22.4)	40 (40.8)	36 (36.7)	98 (99.9)
False	29 (39.7)	28 (38.4)	16 (21.9)	73 (100)
Total	51 (29.8)	68 (39.8)	52 (30.4)	171 (100)

Chi square = 7.27.
Significance = .05 level.
Contingency coefficient = .20621.

mates are unlikely (compared to less experienced ones) to fear for their Safety in institutional environments.

Men who in their younger years experienced environments in which adult supervision was present seem to express more Safety concerns than other men. The absence of familiar support systems can increase one's sense of vulnerability, particularly when peers who did without supports early in life have acquired proficiency in urban jungle warfare.

Two items dealing with the stability of one's past life show relatively high associations with Structure. Table 13-17 (again) tells us that a steady employment pattern carries over into a high Structure concern in the institution. We also discover that experience with major life changes reduces one's dependency on environmental stability.

TABLE 13-15. Personal History Items Relating to Freedom Concerns

| | Freedom Score | | | |
	Low	Medium	High	Total
	No. (%)	No. (%)	No. (%)	No. (%)
Item 23:				
In my teens I was a regular member of a club or organization that had a grown-up who came to meetings (Scouts, School Club, 4-H, Church Youth Club, etc.).				
True	20 (27.8)	35 (48.6)	17 (23.6)	72 (100)
False	16 (15.4)	41 (39.4)	47 (45.2)	104 (100)
Total	36 (20.5)	76 (43.2)	64 (36.4)	176 (100.1)

Chi square = 9.48; significance = .01; contingency coefficient = .22603.

| | Freedom Score | | | |
	Low	Medium	High	Total
	No. (%)	No. (%)	No. (%)	No. (%)
Item 4:				
I have fathered children.				
True	27 (26.7)	45 (44.6)	29 (28.1)	101 (100)
False	8 (10.7)	32 (42.7)	35 (46.7)	75 (100.1)
Total	35 (19.9)	77 (43.8)	64 (36.4)	176 (100.1)

Chi square = 9.437; significance = .01; contingency coefficient = .23155.

| | Freedom Score | | | |
	Low	Medium	High	Total
	No. (%)	No. (%)	No. (%)	No. (%)
Item 22:				
Within the last five years I have spent more than half my time in a mental hospital or prison.				
True	7 (10.0)	30 (42.9)	33 (47.1)	70 (100)
False	29 (27.4)	46 (43.4)	31 (29.2)	106 (100)
Total	36 (20.5)	76 (43.2)	64 (36.4)	176 (100.1)

Chi square = 9.927; significance = .01; contingency coefficient = .23107.

TABLE 13-16. Personal History Items Relating to Safety Concerns

| | Safety Score | | | |
	Low	Medium	High	Total
	No. (%)	No. (%)	No. (%)	No. (%)

Item 23:
In my teens I was a regular member of a club or organization that had a grown-up who came to meetings (Scouts, School Club, 4-H, Church Youth Club, etc.).

	Low	Medium	High	Total
True	19 (28.8)	22 (33.3)	25 (37.9)	66 (100)
False	44 (43.6)	43 (42.6)	14 (13.9)	101 (100.1)
Total	63 (37.7)	65 (38.9)	39 (23.4)	167 (100)

Chi square = 13.046; significance = .01; contingency coefficient = .26918.

| | Safety Score | | | |
	Low	Medium	High	Total
	No. (%)	No. (%)	No. (%)	No. (%)

Item 22:
Within the last five years I have spent more than half my time in a mental hospital or prison.

	Low	Medium	High	Total
True	36 (53.7)	17 (25.4)	14 (20.9)	67 (100.0)
False	26 (26.3)	48 (48.5)	25 (25.3)	99 (100.1)
Total	62 (37.3)	65 (39.2)	39 (23.5)	166 (100)

Chi square = 13.846; significance = .001; contingency coefficient = .27747.

| | Safety Score | | | |
	Low	Medium	High	Total
	No. (%)	No. (%)	No. (%)	No. (%)

Item 5:
Before I was seventeen, I left the home I was raised in and never went back except for visits.

	Low	Medium	High	Total
True	28 (49.1)	22 (38.6)	7 (12.3)	57 (100)
False	35 (32.1)	42 (38.5)	32 (29.4)	109 (100)
Total	63 (38.0)	64 (38.6)	39 (23.5)	166 (100.1)

Chi square = 7.500; significance = .05; contingency coefficient .20792.

TABLE 13-17. Personal History Items Relating to Structure Concerns

	Structure Score			
	Low	Medium	High	Total
	No.	No.	No.	No.
	(%)	(%)	(%)	(%)
Item 16:				
Shortly before I came into jail, there was some major change in my life (other than being imprisoned), such as marriage, the birth of a baby, death, injury, loss of a job, etc.				
True	36	49	32	117
	(30.8)	(41.9)	(27.4)	(100.1)
False	5	19	18	42
	(11.9)	(45.2)	(42.9)	(100.0)
Total	41	68	50	159
	(25.8)	(42.8)	(31.4)	(100)

Chi square = 6.71.
Significance = .05.
Contingency coefficient = .20123.

	Structure Score			
	Low	Medium	High	Total
	No.	No.	No.	No.
	(%)	(%)	(%)	(%)
Item 20:				
I have earned my living for longer than a year at full-time civilian work.				
True	24	38	42	104
	(23.1)	(36.5)	(40.4)	(100)
False	17	29	8	54
	(31.5)	(53.7)	(14.8)	(100)
Total	41	67	50	158
	(25.9)	(42.4)	(31.6)	(99.9)

Chi square = 10.780.
Significance = .01.
Contingency coefficient = .25274.

Of major interest is the fact that adult persons who have limited their social interaction during childhood seem later to be disproportionately concerned with Privacy and unconcerned with Social Stimulation (Table 13-18). Here we have a dramatic instance of adjustment patterns that were developed early in life and continue to govern the habits and concerns of adults in their mature years.

TABLE 13-18. Item Describing Childhood Socialization Pattern Relating to Privacy and Social Stimulation Concerns

| | Privacy Score | | | |
	Low	Medium	High	Total
	No. (%)	No. (%)	No. (%)	No. (%)
Item 11: I hardly ever went over to another kid's house after school or on weekends.				
True	8 (17.0)	18 (38.3)	21 (44.7)	47 (100)
False	34 (28.1)	56 (46.3)	31 (25.6)	121 (100)
Total	42 (25.0)	74 (44.0)	52 (31.0)	168 (100)

Chi square = 6.125.
Significance = .05.
Contingency coefficient = .18755.

| | Social Stimulation Score | | | |
	Low	Medium	High	Total
	No. (%)	No. (%)	No. (%)	No. (%)
Item 11: I hardly ever went over to another kid's house after school or on weekends.				
True	22 (48.9)	16 (35.6)	7 (15.6)	45 (100.1)
False	28 (23.0)	63 (51.6)	31 (25.4)	122 (100)
Total	50 (29.9)	79 (47.3)	38 (22.8)	167 (100)

Chi square = 10.588.
Significance = .01.
Contingency coefficient = .24417.

Profile Dimensions and Self-esteem Clusters

Among the instruments that were administered to the California sample was the Bennett/Cooper Self Esteem Scale (SAI), a derivative of the Coopersmith Self Esteem Inventory (Bennett, Sorensen, and Forshay). In taking this instrument, the respondent classifies fifty statements as either applying to himself ("like me") or not ("unlike me").

Since we had individual responses to the SAI items, we explored the relationship of these items to the PPI dimensions. The result of our analysis is presented in Tables 13-19 through 13-22.

Table 13-19 lists self-satisfaction items that discriminate Low-freedom inmates (who admit that they are not perfect) from other inmates. The items bear on the inmates' amenability to correctional intervention, because they suggest that Freedom concerns go hand in hand with self-classed un-improvability. The one attribute High-freedom inmates do not claim is congenial parents; they also show little pride in their work, which they admit is less than perfect.

A contrasting portrait is that of the High-feedback inmates. Table 13-20 suggests that Feedback concerns often entail a self-conception of weakness of character and of transparent vulnerability. The defenses of these inmates

TABLE 13-19. Relationship of Freedom Scores to Self-Confidence Items from the SAI (California Sample)

		Low		Medium		High	
		No.	(%)	No.	(%)	No.	(%)
Item:							
8. There are a lot of things about myself I'd change if I could.	NO	27	(31.8)	29	(34.1)	29	(34.1)[a]
	yes	103	(45.2)[a]	88	(38.6)	37	(16.2)
15. I'm often sorry for the things I do.	NO	38	(30.4)	54	(43.2)	33	(26.4)
	yes	92	(48.9)[a]	63	(33.5)	33	(17.6)
40. If I have something to say, I usually say it.	no	36	(54.5)[a]	25	(37.9)	5	(7.6)
	YES	94	(38.1)	92	(37.2)	61	(24.7)[a]
19. I give in very easily.	NO	71	(35.0)	85	(41.9)	47	(23.2)
	yes	59	(53.6)[a]	32	(29.1)	19	(17.3)
25. I understand myself.	no	56	(52.3)[b]	33	(30.8)	18	(16.8)
	YES	74	(35.9)	84	(40.8)	48	(23.3)
49. Things usually don't bother me.	no	60	(43.5)	58	(42.0)	20	(14.5)
	YES	70	(40.0)	59	(33.7)	46	(26.3)[b]
39. I'm not as nice look-ing as most people.	NO	90	(37.5)	97	(40.4)	53	(22.1)
	yes	40	(54.8)[b]	20	(27.4)	13	(17.8)
44. I'm a failure.	NO	96	(38.1)	102	(40.5)	54	(21.4)
	yes	34	(55.7)[b]	15	(24.6)	12	(19.7)
Other Items Related to Freedom from the SAI:							
6. My parents and I used to have a lot of fun together.	NO	37	(32.7)	45	(39.8)	31	(27.4)
	yes	93	(46.5)[b]	72	(36.0)	35	(17.5)
18. I'm doing the best work that I can.	NO	23	(37.1)	19	(30.6)	20	(32.3)[b]
	yes	107	(42.6)	98	(39.0)	46	(18.3)

[a]Difference significant > .01 level.
[b]Difference significant > .05 level.

TABLE 13-20. Relationship of Feedback Scores to Self-Criticism Items from the SAI (California Sample)

		Low No.	Low (%)	Medium No.	Medium (%)	High No.	High (%)
			Feedback Score				
Item:							
19. I give in very easily.	no	79	(37.3)[a]	84	(39.6)	49	(23.1)
	YES	23	(20.0)	48	(41.7)	44	(38.3)
31. I can make up my mind and stick to it.	NO	15	(24.2)	19	(30.6)	28	(45.2)[b]
	yes	87	(32.8)	113	(42.6)	65	(24.5)
37. I often feel upset in school.	no	85	(36.0)[b]	86	(36.4)	65	(27.5)
	YES	17	(18.7)	46	(50.5)	28	(30.8)
49. Things usually don't bother me.	NO	35	(24.0)	59	(40.4)	52	(35.6)[b]
	yes	67	(37.0)[b]	73	(40.3)	41	(22.7)
12. I always do the right things	NO	68	(28.0)	97	(39.9)	78	(32.1)[c]
	yes	34	(40.5)	35	(41.7)	15	(17.9)
41. The staff makes me feel I'm not good enough.	no	92	(33.9)[c]	108	(39.9)	71	(26.2)
	YES	10	(17.9)	24	(42.9)	22	(39.3)[c]
8. There are lots of things about myself I'd change if I could.	no	36	(41.9)[c]	28	(32.6)	22	(25.6)
	YES	66	(27.4)	104	(43.2)	71	(29.5)

[a]Difference significant at .001 level.
[b]Difference significant > .01 level.
[c]Difference significant > .05 level.

TABLE 13-21. Relationship of Privacy Scores to Social Rejection Items from the SAI (California Sample)

		Low No.	Low (%)	Medium No.	Medium (%)	High No.	High (%)
			Privacy Score				
Item:							
34. I don't like to be with other people.	no	106	(41.7)	103	(40.6)	45	(17.7)
	YES	17	(25.4)	25	(37.3)	25	(37.3)[a]
44. I'm a failure.	no	108	(42.0)[b]	101	(39.3)	48	(18.7)
	YES	15	(23.4)	27	(42.2)	22	(34.4)[b]
33. I have a low opinion of myself.	no	108	(42.2)[b]	100	(39.1)	48	(18.8)
	YES	15	(23.1)	28	(43.1)	22	(33.8)[b]
10. I'm a lot of fun to be with.	NO	17	(27.4)	23	(37.1)	22	(35.5)[b]
	yes	106	(40.9)	105	(40.5)	48	(18.5)
16. I'm popular with people my own age.	NO	22	(27.5)	35	(43.8)	23	(28.7)
	yes	101	(41.9)[b]	93	(38.6)	47	(19.5)
21. I'm pretty unhappy.	no	96	(42.9)[c]	86	(38.4)	42	(18.8)
	YES	27	(27.8)	42	(43.3)	28	(28.9)
Related Item:							
42. I always tell the truth.	no	79	(44.4)[b]	58	(32.6)	41	(23.0)
	YES	44	(30.8)	70	(49.0)	29	(20.3)

[a]Difference significant at .001 level.
[b]Difference significant > .01 level.
[c]Difference significant > .05 level.

are low, and their change potential is, if anything, too high for their own good.

Table 13-21 shows High-privacy persons who see themselves as unworthy, unamusing, and justifiably undesirable. The positive item associated with Privacy ("I always tell the truth") connotes lack of sophistication or social skill. A very different self-view is that of Social Stimulation inmates, who see themselves as the lives of any party and who admit that they can lie as well as the next man (Table 13-22).

These relationships are merely suggestive and of restricted applicability. But they are useful to us because they place some environmental preferences in context. They suggest that Freedom and Feedback may sometimes place demands on the environment (for "respect" or for "help") that spring from exaggeratedly favorable or unfavorable views of self. Companionship or isolation can be sought by persons who have high or low assessments of themselves as social objects.

TABLE 13-22. Relationship of Social Stimulation Scores to Social Acceptance Items from the SAI (California Sample)

| | | Social Stimulation Score | | | | | |
| | | Low | | Medium | | High | |
		No.	(%)	No.	(%)	No.	(%)
Items:							
44. I'm a failure.	NO	66	(25.2)	112	(42.7)	84	(32.1)[a]
	yes	23	(35.4)	38	(58.5)	4	(6.2)
16. I'm popular with	no	32	(39.5)[b]	36	(44.4)	13	(16.0)
people my own age.	YES	57	(23.2)	114	(46.3)	75	(30.5)[b]
26. It's pretty tough to	NO	46	(23.5)	87	(44.4)	63	(32.1)[c]
be me.	yes	43	(32.8)	63	(48.1)	25	(19.1)
Related Item:							
42. I always tell the	NO	42	(23.1)	82	(45.1)	58	(31.9)[c]
truth.	yes	47	(32.4)[c]	68	(46.9)	30	(20.7)

[a]Difference significant at .001 level.
[b]Difference significant > .01 level.
[c]Difference significant > .05 level.

Environmental Preferences and the Environment "Opportunity Structure"

Our Lexington sample helped us to investigate differences in environmental concerns that could be related not only to inmate backgrounds but also to their responses to different environmental opportunities. To help us get at these relationships, we administered the prison rating scale described in Chapter 1 to each PPI respondent at Lexington.

Compared to ratings of prison by the inmates in Chapter 8, the satisfaction scores of the Lexington clients makes this group appear to be enraptured in Shangri-La rather than languishing as involuntary confinees in a prison. We see in Table 13-23 that the modal scale score is 10, the highest score one can obtain on the scale. The next score in ranking is 9, and more than half the population rated Lexington a 9 or 10 in relation to their needs.

We already know something about the environmental preferences and aversions of inmates in general. For example, we know that Support and Feedback are the two highest-ranking dimensions of the PPI, and that Freedom and Privacy are the two lowest-ranking dimensions. In what ways do these high and low ranking concerns relate to the inmates' assessments of their working and living environment? Once we know this, we can ask whether inmates who have different profiles of concern are happier or unhappier in the same setting.

Tables 13-24 and 13-25 display two different views of the relationship between prison ratings and dimension scores. In Table 13-24, we see Privacy and Freedom as dimensions along which satisfied and dissatisfied Lexington inmates vary. Less-satisfied inmates register higher average Privacy and Freedom scores than more-satisfied inmates. Table 13-25 presents a similar picture. The largest discrepancies in mean scale scores between high and low dimension categories appear in the Privacy and Freedom dimensions, with an additional difference (in the opposite direction) in the Support category. The Lexington environment is clearly fortunate

TABLE 13-23. **Distribution of Prison Rankings for the Lexington Population**

Scale Score	No.	(%)
0	59	11.5
1	0	0.0
2	4	.8
3	17	3.3
4	5	1.0
5	33	6.4
6	19	3.7
7	19	3.7
8	58	11.3
9	71	13.9
10	227	44.3
Total	512	(99.9)

TABLE 13-24. Mean Dimension Scores for Groups with High and Low Prison Ratings

Dimension	Mean for Group with High Ratings (0–8)	Mean for Group with Lower Ratings (9–10)	Mean Score for Total Population
Privacy	6.1	5.2	5.5
Safety	7.2	7.7	7.5
Structure	6.8	6.9	6.9
Support	9.2	9.4	9.3
Emotional Feedback	8.5	8.9	8.7
Social Stimulation	6.4	6.7	6.6
Activity	6.6	6.9	6.7
Freedom	5.6	4.6	5.0

TABLE 13-25. Mean Prison Ratings by Dimension Scores for the Lexington Population

Dimension	Score	Mean Prison Rating
Privacy	Low	7.8
	Medium	8.2
	High	6.9
Safety	Low	7.6
	Medium	7.8
	High	7.9
Structure	Low	7.7
	Medium	7.8
	High	7.8
Support	Low	7.5
	Medium	7.4
	High	8.5
Emotional Feedback	Low	7.5
	Medium	7.7
	High	8.1
Social Stimulation	Low	7.2
	Medium	8.0
	High	8.0
Activity	Low	7.8
	Medium	7.8
	High	7.8
Freedom	Low	8.2
	Medium	7.9
	High	6.9

in one significant respect: The lowest-ranking categories of the PPI (Freedom and Privacy) are prone to make inmates dissatisfied with Lexington. The highest-ranking dimension (Support) predisposes them to contentment.

Profile of the Lexington Climate

What about the impact of the prison climate at Lexington? We can examine the subenvironments (living units) and their associations to our dimensions and to satisfaction levels of the residents. The programs of the Lexington units include Rational Behavior Training, Transactional Analysis, Self-awareness, Group Dynamics, Self-assertive Training, and Group Growth, in addition to individual counseling. In some units these programs are mandatory.

The general impression made by Lexington is that it is a therapeutically oriented institution with programs designed to promote a high level of group interaction, problem sharing, personal disclosure, self-improvement, and accountability to others.

If this portrayal is accurate, Lexington appears to be an environment that should be attractive to High-feedback and High-support inmates. The program offerings seem tailored to inmates who desire intimacy, empathy, and chances for approval or self-improvement. When we subdivide our dimensions into standard categories (high = 10–14, medium = 5–9 and low = 0–4), we find that 48.4 percent of the Lexington population falls in the high-support category and 39.4 percent is in the high-feedback category. Such persons should find a propitious environment in Lexington. The Lexington environment by the same logic should be less inviting when viewed from the perspective of a minority of inmates. As an example, we can visualize a man with a strong Privacy concern at Lexington. In such a man, we have a person who prefers solitude and interpersonal distance. He avoids involvement and overstimulation and (as we know from Chapter 12) he does not really care for Support, Feedback, or Social Stimulation. We see our high-privacy person (Inmate P) in his cell enjoying peace and quiet (at last!) after attending what he considers a very irritating group counseling session. This week it has been his turn to discuss an intimate personal problem, and the group was unimpressed by the amount of personal disclosure he offered. Inmate F stops before P's cell and invites himself in. F's purpose is to help P with his immediate problem, which (as F sees it) is P's aversion to talking about himself in front of a group. P asks F to leave his cell, and F exits convinced that the incident will be appropriate material for the next group meeting. P settles back into his thoughts when a noisy, spontaneous group session begins in an adjacent cell. P is invited to join the group but declines and walks out to the dayroom. He feels and looks irritated and confused. Counselor X approaches P in the dayroom and asks him if everything is all right. P curtly responds "Yes" and returns to his cell. There he sits, silently hoping for a power failure to put out the lights so he can be alone in the darkness.

We note that P's Privacy concern cannot be satisfied because of predictable incursions into his life by people seeking gratification for other concerns. We also notice a Freedom theme emerging when P begins to resent the fact that he is bombarded by interlopers in his personal space. He feels harassed: Why are people interfering with him? Why do they insist? Can't a man run his own life?

In terms of the standard dimension categories, people with high Freedom scores are more rare in Lexington than individuals with high Privacy scores (6.2 percent and 9.7 percent, respectively), and as we saw in Table 13-25, this minority is as unhappy in Lexington as are high-privacy persons. Of course, High-freedom inmates are unhappy in all prisons, because the individual with a strong interest in Freedom wants to be self-governing. When others attempt to make "therapeutic" decisions for such a person, he considers it an infringement of his rights. In the case of Lexington, group assistance may be considered another intrusion and accountability another restriction.

We have suggested that Lexington is an environment that engenders and provides for certain specific needs, and that inmates who express these needs constitute a large part of the Lexington population. The scale ratings for the Lexington population indicate that the majority of the prisoners consider their institutional needs fulfilled and that those individuals who have strong Feedback and Support concerns are especially content. In sum, we infer that Lexington possesses environmental qualities that seem to match the needs and expectations of the majority of its residents.

Transactional Congruence in Subenvironments

We can now consider some of the variables that may be associated with transactional congruence at Lexington. We can survey the level of contentment and the environmental preferences of inmates who reside in the various subenvironments of Lexington. First, a description of the units and of their residents is in order.

The *Comprehensive Health Unit* houses minimum-custody residents who are ill but not immobilized. The purpose of the unit is

> . . . to fill the void that exists between the hospital unit where an individual has 24-hour nursing coverage and the regular unit where an individual is expected to follow the regular routine and work a normal shift and participate in all of the normal activities.

Work assignments in the CHU primarily include chores around the unit, and voluntary programs are "aimed at adjustment to the institution and adjustment to disability." These programs include the Positive Mental Attitude Group, Toastmasters International, and Greater Ideas.

Table 13-26 shows us that the Comprehensive Health Unit is one of the two units at Lexington that houses both men and women; compared to the other living units, the Comprehensive Health Unit has the greatest percentage of residents who are (1) over thirty-five years of age; (2) members of the unit for a relatively short period; and (3) white. The unit's population has also attained a comparatively high education level.

The population of the *Antaeus Unit* is composed of male alcoholics and problem drinkers. The program includes a six-week introductory phase, consisting of four hours of classes per week. Classes are offered in basics of Rational Behavior Training, Transactional Analysis, Self-awareness, and Group Dynamics. The unit has a general requirement of one hour of group counseling and one half-hour of individual counseling each week, in addition to demanding satisfactory performance in an institutional assignment.

The Antaeus population is composed of fairly old, white, uneducated residents who tend to have lived in the unit for more than two months.

Half of the *Women's Unit* contains small private rooms, and the remainder of the rooms house two inmates. There are no program descriptions for the Women's Unit. The inmates housed in the WU are typically young and black and have had some high school education.

The *Renaissance Unit* is another female housing unit. It features programs that "speak to problem areas that are common to most women confined." These program offerings include Self-Esteem Group, Self-assertative Training Group, Domestic Survival, Parental Effectiveness, and training in nontraditional careers for women. The population is demographically similar to that of the Women's Unit but contains an even greater proportion of young and black women.

The *Veritas Unit* houses both male and female prisoners. The unit philosophy places emphasis on

> . . . truth, truthfulness, open communication based upon the philosophy of frankness, consistency and mutual respect, along with assuming responsible behavior.

The program includes a two-week orientation and one mandatory group session per week. Veritas also offers a Planned Parenthood Group and a Self-awareness Group.

The *Younity Unit* contains male drug addicts, twenty-five and older, who are within eighteen to twenty-four months of release. The introductory program at Younity consists of twelve one-and-one-half-hour Human Relation Laboratory sessions in which decision making, communication skills,

TABLE 13-26. Characteristics of the Residents of the Lexington Housing Units

	Comprehensive Health (N=95)	Antaeus (N=48)	Womens (N=101)	Renaissance (N=37)	Veritas (N=67)	Younity (N=59)	Numen (N=55)
Sex							
Female	34.7%	0	100%	100%	61.2%	0	0
Male	65.3	100%	0	0	38.8	100%	100%
Age							
17–25	6.1	4.2	65.6	80.0	65.7	8.5	26.4
26–35	18.9	43.8	30.1	17.1	28.4	71.2	54.7
Over 35	75.0	52.0	4.3	2.9	6.0	20.3	18.9
Length of residence in unit							
0–2 months	35.8	10.4	27.0	22.9	18.5	22.4	23.1
Over 2 months	64.2	89.6	73.0	77.1	81.5	77.6	76.9
Ethnicity							
White	79.1	71.0	35.8	34.4	50.9	41.5	52.2
Black	20.9	29.0	64.2	65.6	49.1	58.5	47.8
Education							
Elementary	20.2	36.7	8.0	2.9	16.4	5.1	11.3
High school	42.6	36.7	68.0	68.6	61.2	55.9	60.4
College	37.2	26.5	24.0	28.6	22.4	39.0	28.3

feedback techniques, and preparation for advanced group counseling are taught. The inmate can choose among the formal programs, which include individual counseling, Group Growth, Transactional Analysis, and a pre-release program.

Compared to the composition of the other units at Lexington, the most distinctive features of the Younity group are a large percentage of members in the twenty-six to thirty-five age group and a disproportionate number of inmates with some college education.

The purpose of the *Numen Unit* "is to provide a resident with a group of significant others who provide consistent behavioral expectations, and who consistently make him aware of his behavior." The program relies heavily on group interaction, but voluntary group and individual counseling are available. The majority of the Numen members are in the middle-age group, and the unit contains males exclusively.

Environmental Preferences and Satisfaction Levels of the Living Unit Groups

Table 13-27 displays the mean dimension scores for the various Lexington living units; the mean prison ratings and the percentages of each group in the high- and low-satisfaction groups are shown in Table 13-28.

The *Comprehensive Health Unit* yields the highest mean for Structure and the lowest for Freedom—7.6 and 4.3 respectively (Table 13-27), and Table 13-28 shows that the group ranks second among units in mean satisfaction and has the largest percentage of people in the highly contented category.

We know from our description of the CH Unit that it contains a greater proportion and absolute number of people in the above-thirty-five age category than any other Lexington subenvironment. We also know that the older inmate has a relatively high concern for Structure and a fairly low concern for Freedom. We can speculate that the Comprehensive Health Unit may have environmental qualities that provide the stability and predictability desired by its predominately older population.

The Comprehensive Health Unit illustrates the results of matching environments with human concerns because, generally, persons with high-structure profiles are not particularly happy at Lexington. Yet here, when we divide the Lexington population by subenvironments, we find a group of older individuals with a relatively strong interest in Structure who are quite content with a highly supportive, low-pressure program.

The members of *Antaeus* appear to value Social Stimulation and Activity and are relatively uninterested in Safety and Support. The Antaeus population comprises predominately older white male residents who have

TABLE 13-27. Mean Dimension Scores by Living Units

	Antaeus	Comprehensive Health	Women's	Renaissance	Veritas	Younity	Numen	Total
Privacy	6.1	5.5	6.1	5.5	5.2	4.7	5.2	5.5
Safety	6.6	7.6	7.0	7.7	8.2	7.8	7.6	7.5
Structure	7.4	7.6	7.0	6.0	6.5	6.7	6.4	6.9
Support	8.3	8.8	9.2	10.0	10.0	9.9	9.3	9.3
Emotional Feedback	8.5	8.8	8.5	8.8	9.0	8.2	9.6	8.7
Social Stimulation	7.4	6.4	6.3	6.2	5.9	6.8	7.3	6.6
Activity	7.5	6.9	6.7	6.6	6.9	6.1	6.3	6.7
Freedom	4.8	4.3	5.4	5.1	5.0	5.6	5.0	5.0

TABLE 13-28. Mean Prison Ratings and Satisfaction Scores by Living Units

A. Mean Prison Ratings by Living Units

Ratings:	Antaeus	Comprehensive Health	Women's	Renaissance	Veritas	Younity	Numen	Total
Mean	7.8	8.1	6.4	7.7	7.2	8.6	7.6	7.5
Rank of mean	3	2	7	4	6	1	5	

B. Satisfaction Scores by Living Units

	Antaeus		Comprehensive Health		Women's		Renaissance		Veritas		Younity		Numen		Total	
	No.	(%)	No.	(%)	No.	(%)	No.	(%)	No.	(%)	No.	(%)	No.	(%)	No.	(%)
Low 0–8	18	(32.1)	30	(27.0)	63	(58.9)	19	(45.2)	35	(47.3)	22	(34.9)	27	(46.6)	214	(41.9)
High 9–10	38	(67.9)	81	(73.0)	44	(41.1)	23	(54.8)	39	(52.7)	41	(65.1)	31	(53.4)	297	(58.1)
Total	56	(100)	111	(100)	107	(100)	42	(100)	74	(100)	63	(100)	58	(100)	511	

Chi square = 27.8.
Significant at .001 level.
Contingency coefficient = .227

been in the unit more than two months. Previous findings showed us a positive association between age and Activity and a negative relationship between age and Support at Lexington. We also found that whites were more strongly interested in Activity and less in Support than blacks. What we see in Table 13-28 is that Antaeus has the third highest satisfaction score mean and that 67.9 percent of the population ranked the institution a 9 or a 10. It appears that Antaeus provides a congenial setting for a group of men who have lived together for some time and who are not only similar in ethnicity and age but share a common experience—the memory of drinking. We also assume that the Antaeus offers its residents ample opportunity to stay occupied but does not feature substantive or vocational training.

The residents of the *Women's Unit* scored higher on Privacy and Freedom than the inhabitants of other units at Lexington. Table 13-27 shows the women of this unit tied on the high Privacy mean score and in second place for the highest Freedom mean score.

It is obvious from what we know about the relationship between Freedom, Privacy, and satisfaction that the Women's Unit contains the toughest clientele at Lexington. We are not surprised to find these inmates to be the most discontented as a group. Available programs may serve some needs, but an average satisfaction score of 6.4 at Lexington is not indicative of inmate–environment congruence.

Although the *Renaissance Unit* houses women, it differs from the Women's Unit in significant ways. There are proportionately more black women housed in the Renaissance unit, the percentage of younger inmates is greater, the population is generally smaller, and special programs are offered.

Table 13-27 suggests that the women of the Renaissance Unit are relatively unconcerned with Structure and that they score fairly high on the Support dimension. It may very well be that the Renaissance program has helped to create a general interest in self-improvement among its women, which may assist in dispelling memories of failure. The unit also may feature spontaneity, intimacy, low pressure, and minimal scheduling in its climate, which invites participation on its clients' own terms.

The members of the *Veritas Unit* score comparatively high on Safety and low on Social Stimulation. They are also an unhappy group in terms of their scale score averages. Veritas is a coeducational unit that contains more women than men, and we have found that women are less concerned with Social Stimulation than men. These facts must be viewed in the context of programming that features confrontations and open communication in a heterogeneous population. Veritas's population scores relatively high on the Support dimension; the programs of the unit must therefore show that they will help inmates adjust to the community, which is not the most plausible purpose of sensitivity training.

Table 13-27 places *Younity* members low on Privacy and relatively high on Support. The Younity Unit has the highest satisfaction mean, with 65.1 percent of its members in the 9 or 10 scale score category.

The Younity Unit contains men who are within eighteen to twenty-four months of release. These men are involved in intensive therapeutic programming, with the emphasis of some of the programs being on promoting post-release success. The focus on preparation for the community may highlight the availability of Support, and it may create an interest in acquiring necessary skills.

The unit's low Privacy average coupled with its low Feedback score suggests preference for intensive interactions that do not entail intimate bonds. Such a profile may. reflect the needs of older addicts for tangible but nonthreatening help.

We know that there is a positive relationship between Support and happiness at Lexington, and a negative association between Privacy and satisfaction. The Younity group therefore fits our general statistical picture of the satisfied Lexington inmate.

A *very* high concern with Feedback and a concern with Social Stimulation characterize the *Numen Unit* residents. Our description of Numen highlights the fact that the program stresses group interactions and counseling, which would hold positive valence for these inmates. Other program emphases (such as behavior feedback and control) might be less well received, since the Numen population ranks relatively low on Structure. The picture is unclear to us, because the unit falls somewhat below the average in the Lexington rating scale. It probably features some junctures of congruence and some of incongruence.

As with the Younity population, the concerns expressed by Numenites match one of our statistical findings. We have found that the highest dimension–dimension correlation at Lexington is between Feedback and Social Stimulation (Table 13-30). Numen residents are among those who desire an environment that provides emotional sustenance and congeniality.

The Relationship of Dimension Scores and Satisfaction within Units

Table 13-29 tabulates average dimension scores against satisfaction levels in the Lexington living units. Our finding that those with high Privacy or Freedom scores are less content with the institution holds for all the units, but the difference is not uniform. The key Privacy issue arises for the Numen Unit, which is sharply polarized along privacy lines. The inmate who is most unhappy in this unit, which provides him with "significant others . . . who make him aware of his behavior," is concerned about viola-

TABLE 13-29. Mean Dimension Scores by Low and High Scale Scores for the Lexington Living Units

Dimension X̄ for	Low (0–8) High (9–10) Satisfaction	Antaeus	Comprehensive	Women's	Rennaisance	Veritas	Younity	Numen
Privacy Mean	Low	6.4	5.9	6.5	5.5	5.9	5.2	6.6
	High	6.0	5.4	5.3	5.5	4.5	4.6	4.4
Safety Mean	Low	6.6	6.9	7.0	7.2	8.0	6.8	7.3
	High	6.5	7.8	7.0	8.2	8.5	8.3	7.8
Structure Mean	Low	7.9	7.6	7.0	5.8	6.5	6.1	6.1
	High	7.1	7.6	6.8	6.1	6.3	6.9	6.6
Support Mean	Low	8.3	9.8	8.5	9.5	9.5	9.8	9.6
	High	8.3	8.6	10.0	10.5	10.4	10.0	9.0
Emotional Feedback Mean	Low	8.2	8.1	8.2	9.2	8.7	8.1	9.0
	High	8.7	9.0	8.9	8.4	9.2	8.2	10.1
Social Stimulation Mean	Low	7.0	6.2	5.9	5.9	5.7	7.4	7.5
	High	7.5	6.4	6.8	6.5	6.1	6.6	7.1
Activity Mean	Low	7.1	6.7	6.8	6.8	6.9	5.3	5.9
	High	7.7	7.0	6.6	6.4	6.8	6.4	6.7
Freedom Mean	Low	5.2	4.7	6.0	5.8	5.6	6.2	5.2
	High	4.6	4.1	4.6	4.4	4.4	5.5	4.7

tions of his Privacy. He is also lower on Feedback than his peers, though his discontent is tempered by an appreciation for the Social Stimulation afforded in the unit.

The Veritas Unit has the next highest difference between happy Low-privacy inmates and a less satisfied High-privacy group. This is not surprising, in view of the unit's stress on "truth, truthfulness, open communication . . . the philosophy of frankness," etc. Persons who are more content in the unit seem to be those who view its confronting climate as sufficiently beneficial (high Support) to risk self-disclosing.

The next highest Privacy difference occurs for the Women's Unit; contented Women's Unit inmates are also less concerned with Freedom issues. Despite its generally tough population, the program appeals to some women who are lower than others in their concern with Freedom and Privacy and who gain more satisfaction than others from Social Stimulation and programs. There is a marked difference in the Support scores of satisfied and dissatisfied residents.

The largest discrepancy in Freedom scores (with the discontent inmates ranking high on Freedom) exists in the Renaissance unit, which is also made up of women. But this unit benefits from a favorable reception of its training programs, as is shown by the high Support scores of its satisfied residents. Renaissance also appears to provide a feeling of security to inmates who prize Safety.

A Lexington unit that stands out as a haven of Safety is Younity, which contains the population of older drug offenders. Younity also offers opportunities for some distracting or cathartic activity for those who need it.

The Comprehensive Health Unit appears to be a psychologically secure (high Safety) climate. However, CHU stands out as a nontraining (low Support) environment. It is the only unit at Lexington in which inmates who prize Support are relatively discontented. On the other hand, the unit furnishes *emotional* support and personal attention. CHU ranks with Numen as a climate in which inmates who prize intimacy, care, and love are relatively content.

Dimensional Patterns and Congruence

Table 13-30 shows the associations between PPI dimensions for all of our samples. We see that the relationships between some of the dimensions are more substantial in the Lexington population than in our other samples. These relationships include (1) the positive correlation between Social Stimulation and Emotional Feedback, (2) the negative association between Structure and (a) Emotional Feedback and (b) Support, (3) the negative correlation between Privacy and Emotional Feedback, (4) the

TABLE 13-30. Dimension to Dimension Correlation Coefficients (Corrected)

	Safety	Structure	Support	Emotional Feedback	Stimulation	Activity	Freedom
Privacy							
California	−.26	−.05	−.62	−.56	−.56	−.26	.35
New York	−.38	−.001	−.45	−.49	−.58	−.22	.22
Connecticut	−.10	.14	−.52	−.42	−.70	−.20	.21
Pennsylvania	−.29	−.11	−.23	−.41	−.61	−.34	.29
Lexington	−.21	.10	−.43	−.68	−.69	−.27	.17
Safety							
California		−.47	−.11	−.09	−.25	−.10	−.52
New York		−.33	.12	.003	−.28	−.36	−.59
Connecticut		−.20	−.25	−.08	−.35	−.33	−.53
Pennsylvania		−.48	−.35	−.10	−.24	−.08	−.35
Lexington		−.23	.10	−.21	−.20	−.32	−.44
Structure							
California			−.16	−.001	−.29	−.25	−.28
New York			−.34	−.33	−.32	−.12	−.001
Connecticut			−.31	−.13	−.55	−.29	−.26
Pennsylvania			−.10	−.06	−.44	−.18	−.16
Lexington			−.57	−.64	−.39	−.13	−.05
Support							
California				−.19	.16	−.14	−.29
New York				−.20	−.23	−.16	−.68
Connecticut				−.18	−.27	.13	−.38
Pennsylvania				−.06	−.22	−.06	−.36
Lexington				−.12	−.23	−.07	−.45
Emotional Feedback							
California					−.05	−.36	−.45
New York					.06	−.48	−.42
Connecticut					.14	−.55	−.30
Pennsylvania					−.13	−.58	−.49
Lexington					.31	−.16	−.35
Social Stimulation							
California						−.23	−.09
New York						−.09	−.13
Connecticut						−.15	−.05
Pennsylvania						−.01	−.06
Lexington						−.30	−.33
Activity							
California							−.33
New York							−.16
Connecticut							−.21
Pennsylvania							−.29
Lexington							−.51

negative relationship between Freedom and Activity. The negative association between Emotional Feedback and Activity is weaker in the Federal data than for other samples.

These patterns make sense of the congruence we seem to find between the Lexington environment and the PPI profiles of its inmates.

Lexington is a therapeutic milieu. Sociability and the open expression of feelings in the programs (Social Stimulation and Emotional Feedback) run hand in hand. Therapy and training are offered in an informal, quasi-spontaneous fashion (Structure is negatively related to Feedback and Support). Inmates share their experiences and reveal their motives in therapeutic interactions (negative correlation between Privacy and Feedback). In their spare time, the inmates are free to engage in extracurricular pursuits (Freedom is negatively correlated with Activity). Extracurricular pursuits, however, are not really integrated with the therapeutic milieu (weak negative correlation between Emotional Feedback and Activity).

Our point would be that, while this portrait is a somewhat idealized description of the Lexington milieu, the correlations are associations that we find in the PPI matrix. The congruence we describe is not one-to-one dimensional correspondence, but suggests a *patterned* relationship between the *climate* of an environment and the *profile* of its inhabitants' concerns.

The Interview Results and the PPI Data

In Chapter 8 we reviewed the results of our effort to code open-ended inmate interviews for the prevalence of transactional themes. The content analysis yielded a frequency profile that can be compared to the PPI profile.

Figure 13-1 depicts both of the profiles and shows their similarities and differences. We see that Freedom and Activity appear differently in the two sets of data: Freedom is a frequently mentioned concern of interview subjects, but it ranks low among the PPI concerns. Activity is on the other hand comparatively rare in interviews, but salient on the PPI. In other respects, the distributions are similar.

With respect to demographic profiles, we recall that several relationships emerged from our analysis of interview themes:

1. In comparison to whites, blacks expressed greater concern for Support and Freedom (Table 8-3).
2. Whites were more interested in Safety and Activity than blacks (Table 8-3).
3. Young inmates showed a concern for Privacy and concern about Safety, while older inmates were interested in Structure (Table 8-6).

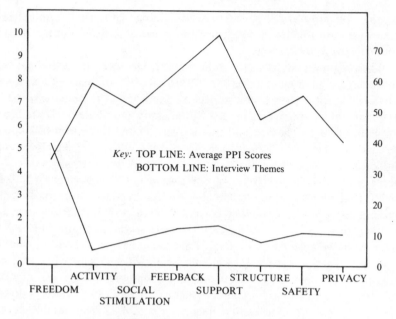

Figure 13-1. Comparison of the Average PPI Dimension Scores for the Combined Sample and the Distribution of Primary Themes for the Total Interview Sample

4. Compared to single inmates, married prisoners expressed a strong need for Emotional Feedback but showed limited interest in Freedom (Table 8-7).

A number of these findings also appear in the present chapter. We find black inmates more concerned with Support and Freedom; we see older inmates ranking high on the Structure dimension; we describe the concern of married men with Emotional Feedback. In the Lexington data, we replicate the relationships of prison satisfaction with Support and Freedom.

While we welcome any findings that recur, we need not be surprised where some do not, because an interview taps the mind differently from a forced choice inventory. Different methods of inquiry provoke different associations at different levels of awareness for different people. The phenomenon is similar to the results of using surgery and radiotherapy with carcinoma; if one method cures a patient, this does not invalidate the other.

What is figure in one inquiry, is sometimes ground in another. Freedom is prominent in prison interviews because it is a salient theme in prisons. The interview comes closer to depicting the Freedom in "cognitive maps" or the "phenomenal field" of prisons than does the questionnaire. By the same token, the interview sacrifices discriminating power, because too many inmates mention Freedom too often. In responses to the PPI, Freedom comes up where it appears as a *specific* concern matched with other specific concerns, and it is otherwise stipulated. The PPI discriminates inmates who are concretely concerned about Freedom from inmates who are routinely concerned about it.

Activity concerns are rare in interviews, because they are often taken for granted. We know that we like to be busy, but we do not conceptualize this fact as a concrete theme of our personalities. In this sense, the PPI helps to surface the dimension for us. In reacting to Activity items, we define a trend in ourselves where we ordinarily don't think of a trend.

The interview helps where a concern is complex and where we wish to describe it. The inmate who is obsessed with Safety problems can tell us about them in an interview. In the PPI, the inmate must range widely and is confined to a few Safety items. He cannot inform us about the substance of his concerns, which is crucial to programming decisions.

The PPI and the interview are valid sources of overlapping data. The decision about which to use, and when to use it, is a practical one. We shall examine the issue in this way in our final chapter.

14

Classification for Inmate Survival

THERE ARE MANY JUNCTURES at which society engages in social engineering, sometimes to further institutional purposes, often "for a person's own benefit," and frequently for combined ends. We assign children to grade levels, find jobs for the unemployed, commit people to hospitals or asylums, and send men to war. We pretend to do these things "objectively" by matching people with available challenges or opportunities on the basis of relevant data.

We find as we look at the classification process that it can reflect dichotomous views of its clients and their settings. "Matching" people and placements can come to mean matching data about the person as an independently defined set of traits with information about the placement, defined purely in "structural" terms.

In limited respects, this procedure works. If we know that a man has manual dexterity, we can appropriately assign him to an electronics wiring room, where we know that nimble fingers are deployed. If a man tells us he hears voices, it seems legitimate to consider sequestering him in a facility for psychotics. A child of six who reads Shakespeare may be well placed in an accelerated classroom.

But such categorizations are imperfect. Our electronics "match," for instance, may be unimpeachable with respect to ability (which we can measure) and job requirements (which we can assess). It may be destructive, however, in relation to issues we do not address through conventional measurement. Our technician-elect, for example, may be bored to death by replicated tasks, may crave communication, and may feel alienated in assembly lines. Our psychotic can feel threatened by other psychotics or may panic in confinement. Our prodigy may react to competition by developing a speech defect.

The problem lies in the fact that what we know about job candidates, patients, and students predates their transactions with the environments to which we assign them and relates to personal traits (aptitudes, cognitive states, etc.) that may be overshadowed and neutralized by reactions to environmental presses. If we do not consider the individual's probable reactions to the attributes of an environment, we risk, *at best,* a fair amount of unhappiness or concrete problems of adjustment. At worst (as in a carefully certified sharpshooter who is fearful of war) we ignore predictable and preventable stress.

To the social engineer—the person engaged in classifying and assigning people—unhappiness among his clients may be an acceptable trade-off, a price well paid for straight shooting, fast learning, or effective therapy. But stress and human breakdown ultimately prevent us from achieving our aims. Stress is therefore too high a price to pay for both classifiers and clients, and for society at large.

I am not implying that such damage is routinely or frequently done in classifying people. But if more damage is not done, it is not because the process of classification is harmless, but because it is ignored. Most assignments in life are not made on the basis of test scores but in response to population pressures. Classifiers abound, but opportunities do not. Classification has outstripped the options available to consumers of classification, to the point that recommendations may be routinely aimed at nonexistent options.

A person with a problem has little difficulty finding someone who is willing to certify and describe his or her problem. But the dispensers of solutions are few. The assignment of clients to resources is more likely to take place from waiting lists than from classification rosters. And the classifier's contribution is increasingly that of adding useless documents to overflowing files.

It would be different, I suspect, if classifiers were "tuned in" to the real world and to their clients' chances in it. It is harder to ignore an argument for environmental fit ("Here is a man for your opening.") than it is to overlook criteria of questionable relevance ("I don't know what kind of job you've got, but I have a man here with four college degrees."). A transactional view remedies this problem. It supplements the usual "trait" model by classifying people *proactively,* making a case for closeness of fit between client needs and available resources.

Inmate Classification as a Case in Point

The 1967 Task Force on Corrections noted that some ways of classifying inmates "are of immediate relevance to corrections, either in determining treatment or enabling more efficient and effective management of offenders in institutions. *Some have less immediate implications"* (President's Commission, p. 20, emphasis added).

In theory, the objectives of any classification in prisons are (1) to determine the personal requirements and assess the needs of individual inmates, and (2) to *match* requirements and needs with existing correctional resources (National Advisory Commission, p. 197).[1]

The problem that arises in practice is that the diagnostic and classification centers that engage in the assessment of personal needs describe inmates in ways that carry no program implications or, to put it more fairly, are not easily converted into assignment options. Inmate folders contain MMPI and other test scores, social histories, and categorizations of mental health that are partly derived from previous classifications and are quoted by subsequent classifiers.[2] It is no help when special experts (such as psy-

---

[1] An authoritative definition of classification is endorsed by the *Manual of Correctional Standards* (1966): "Classification . . . contributes to a smoothly, efficiently operated correctional program by the pooling of all *relevant* information concerning the offender, by devising a program for the individual *based upon that information* and by *keeping the program realistically in line with the individual's requirements*. It furnishes an orderly method to the institution administrator by which the varied *needs and requirements* of each inmate *may be followed through* from commitment to discharge. Through its diagnosis and coordinating functions, classification not only contributes to the objective of rehabilitation, but also to custody, discipline, work assignments, officer and inmate morale, and the effective use of training opportunities. Through the data it develops, it assists in long range planning and development, both in the correctional system as a whole and in the individual institution." (Emphasis added.)

The *Manual* asserts that "the primary objective of classification as a systematic process is the development and administration of an integrated and realistic program of treatment for the individual, with procedures for changing the program when indicated. . . . Classification [is] . . . the process through which the resources of the correctional institution can be applied effectively to the individual case. . . . Classification may be conceived of as the process of pooling all relevant knowledge about the inmate so that important decisions and activities affecting him may be better coordinated. . . . Upon the basis of classification findings, the planning of the correctional system is assisted through knowledge of what types of programs and institutions are needed" (American Correctional Association, p. 353). The *Manual* makes specific recommendations, but these involve the usual bifurcated system of diagnostic units and classification boards, with inmate folders flowing from the former to the latter.

[2] Glaser points out that classifiers tend to be rated on the "quality" of their "reports." The judges of "quality" (e.g., supervisors) are rarely acquainted with the persons who are classified and read reports by comparing them against other information on file. According to Glaser, "they can judge the validity of these reports only by their styles and by their consistency with the other contents of the inmate's file. Therefore, the caseworker's efforts at 'interviewing the file' and 'polishing the report,' as they sometimes express it, may be more important in the impression he creates than his efforts to know each inmate's prison conduct and experience as perfectly as possible. When this condition prevails it greatly reduces the practical value of 'observation in prison' as a basis for diagnostic and prognostic knowledge of prisoners, although classification and parole policy assumes that much is learned about a man when he is imprisoned" (Glaser, p. 194). Wherever reliability becomes the criterion of validity in classification, we can expect to discover considerable redundancy.

chiatrists) are invoked. Such experts not only paraphrase each other prodigiously, but they construct taxonomies that are of exclusive interest to the next sorter down the line. Such activity is incestuous and largely sterile. True, classifications affect a man's sentence and may delay or advance his parole date, and sometimes may bring a person mental health care if he has been classed as disturbed. But the man's prison life—the nature of his assignments—is apt to be uninfluenced by most data in his file.

Where the deployment of resources is contaminated by some data, the data involved (education, extent of record, age) could easily be recorded on a 3″ × 5″ card. Information used in making assignments is more often the experience accumulated by staff through previous assignments than the recommendation of classifiers. A man receives a work assignment because "his supervisor says he is a good worker", with (understandable) disregard of the "Runkelhauser Vocational Aptitude/Interest Inventory (Third Revision)" scores in his folder.

Most generally, moreover, assignments are based on information that is unrelated to the inmate, such as the availability of cell space or classroom seats. This situation is not the fault of assignment staff or of classification personnel. Each person may do his or her job conscientiously, responsive to his or her mandate and to organizational constraints. And, while classification-diagnostic personnel go about their task of filling folders, and assignment staff juggle slots to accommodate warm bodies, the hope lingers that somewhere, sometime, the twain will meet.

Over the rainbow, in the correctional Land of Oz, when population pressures decrease, when budgets are smiled upon, when administrations don't change and crises cease, staff expect to rethink and streamline classification procedures. They also sometimes assume that in the Land of Oz computers will assure maximum match of inmate needs and prison assignments. The requirement for achieving this millennium is to translate what we know into uniform, machine-codable tabulations.

Rainbows, unfortunately, are unbridgeable, as is the gap between *autonomous* diagnostic and assignment procedures. While classification personnel collect information that carries no practical implications, and while assignments are made without worrying about what sorts of people are most appropriate for a given placement, no "matches" are possible. Computerization perpetuates the cumulation of ritualistically gathered information and gives an illusion of science and accuracy while decisions are made on traditional intuitive grounds.

The point is that the business of matching people and opportunities cannot be diagnosis *plus* assignment but must ideally be a *diagnosis–assignment transaction* in which one always implies the other, and neither ever occurs separately. This does not mean that classification must keep one eye on the assignment process, and that assignment must use one or two juicy items from bulky folders. It means that data must not get collected if they cannot be translated and used in decisions and that no person may be placed anywhere without concern about whether we know enough about him or her, and his or her placement, to insure the best possible match. Where relevant information is not now available, it should be requested and collected, which can be done if we redirect energy deployed in collecting information nobody needs, to plow this energy (and our underworked ingenuity) into finding data that help us relate people to settings.[3]

Ingenuity is critical, because we must necessarily depart from familiar modes of thought. We must ask ourselves whether data we have seen as exclusively relevant are the only kind of information at issue, and whether the select facts we now consider are critical or useful. We send inmates to an institution, for example, to meet educational needs at a given physical security level. Do we know whether a learning climate exists that matches the formal program options? Do we know whether inmates feel it is profitable to participate in the program? Do we know whether a social setting exists (or is being created by us) that prevents exploitation or that groups compatible persons? Do we know whether living arrangements make study possible? Do we know whether civilian and custodial supervision is matched with the expectations and needs of inmates?

We send long-term inmates to a given institution. Are we assured that this institution does not also contain young inmates who'll grate on our assignees' nerves? Are we certain that inmates with long sentences will be kept busy to make their time easier? That counseling is available to deal with despondency? That a law library furnishes hope or life-giving illusion?

The point here is not only that we must know more about the inmates than we know now but also that classifiers must know a great deal about the settings that inmates are assigned to.[4] We must ensure that information

---

[3] The National Advisory Commission notes approvingly that "Corrections personnel from necessity have become interested in the possibility of dealing with programs and persons *simultaneously*; that is, utilizing a classification system that would make it possible to *match* subjects and programs. Experience suggests that when such differential programming is inaugurated, the overall success rate achieved by offenders may be increased, particularly, when the offender is included in determining the direction and extent of his program" (National Advisory Commission, p. 201. Emphasis added.).

[4] Glaser suggests that classifiers be assigned to cases that derive from the same environments or subenvironments, so that they can observe their clients in context: "One of the major deficiencies of the prevailing system of casework operation is that, by randomizing his caseload through the last number assignment system, the caseworker in a larger prison inadvertently reduces his chances of knowing the social environment in which his clients live. By scattering his caseload throughout the prison population, the caseworker minimizes the probability of his also knowing the cellmates or dormitory colleagues, coworkers, recreational partners, or other close inmate friends or associates of any specific client. By having the caseload distributed over all assignments, the caseworker in the large institution reduces to an absolute minimum his ability to learn the special competencies, personal styles, or individual standards of the work supervisors and unit officers who submit reports on his clients. Also, when the caseload is scattered, it clearly becomes more diffi-

is shared along the line. This means that diagnostic personnel must have data about available settings to make specific recommendations; and it means that assignment staff must be abreast of all we know about the relationship between types of inmates and types of settings.

Day-to-day evaluation is critical, because it tells us not only about routine matches and mismatches but about subsurface problems that are easy to miss. In prison we are cognizant of inmates for whom "routine" classification is inappropriate, such as psychotics, chronically aggressive inmates, or men who are infirm. But prison settings (and other settings) are often stressful for persons who do not bloom into psychoses and burst into extreme violence. These persons do not usually demand our attention until it may be too late. Such inmates constitute a "gray area" in the population for whom primary prevention is appropriate. Special assessment must be invoked wherever and whenever the need for it is indicated, such as in situations of personal stress. In prisons, this entails staff sensitivity to stress cues, and requires a flexible administrative arrangement in which transfers and reassignments can be mobilized and completed speedily and in coordinated fashion.

It is crucial to stress this point, because it affects what we usually do. Ordinarily, we respond to needs that show up in statistics or explode in crises. Short-term inmates can get more help than long-term inmates because there are so many of them; if we did not address their illiteracy or their lack of vocational skills, our computers would complain loudly or would flash red lights. If we did not keep short-termers occupied, hundreds of them would noisily mill around prison yards looking unhappy. We have no choice, either, about helping our more visible minorities, the most vociferous psychotics, the helplessly and blatantly feebleminded, the persistently and severely disruptive. Such persons earn the benefit or brunt of special programs so that we can go on about our business elsewhere. We cannot run prisons in which men need help getting dressed, proclaim themselves kings, or attack fellow-inmates. But we can run prisons in which inmates unobtrusively and very gradually waste away.

---

cult for the caseworker to see his client's customary behavior in the institution, away from the casework interview" (Glaser, p. 193).

Glaser adds that, "by having the entire population in a work or quarters unit as his caseload, each caseworker would know the other inmates and staff workers in the immediate environment of each of his clients, and he could observe them at work, residence, or play more readily.... These caseload and office location arrangements... would enable the caseworker to observe the behavior of his clients much more adequately, and to understand their problems in the institution... the caseworker would be expected to describe in more detail than he generally can at present the nature of an inmate's relationships to other inmates and to his work and unit officers. The reports could also summarize the gist of the caseworker's conversations with other officials, indicating the variety of considerations raised by each and the extent of consensus achieved. This would contrast with the present verbose narrative listing of grades, scores, or numerical ratings which can be more concisely communicated in a tabular form" (*ibid.*, pp. 195, 198).

Both "routine" and "special" assignments call for more knowledge than we now possess and for the systematization of whatever "informal" knowledge we may have. We must know which inmates have compatible habits, which staff are best suited for dealing with which inmates, which physical settings are least stressful for whom, and which activities are necessary for survival and growth. Where our aim includes therapy (no matter how loosely we define it) we must know what the "therapeutic" and "antitherapeutic" properties of our settings may be (Redl; Bettelheim, 1975).

We have tried to show that relevant data can be obtained by measuring one transactional realm, that of *congenial and uncongenial living environments*. We assume that any inmate finds it "easier" or "harder" to do time in some assignments than in others, depending on types of fellow inmates, types of staff, personal routines, and other aspects of the environment. We assume that whether an inmate will be content in a given institution, program, work or living assignment depends on his psychological makeup, his cultural background, his institutional experiences, and the type of sentence he must serve. The precise relationship of such factors to environmental adjustment is one that we have tried to explore.

We have suggested that measures of environmental concerns have "routine" and "special" uses. "Routine" matches of inmates and environments have to do with making it *easier* for the inmate to adjust to prison and to serve time. Such matches provide some inmates with intensive staff contact and others with nonobtrusive supervision; they furnish congenial peers for some persons and privacy for others; they meet the aspirations of those intent on self-advancement and the need of others for intense contact with outsiders; they furnish stable routines for those who need them most and an active life for those who prize keeping busy.

"Special" matches make it possible for "special" inmates to *survive*. They provide solitude for those who find crowding painful; they furnish safety for men who are panic stricken and concern for those who feel lost; they cement corroding bonds with relatives and spouses.

Classification of both kinds requires a mapping of the concerns that inmates have with aspects of the environment. It requires a way of highlighting the qualities of a prison setting that the inmate or prospective inmate may prefer or require, may find uncomfortable, painful, or noxious. Such information is not currently sought.

To say that such information is not currently sought carries no pejorative implication, because these data are not easily available. In writing this book, we have in part responded to this vacuum. We have done so because we assume that, if needs are stated *in terms of environmental dimensions,* it is easier to make appropriate assignments. Information about a person's needs is of course not enough: to respond to a man's needs, classifiers must be familiar with the attributes of environments that can satisfy needs. Prison staff must know where in their institutions one finds quiet or laughter, solitude or friends, advancement or activity. They must know the front-line staff individually, particularly their strengths and idiosyncrasies. They must know where to find places for inmates to feel safe, let off steam, regroup, seek personal help, find distraction, recognition, support.

The view we need here is consumer-centered. Front-line worlds are different from the "ideal type" worlds that are featured in program manuals, organization tables, recruiting posters, five year plans, and annual reports. A sailor who swabs decks or who peels potatoes is not "seeing the world" or "joining the electronic age of the Modern Navy." A tired police officer who spends hours driving through deserted, dingy, snowy streets is not "waging Vigorous War on crime." A student facing solitary weekends of reviewing statistics is not savoring "a stimulating scholarly atmosphere" or enjoying his "active student social life."

Settings that contain stressors have a very special obligation to catalog the *impinging* and the *experienced* environment, rather than the few "highlights" that distinguish the administrator's world. "Innovative programs" or "progressive offerings" may exist for the few, while most clients (or staff) face boredom, loneliness, frustration, or fear. We may be "surprised" by eminently foreseeable stress because we discount our impinging stressors and ignore what impact they have.

Attributes of the PPI

The PPI yields a profile of concerns that covers eight aspects of the environment. Profile scores have significance relative to each other, since they are obtained through comparisons. A "high" in Dimensions A and B and a "low" in Dimension E signify that A and B are of more significance—and E of less significance—than other dimensions. The scores do not mean that the person's ideal world is comprised of A and B and that he couldn't care less about E. It is possible for a person to be highly concerned (or unconcerned) with all aspects of his milieu but to be more interested or involved in some issues than in others.

Like all instruments, the PPI measures what it measures at the point in the person's career where he responds to the questionnaire. A prison at the entry point may have different meanings from those at the midpoint of a long stay, and a man in his first institution may react differently than he will as a fourth-termer. It is obvious that concerns may be responsive to situational presses. A self-assured inmate may become less self-assured if he is solicited in the shower room and harassed in his cell. Such an inmate's Safety score may quickly increase, and his Freedom score may decrease overnight. A lifer may reach the end of his Support concern after undergoing six training cycles and discovering that he faces eight more years in prison.

For any population, we can speak of a "modal" profile for the population as a whole, of "modal" profiles for subpopulations (age groups, ethnic groups, offender groups, etc), and of "deviant" profiles. Deviant profiles belong to persons who respond differently from other persons, including those in their subpopulation. Modal profiles pose "routine" classification problems, and deviant profiles point to "special" classification issues.

The PPI is an instrument that, like any instrument, taps a specific "level" of thought, feeling, and personality. We know of one dimension (Freedom) that is "pulled" by the PPI to a lesser extent than it emerges in open-ended interviews. We assume that there are other dimensions that would become more salient if they were differently invoked. A projective test might uncover Emotional Feedback concerns that tough young men might not reveal at the PPI "level."

We know from our data that environments and subenvironments have "modal" profiles and others that are "deviant." The "modal" prison can supply Support but it may yield limited Privacy. Some prisons are high on the Structure dimension, and others are not. Protection tiers may be long on Safety and short on Activity. Niches may maximize almost any dimension available in a larger setting.

Environmental profiles can be altered through interventions. Nightly phone calls and regular furloughs can increase a prison's capacity for responding to Emotional Feedback concerns. New hobby shops and a circulating library may lead to more chances for Activity, while a lockdown reduces the arena of Freedom and rule changes decrease Structure. Most interventions have multiple impact: To institute nightly recreation may lower Privacy and boost Activity. Quiet periods may provide Privacy at the expense of Activity or Freedom.

The last point we made about persons holds for settings. The salience of environmental dimensions varies with one's level of observation. A gruff guard may personify low Freedom in public encounters and may become high Feedback in private. Such a guard may defy the Freedom of some and supply Emotional Feedback to others.

The "play" in environment profiles makes "matching" more complicated but also more flexible. If Guard Scrooge has a low-freedom–high-structure (pre-Christmas) façade, but can take a high-feedback–high-safety (post-Christmas) stance, we may invoke either profile when we assign Inmate Timothy Cratchet to his care.

A static view of environments invites cynicism. Such a view sees no Privacy while we service many clients and furnishes no hope of Freedom till we can "break down walls." To assume subsurface profiles in our environments gives us transactional potential and new options. It lets us create settings by encouraging responses that the environment is capable of but may not routinely invoke.

Profile Intersections

In social environments, one man's profile forms part of another's milieu. A's Activity invades B's Privacy, and C's Freedom threatens D's Safety or E's Support. A PPI respondent who records disdain for "inmates who are rats" (Freedom item) may be referring to another respondent who seeks "staff who help a man who's depressed" (Emotional Feedback). A man who requests "rules that tell me what to expect" (Structure) may offend the man who wishes "as few rules as possible" (Freedom).

Classification not only entails matching needs with environments but means orchestrating various profiles to maximize harmony and to minimize dissonance among them. In extreme cases this involves segregating and homogenizing subpopulations.

To "match" in our sense means to achieve the best fit we can, rather than to attain a perfect fit. If necessary, we must satisfy some profile dimensions at the expense of others, though such solutions may be unstable. The Roman empire for example, supplied Activity (circuses) in lieu of Support (bread) and discovered that the formula was not a long-run solution.

The PPI as a Classification Tool

We have implied that the PPI has two separable uses. The first is as an *ancillary* classification tool to help "match" inmates with institutional programs, with staffing patterns, and client groupings. Support and Activity, for instance, are program-relevant dimensions, and so—sometimes—is Emotional Feedback. Support refers to tangible opportunities, while Activity means things to do. Emotional Feedback may mean warmth in the environment or bridges that lead to the outside. Structure and Freedom dimensions are linked to the exercise of authority, to its consistency and its (relative) nonassertiveness. Social Stimulation relates to peer groups and to chances for friendly gregariousness. Safety and Privacy are dimensions that combine physical, staff, and peer variables.

In each case the availability of environmental dimensions must be assessed in the transactions of clients. Support cannot be documented in lists of programs, Structure is not the printed rule book, and Emotional Feedback is not ensured by having counselors on one's staff. Environmental profile dimensions are responses to personal profile dimensions. They entail the responses to concerns in concrete transactions. A horse led to water is not necessarily a participant in a drinking transaction. If the horse does not drink (and if we know the horse is thirsty), the water may be polluted or the trough too high. It may also be possible that the situation is unsafe, so that the horse is caught in a double bind, as is the Support-thirsting inmate whose classroom and living environment are jungles.

A high-support institution may have a young, aggressive population and may be unable to provide Safety or Privacy, which an inmate may need conjointly with Support. The high-support institution may also feature a routine that has much leeway (low Structure) or calls for tight discipline (low Freedom). It may be a "cold" environment (low Emotional Feedback) or provide few chances for hobbies or for spare-time occupations (low Activity). The inmate's profile as a whole must be matched as well as possible to the institution's "environment profile."[5]

The issue of profile intersections raises classification problems that are difficult to solve. No matter how we address these problems, we face human, ethical, legal, and practical consequences that are troublesome.

In schools, slow learners are separated from fast learners in homogeneous "tracks" or learning environments. Such differentiation is hard to achieve without producing status differentials for pupils and teachers. Status differentials are a problem elsewhere in education, because they

---

[5] Examples of such institutional profiles are furnished by Stern. He describes the "environmental press characteristics" of the liberal arts program of Syracuse University with the following vignette:

"I. *Intellectual Climate.* Many of the professors in both the natural and social sciences are engaged in research. Tutorial or honors programs are available for qualified students. There are student organizations actively involved in campus or community affairs. Many famous people are brought on campus for lectures, concerts, students discussions, etc. There are many foreign students on campus, and a great variety in nationality, religion and social status.

"II. *Nonintellectual Climate.* Students quickly learn what is done on this campus. Papers and reports must be neat. The college offers many really practical courses in typing, report writing, etc. The future goals for most students emphasize job security, family happiness, and good citizenship.

"There is plenty to do here besides going to classes and studying. Students have many opportunities to get together in extracurricular activities. There are many fraternities and sororities, and lots of dances, parties, and social activities. There is an extensive program of intramural sports and informal athletic activities. Students frequently go away for football games, skiing weekends, etc. Every year there are carnivals, parades, and other festive events on campus. There is a lot of excitement and restlessness just before holidays.

"Student gathering places are typically active and noisy. There are several popular spots where a crowd of boys and girls can always be found. Students spend a lot of time together at the snack bars, taverns, and in one another's rooms. There is a lot of informal dating during the week—at the library, snack bar, movies, etc. It's easy to get a group together for card games, singing, going to the movies, etc. Jazz bands and novelty groups are more popular here than society orchestras. Bermuda shorts, pin-up pictures, etc., are common on this campus. There are paintings or statues of nudes" (p. 125).

exist in the *de facto* segregation of urban school systems. This problem has been addressed through efforts at integrating environments (busing), which are often resented. The strategy entails inconvenient logistics, the disruption of familiar settings, the creation of new profile intersections, and the challenge to Freedom of a *justicius ex machina* approach to environmental reform.

In prisons, dissonant profiles occur along intersections of age groups, ethnic groups (which are hard to distinguish from rural–urban intersections), and groups with disparate sentences. The most simplistic solutions entail separating incompatible groups by segregating them spatially; more sophisticated solutions involve arranging nonintersecting schedules over space and time. If groups must physically coexist, some select facilities (such as shops and classrooms) may be converted into reservations or enclaves, with environmental profiles that are homogeneously responsive to modal needs.

Such strategies, however, tax resources and run the risk of being antidemocratic and discriminatory. Moreover, homogeneity is sometimes destructive. We have seen, for example, that young inmates often feel themselves victimized by milieus designed for the average youth, whom they view as "immature."

We know that demographic differences involve overlapping concerns and attitudes. While our data show that cultural backgrounds are psychologically important, the data leave room for different variables and for the interaction of variables. Many young urban black inmates may prize Freedom, but others are saliently concerned with Support, which is negatively correlated with an interest in Freedom.

If we use PPI profiles to group and separate people, we produce disproportionate representations of demographic backgrounds. But we ameliorate the more blatant bias entailed in demographic "tracking." Moreover, it is one thing to sort people because of who they *are,* and another to assign them in terms of what they *want.*

Special Classification

The PPI can identify persons who need "special" or individualized attention. Such persons are people who either (1) have statistically deviant PPI profiles or (2) have heavily skewed dimensional distributions.

A deviant profile does not necessarily point to a man in trouble, but raises the possibility or presumption of trouble. The unusual profile may mean a person in conflict, a person who does not "fit in" socially, or a person who is uncomfortably aware of being a square peg in a round hole who is surrounded by round pegs. The PPI functions as a "red flag" index, which points to individuals we must interview for further information about their needs. The PPI also points to some subject matter areas that may be profitably explored in interviews.

Deviance is an arbitrary construct. Diagnoses of deviance are arrived at by talking about "significant differences" from population norms. The difference we call significant relates to the amount and type of flexibility we have in our assignment system and to the adjustment problems among our clients. If we know that we have a large number of persons who in our current system have trouble surviving (Type I error), we must be willing to consider modest danger signals as possibly relevant. On the other hand, if we discovered we were identifying appreciable numbers as "special" for whom we had no resources (Type II error), we would have to raise our "standards." The advantage of employing an instrument like the PPI is efficiency. It isolates possible problem people quickly and economically and allows us to allocate limited resources to those who have specific needs.

Skewed PPI profiles are always important, because they suggest strong needs. If these needs "match" our resources, we can use them to set priorities in assignments. Where strong needs are not "matched" to modal environment profiles, special classification is indicated.

In evaluating assignments, the criterion is the congruence or incongruence of environmental transactions. In our survey of the Federal institution at Lexington, for example, we used the self-anchoring scale in an effort to determine the degree of congruence. Our data showed that, although inmates with high Privacy and/or Freedom scores were generally unhappy, they were less discontent in some subenvironments than in others. This is the type of information that permits humane and rational decisions. In order to obtain such data, one must survey institutional settings by using a measure like the PPI and some indicator of satisfaction and/or adjustment.

Wherever we engineer environmental transactions we must conscientiously hedge our bets and check our hunches. At this stage of our knowledge it is unthinkable for us to place people in settings without carefully ascertaining how they fare there. We must observe our clients, talk to them, and keep contact with the custodians of their milieus in order to verify or to disconfirm our assumptions about our clients' personal needs and about our responsiveness to these needs.

If we have achieved congruent transactions, we must be sensitive to changes in people and settings. Reviews or reclassifications are vital, particularly where people have career patterns, where settings are dynamic, or where people stay in the same milieus over long periods of time. This flow review has important scientific implications, because it sheds light on the dynamics of ecological change.

Knowledge about change is of practical importance. It tells us about the result of what we do, so that we know when we can keep doing it and when me must shift strategies. We engineer futures based on the impact of people's pasts. But the future becomes the past as it is lived. The second-grade graduate becomes a third-grader, the inductee a veteran, and the convicted offender turns into the seasoned inmate. The environments we help arrange build past experience that molds and modifies people.

If we deal with static indicators, we cannot be tuned into the problems encountered by a person, because our tests do not measure them. The alienated worker may continue to sparkle on the Hackfleisch Clerical Aptitude Scale, but the same worker may be nearing a nervous breakdown or may resign. The certified sharpshooter may shoot accurately, though he breaks out in cold sweat or may shoot his lieutenant in the back. When our assignments boomerang, we invoke new static tests, such as mental health inventories, exit interviews or alienation scales.

Transactionally oriented measures must be differently used, because we expect to see shifts in the impact of environment-oriented concerns under the impact of stimuli. We expect such shifts even with congruent environments, because (as Maslow points out) congruence leads to growth. New environmental concerns arise as old ones are satisfied.

Anticipated congruence is not real congruence. Measures like the PPI are make-believe, but environments such as prison are real and may be different from a person's previous milieus in unanticipated ways. A man who is tolerant of crowding at home may find crowds noxious in a cell block; an inmate may react to correctional officers differently than to authorities in his past.

We pay for our failures to accommodate adjustments to new environments. Nonproactivity has made many of our environments inhospitable to those who must enter them and continue to live in them. A couple that enjoys an idyllic trial marriage may find itself less well matched when it is surrounded by screaming children. And long-term institutionalization is always qualitatively different from a hypothetical series of short-term commitments.

Reassessments of personal adjustment are vital to the rational, systemic use of institutions. Periodic reviews permit the deployment of resources where they are most needed rather than at arbitrary but visible junctures, such as at intake into a system. A longitudinal view gives us a better chance of reducing the undesirable impact of stressful environmental impingements and of maximizing the benefits of growth-promotive congruence. With prisons, we can at least ensure that the inmate does time as well as he can. We can prevent a person from adding a new experience of failure to a career that may be saturated with past failures.

APPENDIXES

We have developed the Prison Preference Inventory hoping that it might be used by prison staff to help inmates, and by researchers to secure knowledge. The instrument is considered in the public domain; there is no objection to its deployment—in whole, in part or in adapted form—for basic and applied inquiry.

I. Prison Preference Questionnaire

NO ONE LIKES DOING TIME. But there are some things that can make life in prison EASIER, and some that make it HARDER.

We'd like to know some of the things you LIKE MOST and DISLIKE MOST about prisons. First, we'll give you a list of things you can choose from, and we'd like to know which of them you PREFER.

Here is an example:

I'D PREFER

A parole date   Chicken next Sunday

We'd like you to CIRCLE the one *you* prefer. If you are like most people, you'll want the parole date. If you do, please circle it; your answer will look like this:

I'D PREFER

(A parole date)   Chicken next Sunday

Some of the choices will be tougher than this one, but please try your best. Even if you have a hard time deciding, or you have only a SLIGHT preference, let us know which way you lean.

Remember to CIRCLE the one you LIKE BEST, and DON'T SKIP ANY.

I'D PREFER

1. Guards who are consistent   Housing that keeps out noise

2. Housing in which no one can   Staying away from guards
   harm me

3. Inmates who know their rights   Inmates who make no noise

4.	Housing where people rap	A friend who shares my problems
5.	Knowing my people still love me	A guard who overlooks infractions
6.	Educational advancement	Protection from danger
7.	Staff who stick to their rules	Staff who care how I feel
8.	Staff who let me run my life	Staff who are honest
9.	Staff who help a man who's depressed	A shop where they teach you skills
10.	Being by myself	Learning something
11.	Inmates I know well from the streets	Guards who act the same every day
12.	Getting a good job in prison	Being safe in prison
13.	Knowing that I'm loved	Getting peace and quiet
14.	Staying in my cell	Feeling safe
15.	Having no guards around	Having lots of friends
16.	A place with no crowds	A place where you are safe
17.	Keeping active	Loving someone
18.	A job where I have friends	A job where I work alone
19.	Staff who advance my interests	Not having a boss
20.	Having a good time	Being close to someone
21.	Having consistent rules	Being busy all day
22.	Teachers from whom I learn	Guards who protect me
23.	Housing where I know everybody	Housing in which I keep busy
24.	Rules that tell me what to expect	As few rules as possible
25.	A place with friends	A quiet place
26.	A very busy day	A message of love
27.	A friendly game	No supervision
28.	An active program	Time by myself
29.	No one to disturb me	No one to forget me

30.   No one checking up on me   No time to be bored

We'll ask you about some things now you probably DON'T like. What we want to know is which of two things you like LEAST.

For instance, if you were forced to live with

An inmate who snores all night   or   An inmate who reads all day

Which would bother you more? If you sleep nights and you have good ears, you'd probably say, "an inmate who snores all night." Your answer would be:

I'D BE MORE BOTHERED BY

(An inmate who snores all night)   An inmate who reads all day

Here are some other pairs like this. In each case, please CIRCLE the one you LIKE LEAST:

I'D BE MORE BOTHERED BY

31.	Too much time to think	Too much talk and noise
32.	Housing where people could trap me	Housing where no one knows me
33.	Sitting around	Getting nowhere
34.	Inmates who are always noisy	Staff who are on my back
35.	Having no friends	Having enemies
36.	Feeling unsafe	Feeling unloved
37.	Having nothing to do	Learning nothing new
38.	Having few friends	Having no money
39.	A prison with no protection	A prison with no rules
40.	Not knowing the rules	Not feeling safe
41.	Being depressed	Being confused
42.	Inmates who are dangerous	Inmates who are rats
43.	Guards giving petty orders	Family who forget you
44.	People who talk loud	People who use me
45.	Inmates who pick fights	Inmates who are squares
46.	Not knowing anyone	Thinking too much
47.	No visits from home	Tension in prison

48.	Lots of dangerous people	Lots of idle time
49.	Being used	Being told what to do
50.	Being bored	Having rules changed
51.	An uncertain assignment	Programs that don't help me enough
52.	Noisy tiers	No rules at all
53.	A lot of rules	A lot of boredom
54.	A prison with changing rules	A prison with no friends
55.	Programs that don't help me make parole	Staff who keep changing rules
56.	Staff who won't teach you skills	Staff who don't care how you feel

II. Scoring Key for the PPI

1. STRU	PRI		29. PRI	FEED
2. SAF	FREE		30. FREE	ACT
3. FREE	PRI		31. ACT	PRI
4. SOC	FEED		32. SAF	SOC
5. FEED	FREE		33. ACT	SUP
6. SUP	SAF		34. PRI	FREE
7. STRU	FEED		35. SOC	SAF
8. FREE	STRU		36. SAF	FEED
9. FEED	SUP		37. ACT	SUP
10. PRI	SUP		38. SOC	SUP
11. SOC	STRU		39. SAF	STRU
12. ACT	SAF		40. STRU	SAF
13. FEED	PRI		41. FEED	STRU
14. PRI	SAF		42. SAF	FREE
15. FREE	SOC		43. FREE	FEED
16. PRI	SAF		44. PRI	SUP
17. ACT	FEED		45. SUP	SOC
18. SOC	PRI		46. SOC	ACT
19. SUP	FREE		47. FEED	SAF
20. SOC	FEED		48. SAF	ACT
21. STRU	ACT		49. SUP	FREE
22. SUP	SAF		50. ACT	STRU
23. SOC	ACT		51. STRU	SUP
24. STRU	FREE		52. PRI	STRU
25. SOC	PRI		53. FREE	ACT
26. ACT	FEED		54. STRU	SOC
27. SOC	FREE		55. SUP	STRU
28. ACT	PRI		56. SUP	FEED

Bibliography

AMERICAN CORRECTIONAL ASSOCIATION. *Manual of Correctional Standards.* College Park, Md.: American Correctional Association, 1966.

APPLEY, M. H., AND R. TRUMBULL. *Psychological Stress.* New York: Appleton, 1967.

BARTOLLAS, C.; S. J. MILLER; AND S. DINITZ, *Juvenile Victimization: The Institutional Paradox.* New York: Halsted Press, 1976.

————. "The White Victim in a Black Institution." In Riedel and Vales, eds., *Treating the Offender: Problems and Issues.* New York: Praeger, 1976.

BENNETT, L. A.; D. E. SORENSEN; AND H. FORSHAY. "The Applicability of Self-Esteem Measures in a Correctional Setting: I. Reliability of the Scale and Relationship to Other Measures." *Journal of Research in Crime and Delinquency,* 8 (1971): 1–10.

BETTELHEIM, B. *The Informed Heart.* Glencoe, Ill.: Free Press, 1960.

————. *A Home for the Heart.* New York: Bantam Books, 1975.

BUFFUM, P. C. *Homosexuality in Prisons.* NILECJ Monograph. Washington: U.S. Government Printing Office, 1972.

CANTRIL, H. *The "Why" of Man's Experience.* New York: Macmillan Co., 1950.

————. *The Politics of Despair.* New York: Basic Books, 1958.

————. *The Pattern of Human Concerns.* New Brunswick, N.J.: Rutgers University Press, 1965.

CARTER, M.; D. GLASER; AND L. T. WILKENS, eds. *Correctional Institutions.* Philadelphia: J. B. Lippincott, 1972.

CRONBACH, L. J. *Essentials of Psychological Testing.* New York: Harper & Row, 1970.

DAVIES, J. C. "Toward a Theory of Revolution." *American Sociological Review,* 27 (1962): 5–19.

DAVIS, A. J. "Sexual Assaults in the Philadelphia Prison System and Sheriff's Vans." *Trans-Action,* 6 (1968): 8–12.

DEWEY, J., AND A. F. BENTLEY. *Knowing and the Known.* Boston: Beacon Press, 1949.

FISHER, S. "Social Organization in a Correctional Residence," *Pacific Sociological Review,* 4 (1961): 87–93.

FLYNN, EDITH. "The Ecology of Prison Violence." In A. K. Cohen, G. F. Cole, and R. G. Bailey, *Prison Violence.* Lexington, Mass.: Heath, Lexington Books, 1975.

GIALLOMBARDO, R. *Society of Women: A Study of Women's Prison.* New York: John Wiley & Sons, 1966.

GLASER, D. *The Effectiveness of a Prison and Parole System.* Indianapolis: Bobbs-Merrill, 1964.

GOFFMAN, E. *Asylums: Essays on the Social Situation of Mental Patients and Other Inmates.* Garden City, N.Y.: Anchor Books, 1961.

HAYAKAWA, S. I. "Why the Edsel Laid an Egg: Motivational Research vs. the Reality Principle." in S. I. Hayakawa, ed., *The Use and Misuse of Language* (Greenwich, Conn.: Fawcett Publications), 1962.

HEFFERMAN, E. *Making It in Prison: The Square, the Cool, and the Life.* New York: Wiley-Interscience, 1972.

HUFFMAN, A. V. "Problems Precipitated by Homosexual Approaches on Youthful First Offenders." *Journal of Social Therapy,* 7 (1961): 170–181.

IRWIN, J. *The Felon.* Englewood Cliffs, N.J.: Prentice-Hall, 1970.

ITTELSON, W. H.; H. M. PROSHANSKY; L. C. RIVLIN; AND G. H. WINKEL. *An Introduction to Environmental Psychology.* New York: Holt, Rinehart & Winston, 1974.

JONES, M. *The Therapeutic Community: A New Treatment Method in Psychiatry.* New York: Basic Books, 1953.

KELMAN, H. C. "Processes of Opinion Change." *Public Opinion Quarterly,* 25 (1961): 57–78.

KINZEL, A. F. "Body-buffer Zone in Violent Prisoners." *American Journal of Psychiatry,* 127 (1970): 59–64.

LAZARUS, R. S. *Psychological Stress and the Coping Process.* New York: McGraw-Hill, 1966.

LOVE, E. G. *Subways Are for Sleeping.* New York: Harcourt Brace, 1957.

MATHIESEN, T. *The Defences of the Weak: A Sociological Study of a Norwegian Correctional Institution.* London: Tavistock, 1965.

McCLELLAND, D. C. *The Achieving Society.* Princeton, N.J.: Van Nostrand, 1961.

McGRATH, E., ed. *Social and Psychological Factors in Stress.* New York: Holt, Rinehart & Winston, 1970.

McGREGOR, D. *The Human Side of Enterprise.* New York: McGraw-Hill, 1960.

———. "Conditions of Effective Leadership in the Industrial Organization." *Journal of Consulting Psychology,* 7 (1944): 55 ff.

MILGRAM, S. *Obedience to Authority.* New York: Harper & Row, 1974.

MOOS, R. H. *Evaluating Treatment Environments: A Social Ecological Approach.* New York: John Wiley & Sons, 1974.

MORRIS, N. *The Future of Imprisonment: Studies in Crime and Justice.* Chicago: University of Chicago Press, 1974.

MURRAY, H. A., AND COLLABORATORS. *Explorations in Personality.* New York: Oxford, 1938.

————, AND C. D. MORGAN. "A Clinical Study of Sentiments." *Genetic Psychology Monographs,* 32 (1945): 3–311.

NAGEL, W. G. "Environmental Influences in Prison Violence," in A. K. Cohen et al., *Prison Violence.* Lexington, Mass.: Heath, Lexington Books, 1976.

NATIONAL ADVISORY COMMISSION ON CRIMINAL JUSTICE STANDARDS AND GOALS, *Corrections.* Washington: U.S. Government Printing Office, 1973.

NUNALLY, J. *Psychometric Theory.* New York: McGraw-Hill, 1967.

PARKS, C. "Psycho-social Transitions." *Social Science and Medicine,* 5 (1971): 101–115.

PERVIN, L. "Performance and Satisfaction as a Function of Individual–Environment Fit." *Psychological Bulletin,* 69 (1968): 56–58.

PRESIDENT'S COMMISSION ON LAW ENFORCEMENT AND ADMINISTRATION OF JUSTICE, *Task Force Report: Corrections.* Washington: U.S. Government Printing Office, 1967.

PROSHANSKY, H. M.; W. H. ITTELSON; AND L. G. RIVLIN, "Freedom of Choice and Behavior in a Physical Setting." In J. F. Wohlwill and D. H. Larson; *Environment and the Social Sciences: Perspectives and Applications.* Washington: American Psychological Association, 1972. Pp. 29–43.

REDL, F. "The Concept of a 'Therapeutic Milieu.'" In F. Redl, *When We Deal With Children.* New York: Free Press, 1966.

REMARQUE, E. M. *All Quiet on the Western Front.* Greenwich, Conn.: Fawcett, World, 1969.

SARTRE, J. *Being and Nothingness.* New York: Citadel Press, 1965.

SCACCO, A. M. *Rape in Prison.* Springfield, Ill.: Thomas, 1975.

SIMIRENKO, A. Review of H. Toch, *Men in Crisis: Human Breakdowns in Prison.* (Chicago: Aldine, 1975). *Annals of the American Academy of Political and Social Science,* May 1976, vol. 425.

STERN, G. G. *People in Context: Measuring Person–Environment Congruence in Education and Industry.* New York: Wiley, 1970.

SYKES, G. M. *The Society of Captives: A Study of a Maximum Security Prison.* New York: Atheneum, 1966.

SZE, M. *The Way of Chinese Painting.* New York: Random House, 1959.

TOCH, H. "The Convict as Researcher." *Trans-Action,* 4 (1967): 72–75.

————. *Violent Men: An Inquiry into the Psychology of Violence.* Chicago: Aldine, 1969.

————. *Men in Crisis: Human Breakdowns in Prison.* Chicago: Aldine, 1975.

————. "A Psychological View of Prison Violence." In A. Cohen et al., eds., *Violence in Prison.* Lexington: Lexington Books, 1976.

————, and H. Cantril. "A Preliminary Inquiry into the Learning of Values." *Journal of Educational Psychology,* 48 (1957): 145–156.

WECHSLER, H., AND J. F. PUGH. "Fit of Individual and Community Characteristics and Rates of Psychiatric Hospitalization." In H. Wechsler, L. Solomon, and B. M. Kramer, eds. *Social Psychology and Mental Health.* New York: Holt, Rinehart & Winston, 1970.

WERTHAM, C., "The Functions of Social Definitions in the Development of Delinquent Careers." In President's Commission on Law Enforcement and Administration of Justice, *Task Force Report: Juvenile Delinquency and Youth Crime.* Washington: U.S. Government Printing Office, 1967. Pp. 155–170.

———, AND I. PILIAVIN. "Gang Members and the Police." In D. J. Bordua, ed., *The Police: Six Sociological Essays.* New York: Wiley, 1967.

WHITE, R. W., ed. *The Study of Lives.* New York: Atherton Press, 1963.

WING, J. K. "Evaluating Community Care for Schizophrenic Patients in the United Kingdom." In L. M. Roberts, S. L. Halleck, and M. B. Loeb, *Community Psychiatry.* New York: Doubleday Anchor, 1969. Pp. 138–169.

WOODWORTH, R. S. *Experimental Psychology.* New York: Henry Holt, 1938.

ZIGLER, E., AND L. PHILLIPS. "Social Effectiveness of Symptomatic Behaviors." *Journal of Abnormal and Social Psychology,* 65 (1960): 607–618.

Index

Index